A Grand Tour of Asia

1910

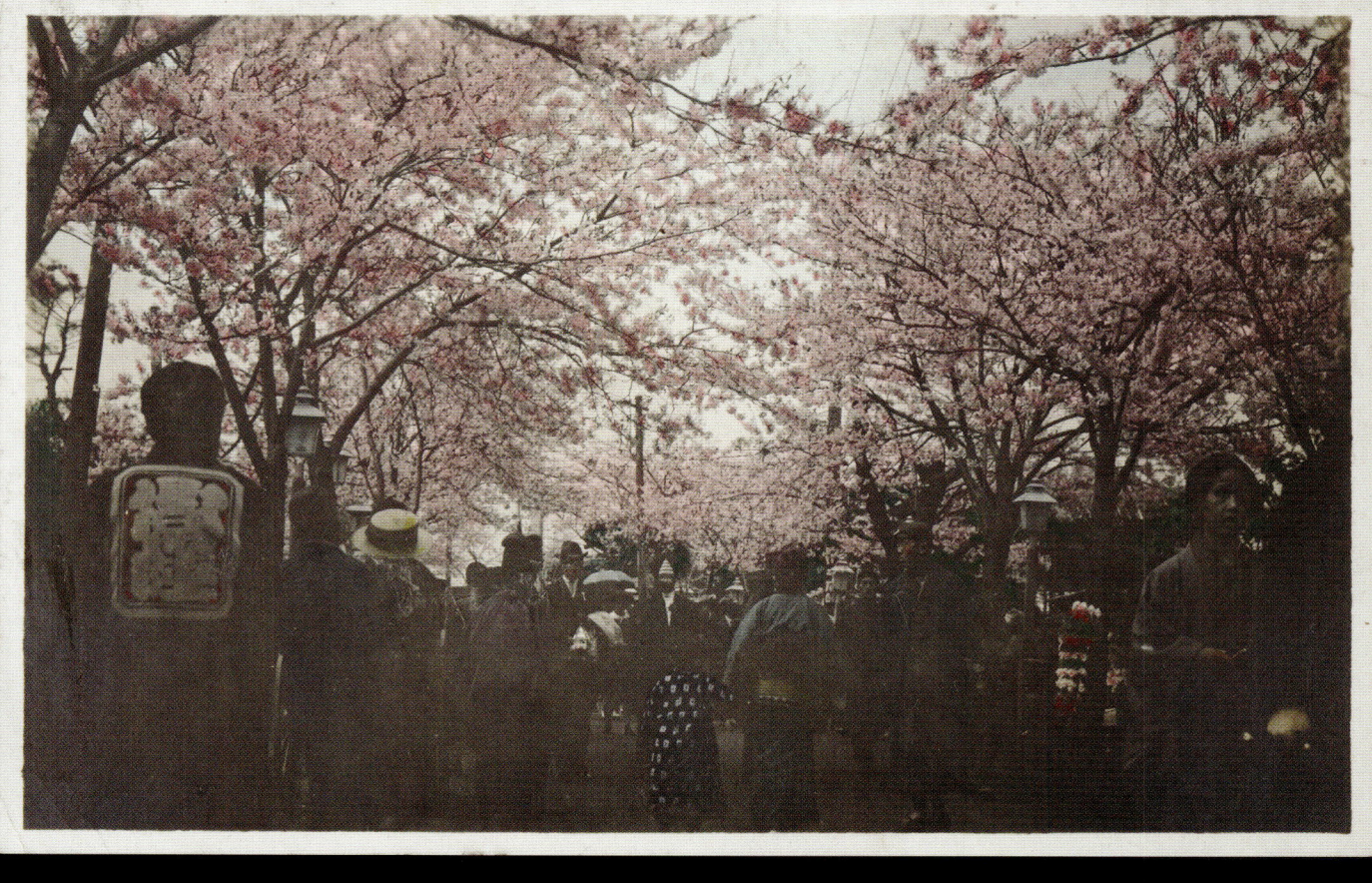

Japan April 9th — April 29th 1910

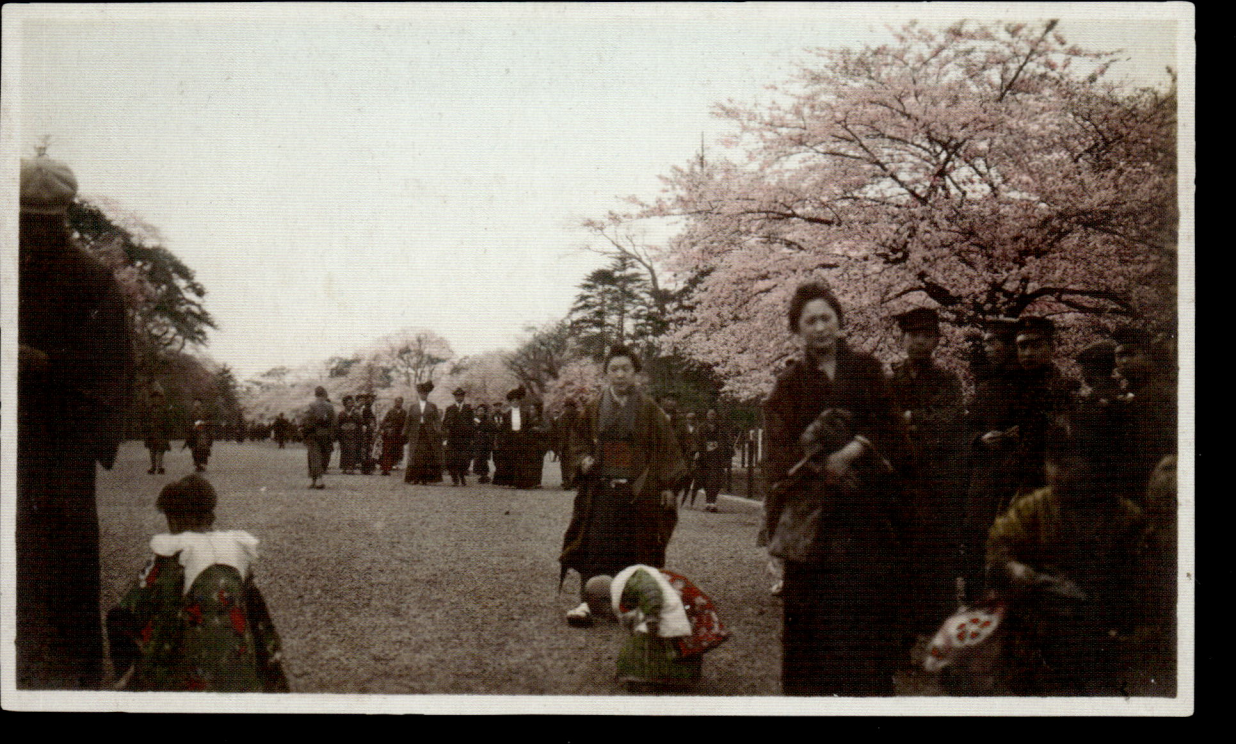

How fortunate we were to start our tour during Cherry Blossom time. A Japanese man, who spoke very good English, told me Japan has 400 varieties of cherry trees. Tokyo—4/10/1910

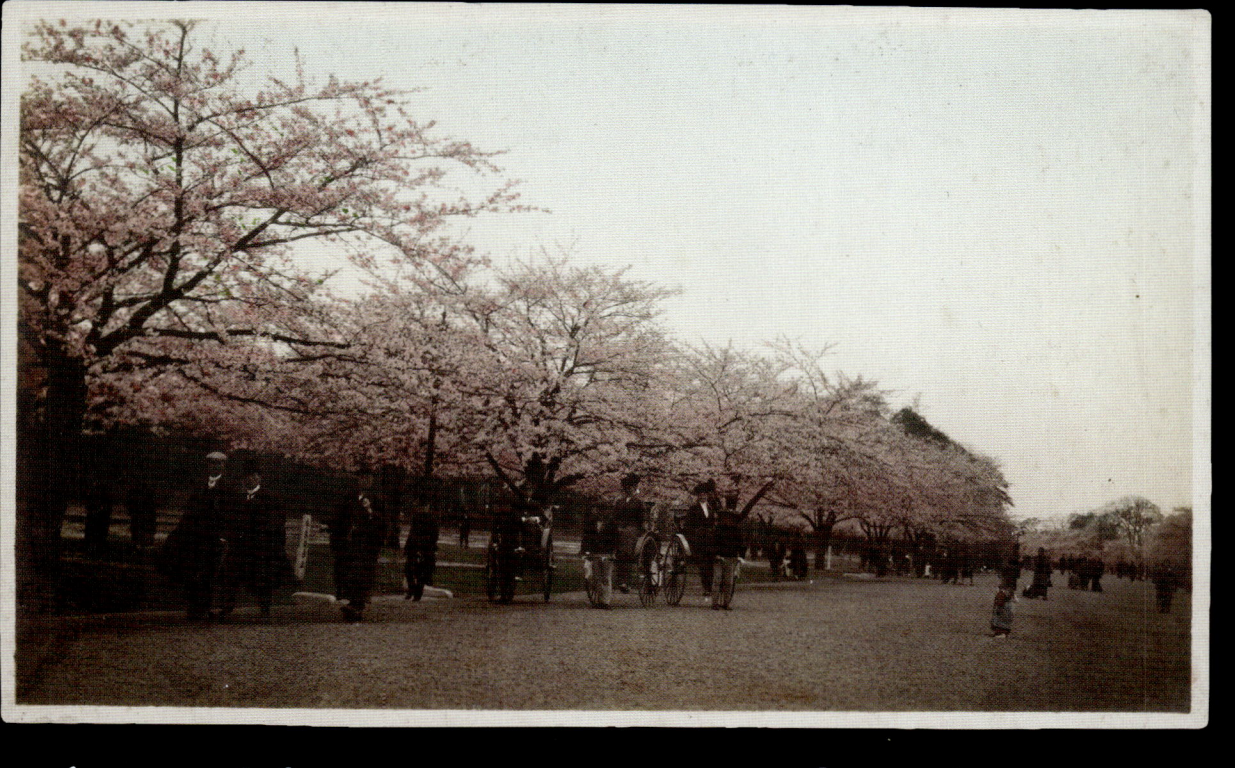

The wealthy Japanese, as well as the poor, promenaded beneath the enchanting pink trees during the Cherry Blossom Festival. Many dressed in their best kimonos for the event.

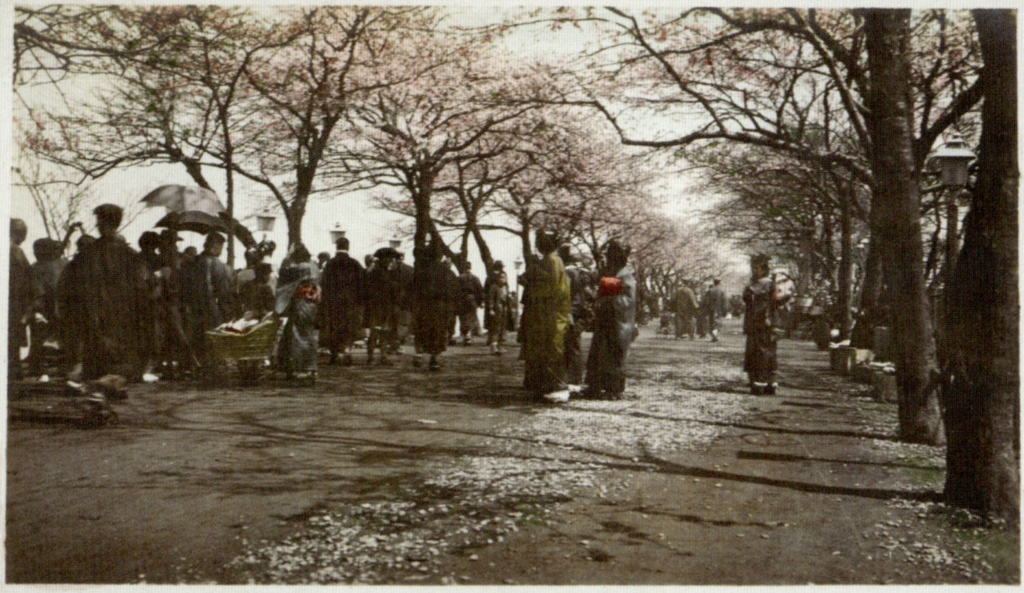

Families gathered along the river embankment for the Festival.

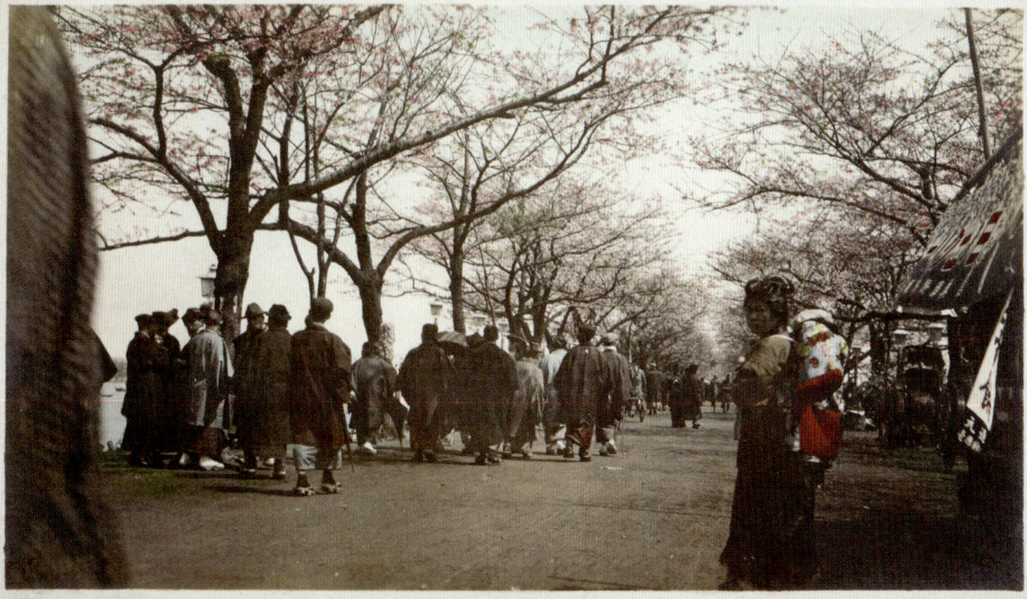

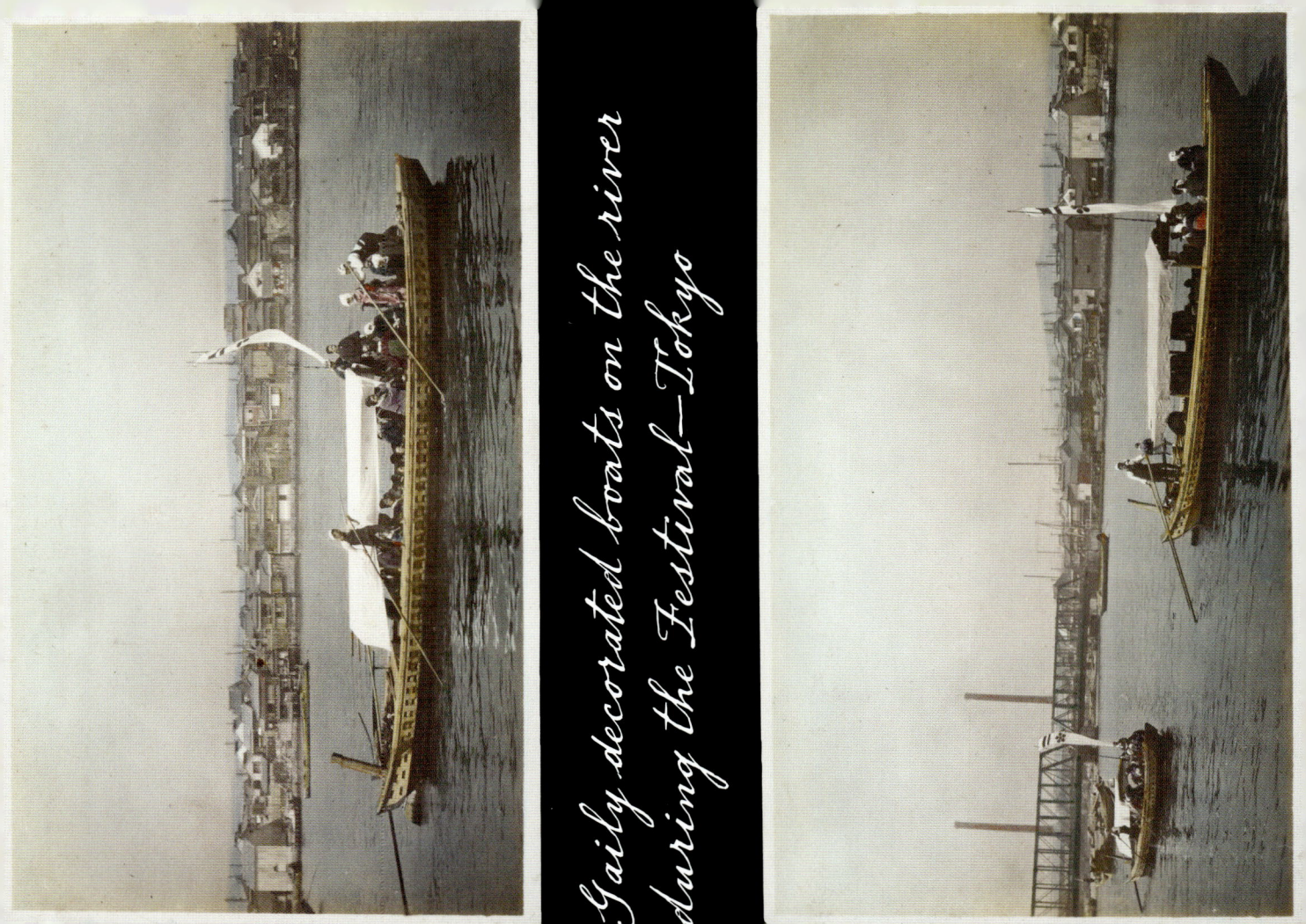

Gaily decorated boats on the river during the Festival—Tokyo

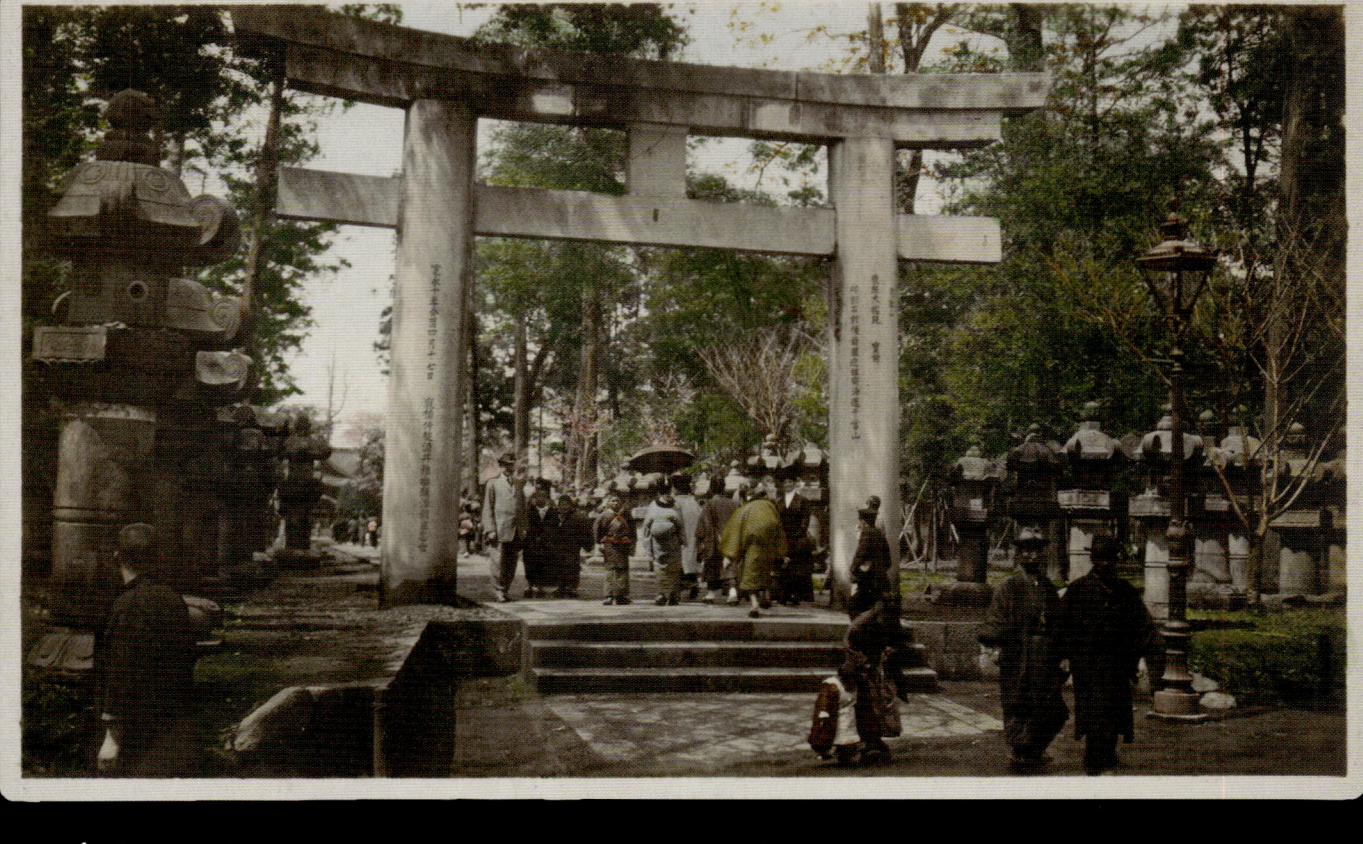

A handsome Torii gate at the entrance to a temple in Ueno Park—4/13/1910

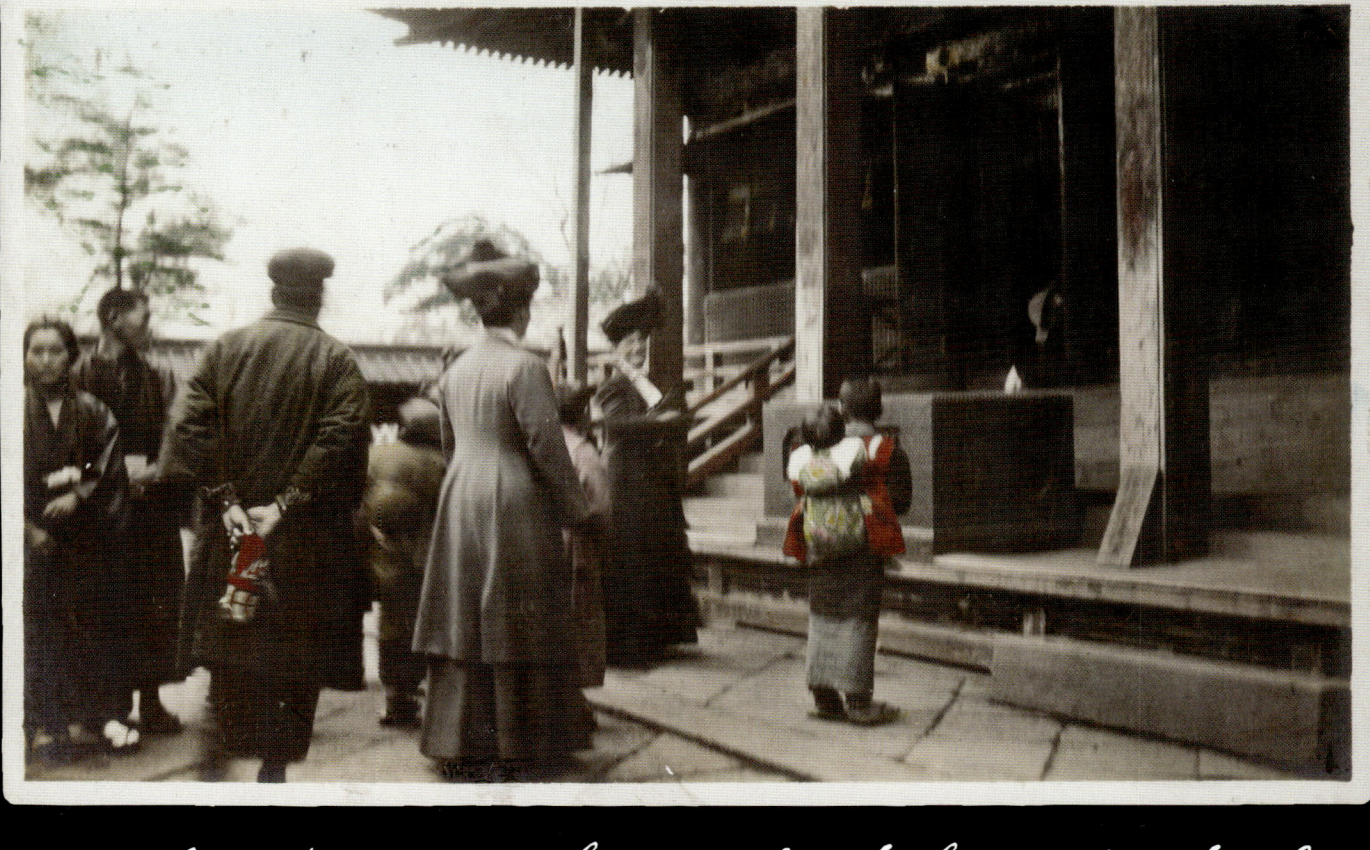

We followed a young boy with a baby on his back to a crowded Shinto Temple.

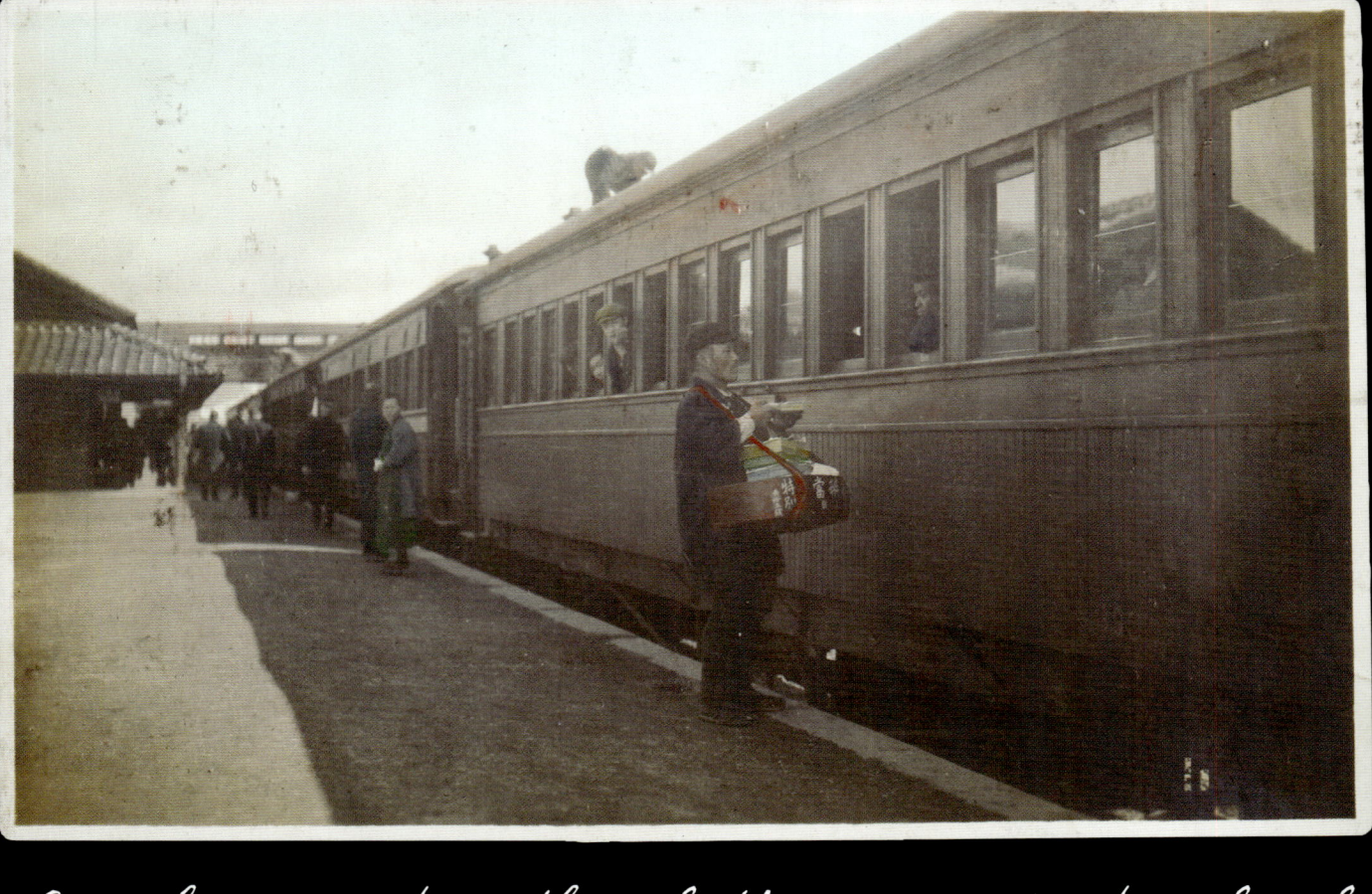

Lunch arrived on the platform wrapped in lovely little boxes.

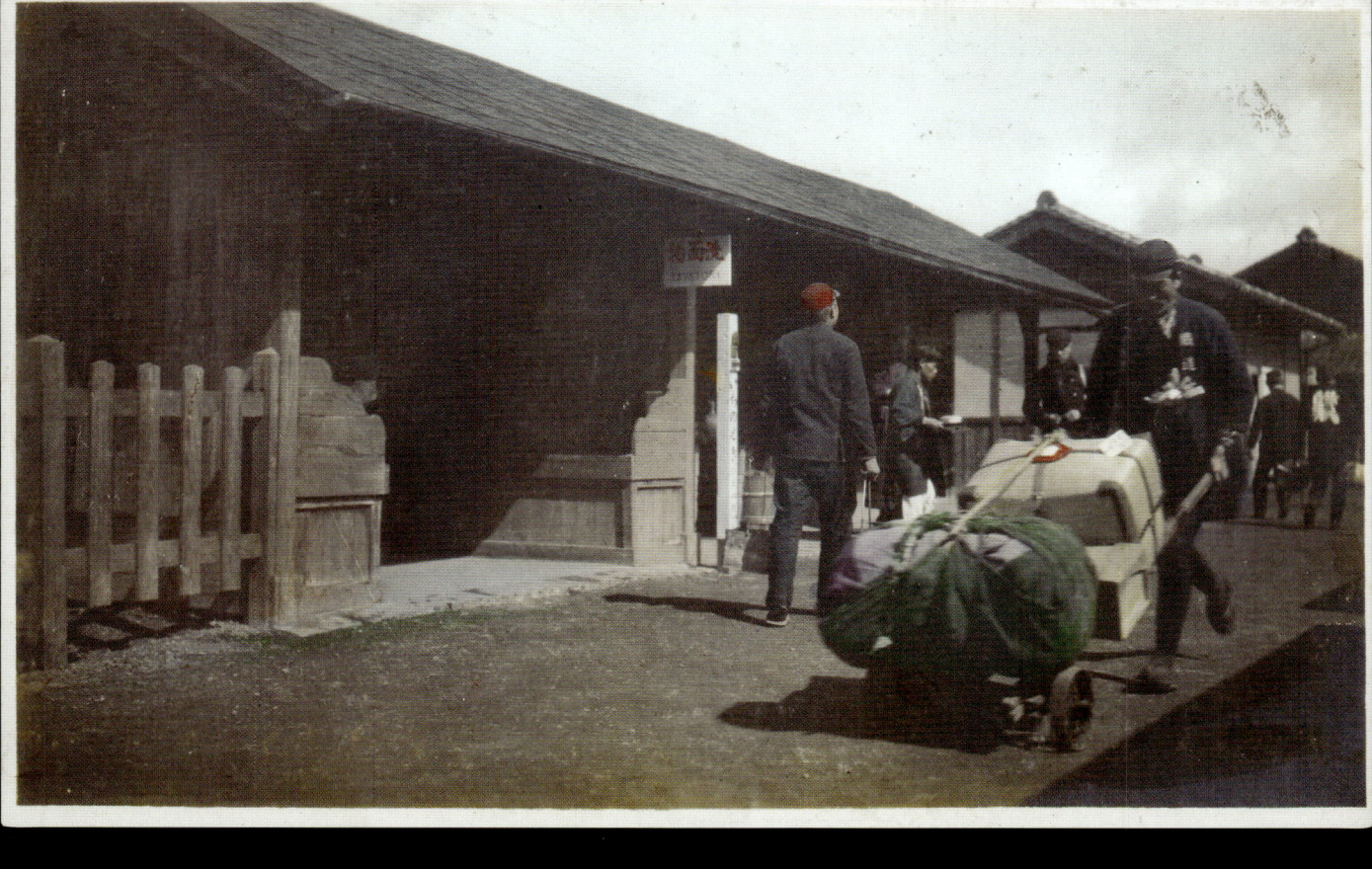

Traveling by rail in Japan was fast and efficient.

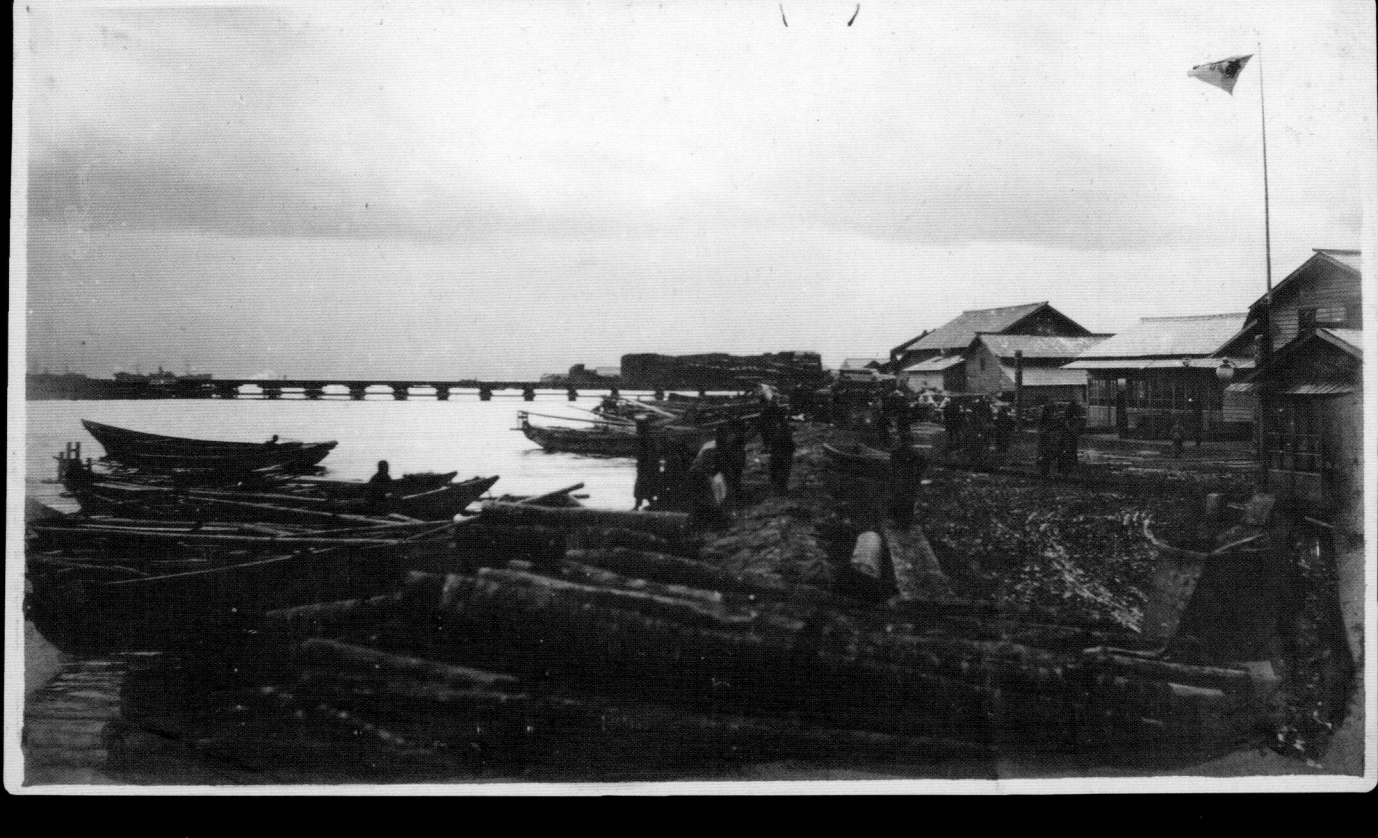

Small vessels moored along the wharf—Otaru

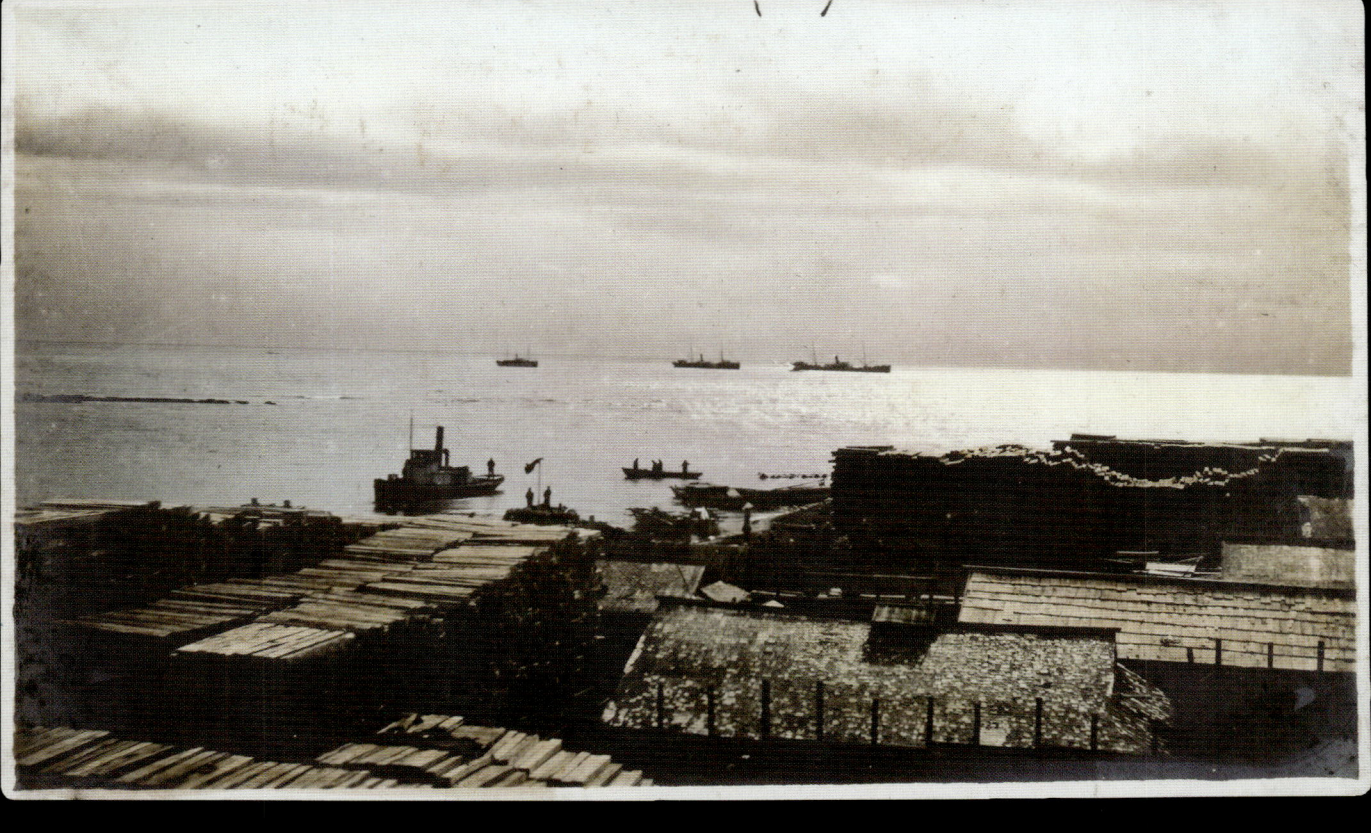

Lumber destined for foreign ports—Otaru

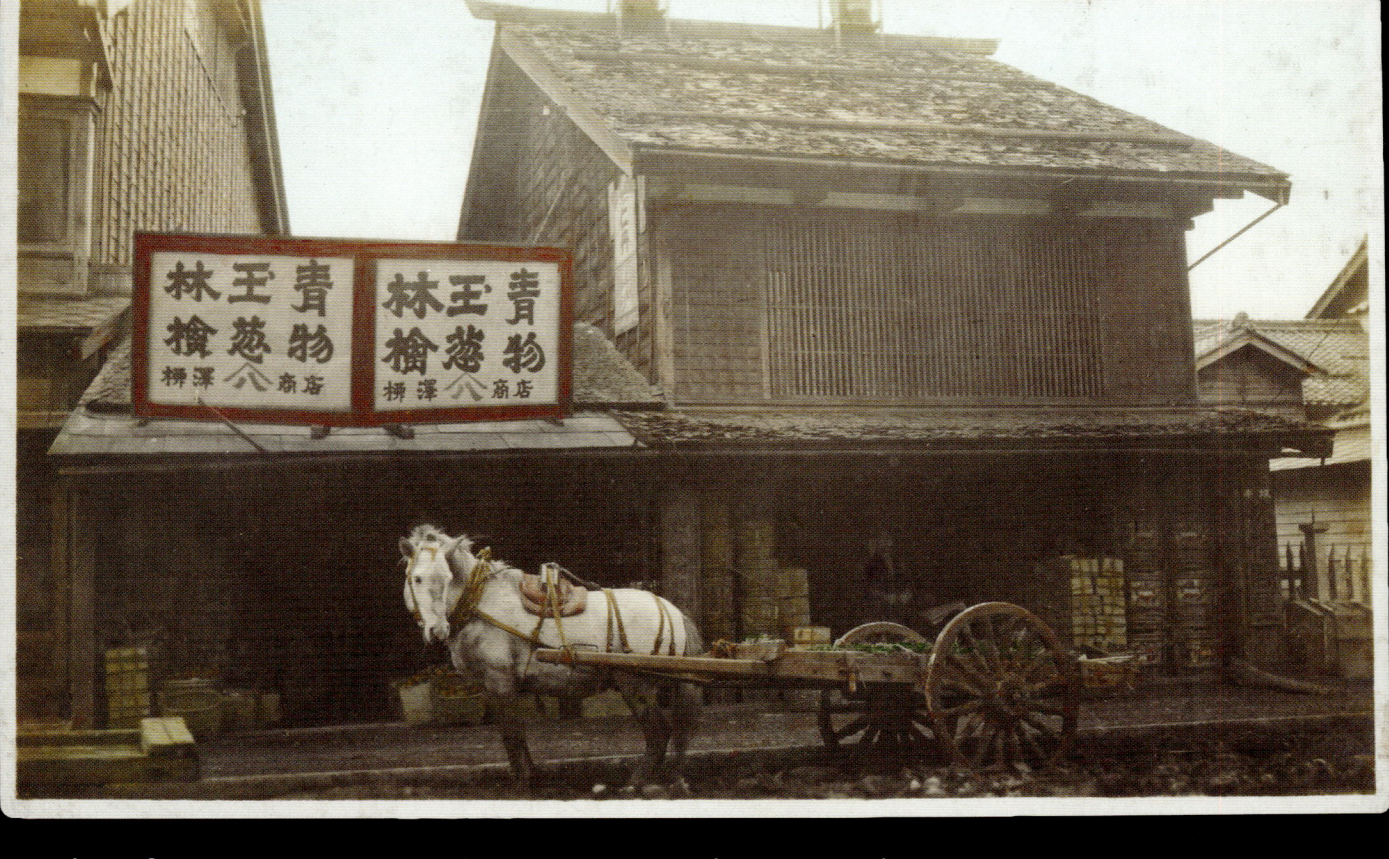

The horse waited patiently for his owner to return.

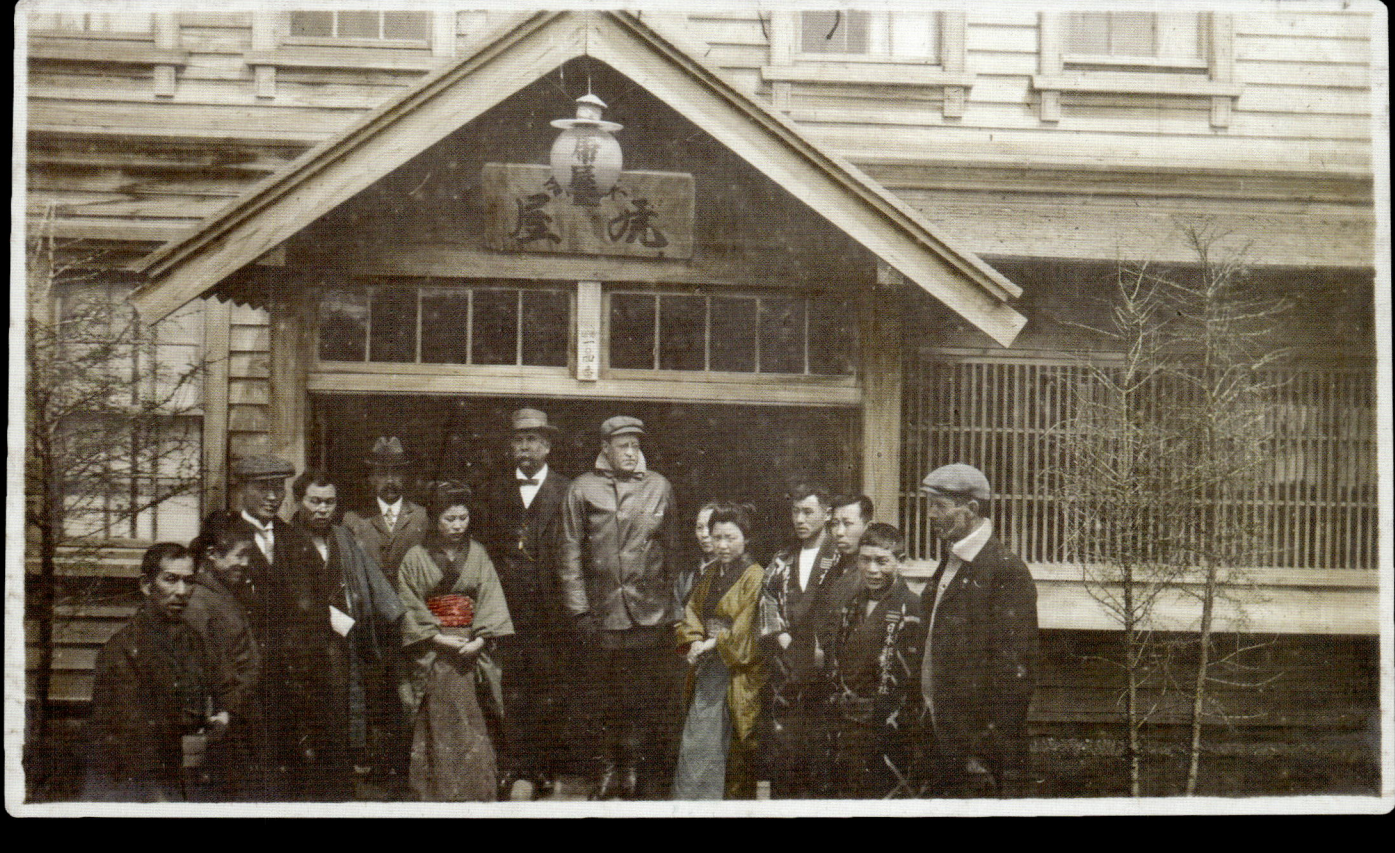

The inn at Otaru was quite pleasant.

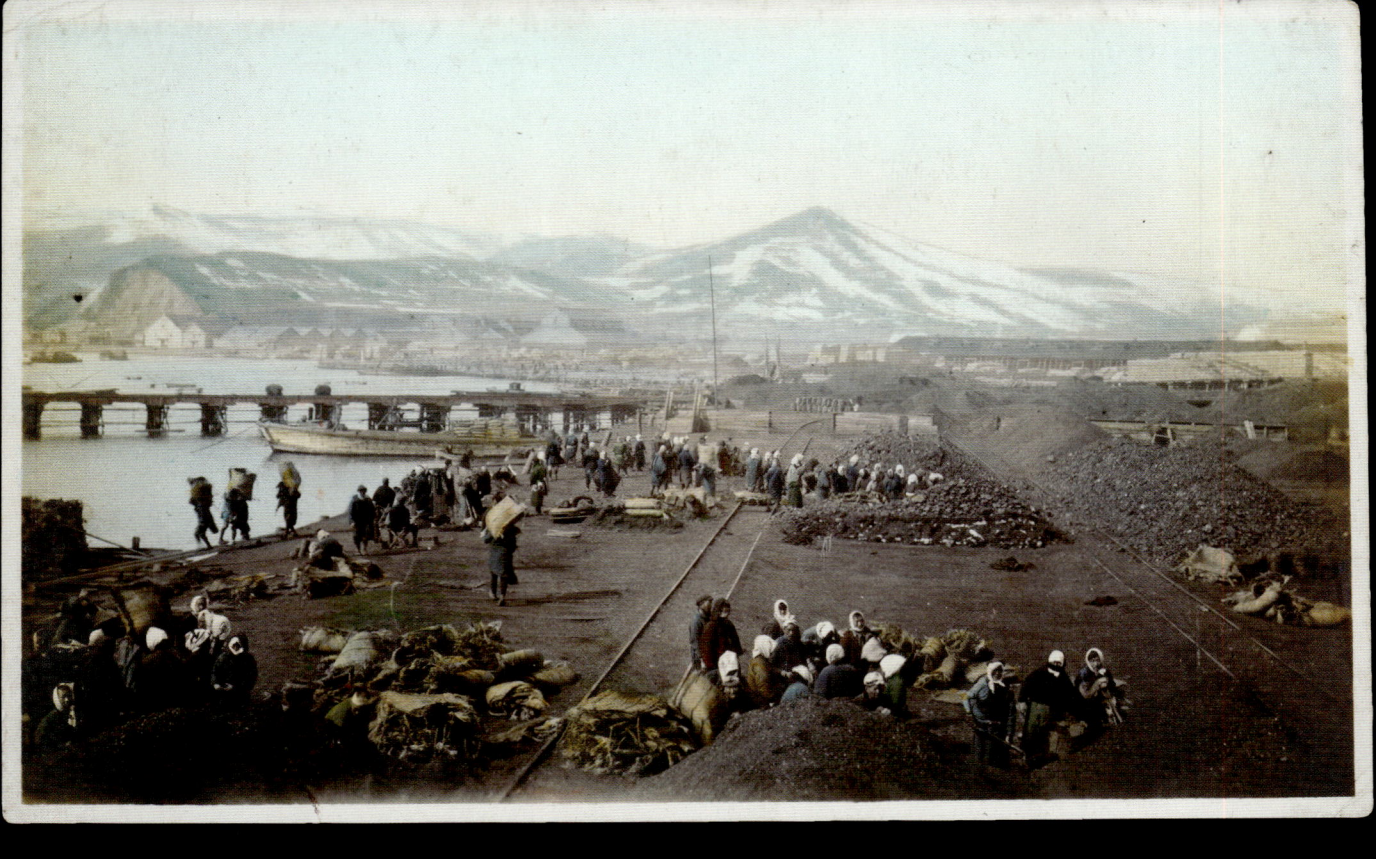

Women supply coal to the waiting steam ships.

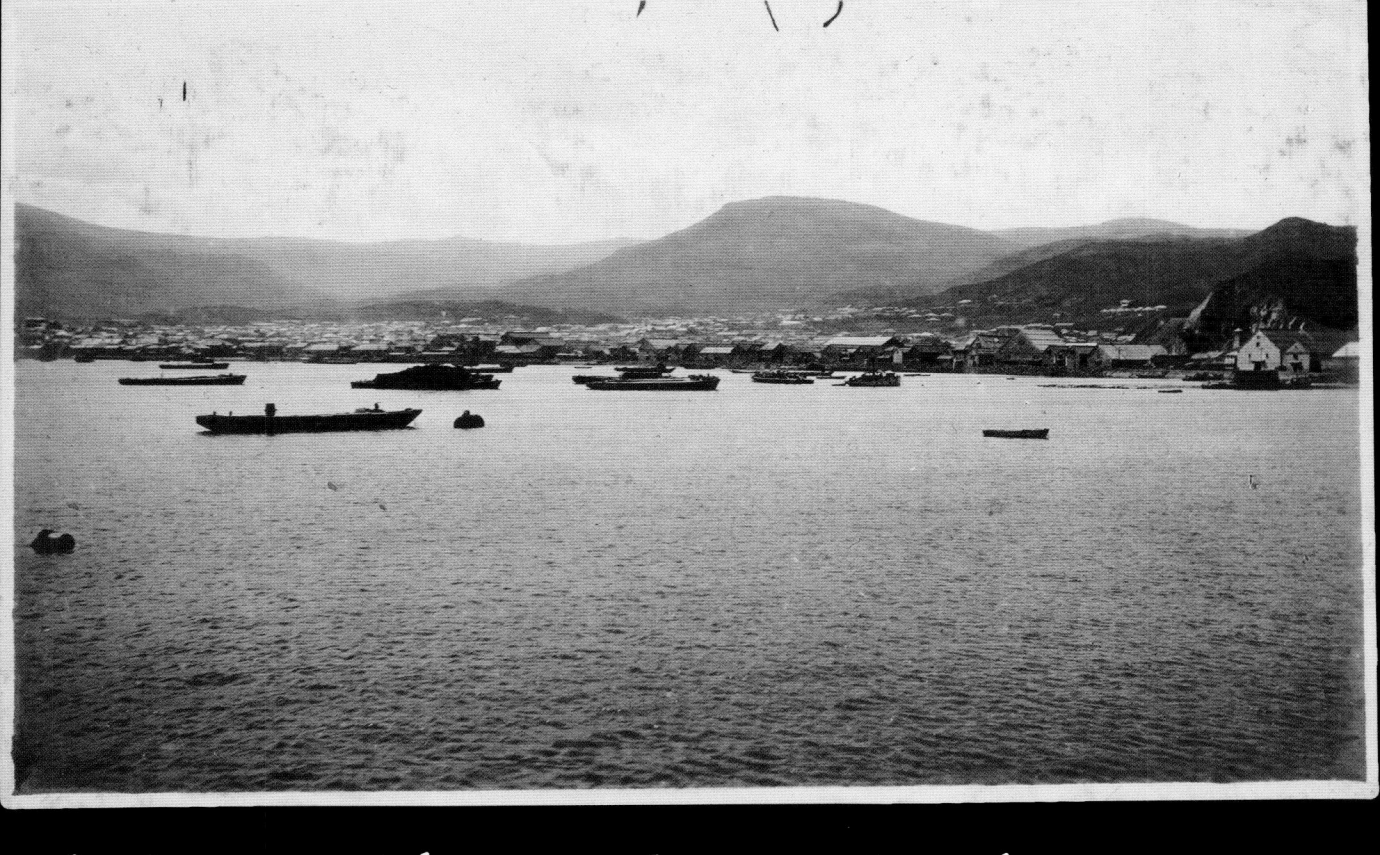

The large and beautiful natural harbor at Otaru.

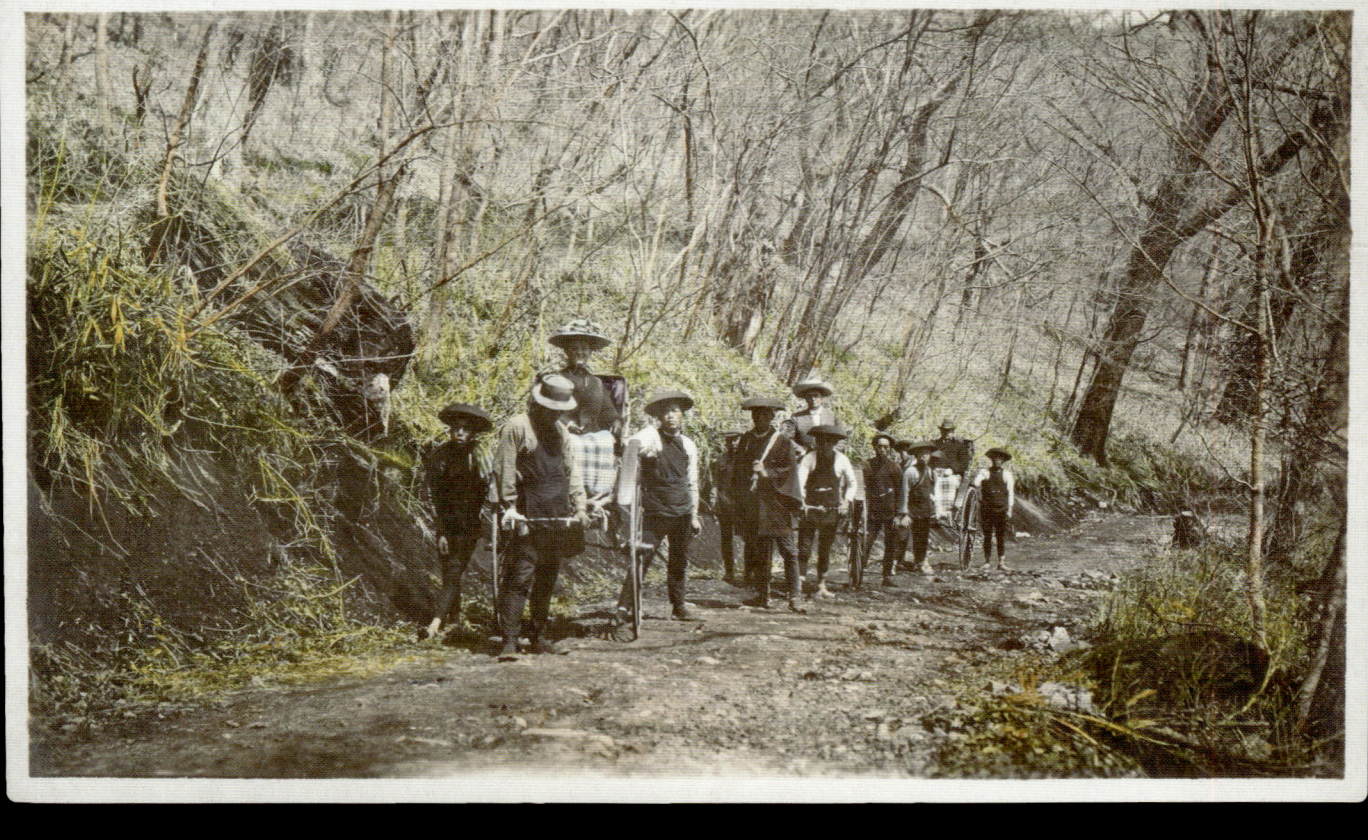

Along the road between Nikko and Lake Chuzenji—4/14/1910

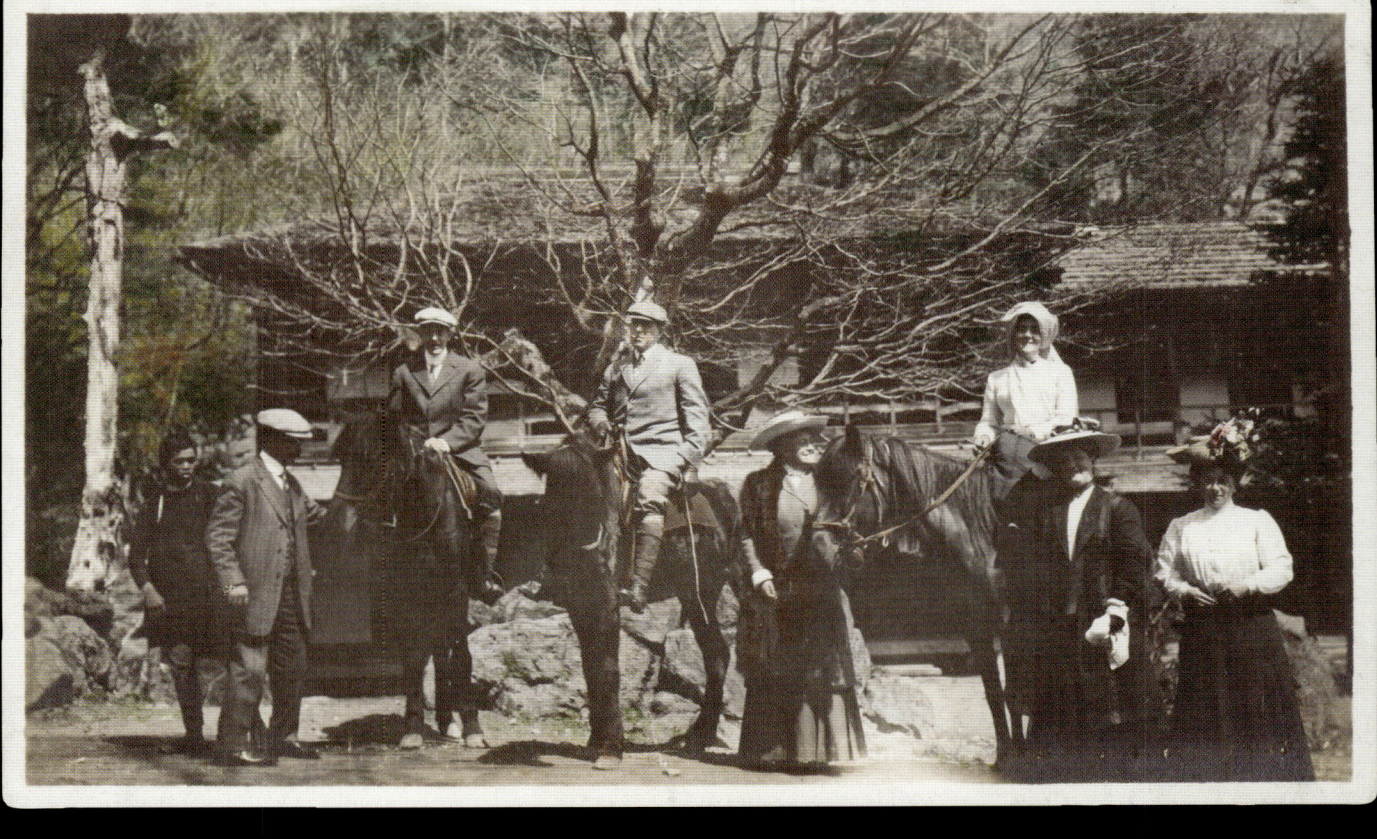

We stopped at the tea house between Nikko and Lake Chuzenji.

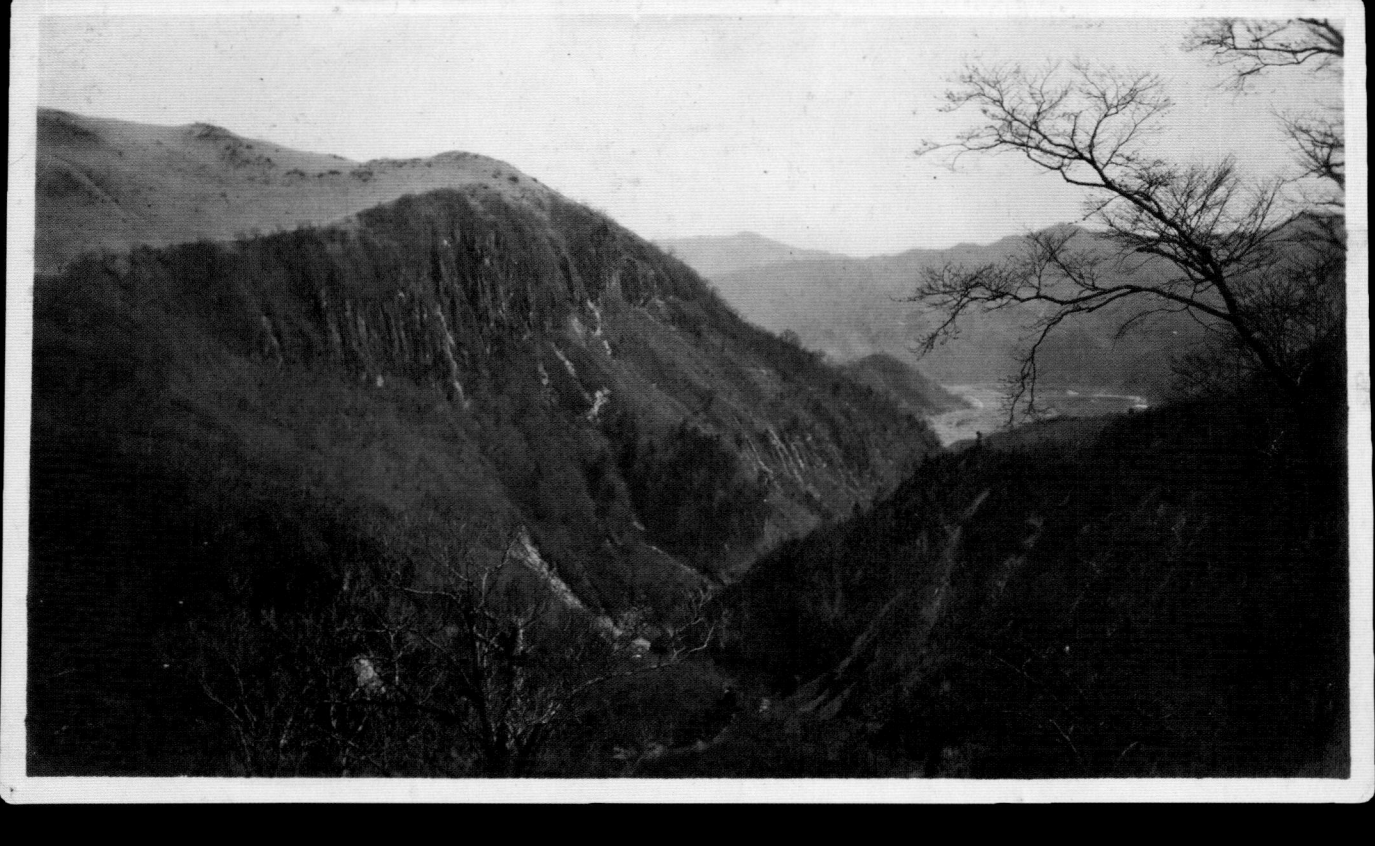

First view of the Lake through a mountain gorge.

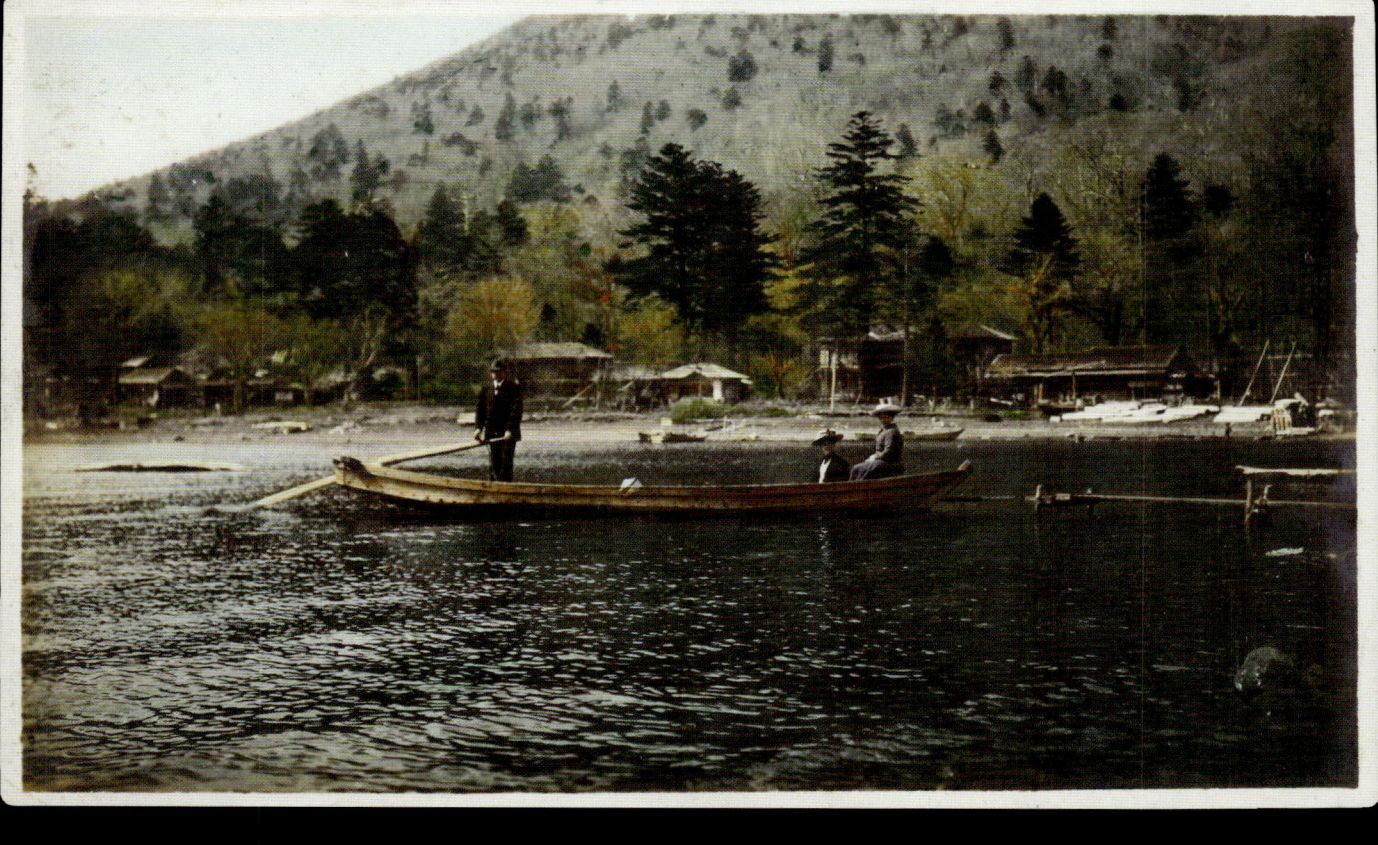

A serene afternoon of boating on Lake Chuzenji.

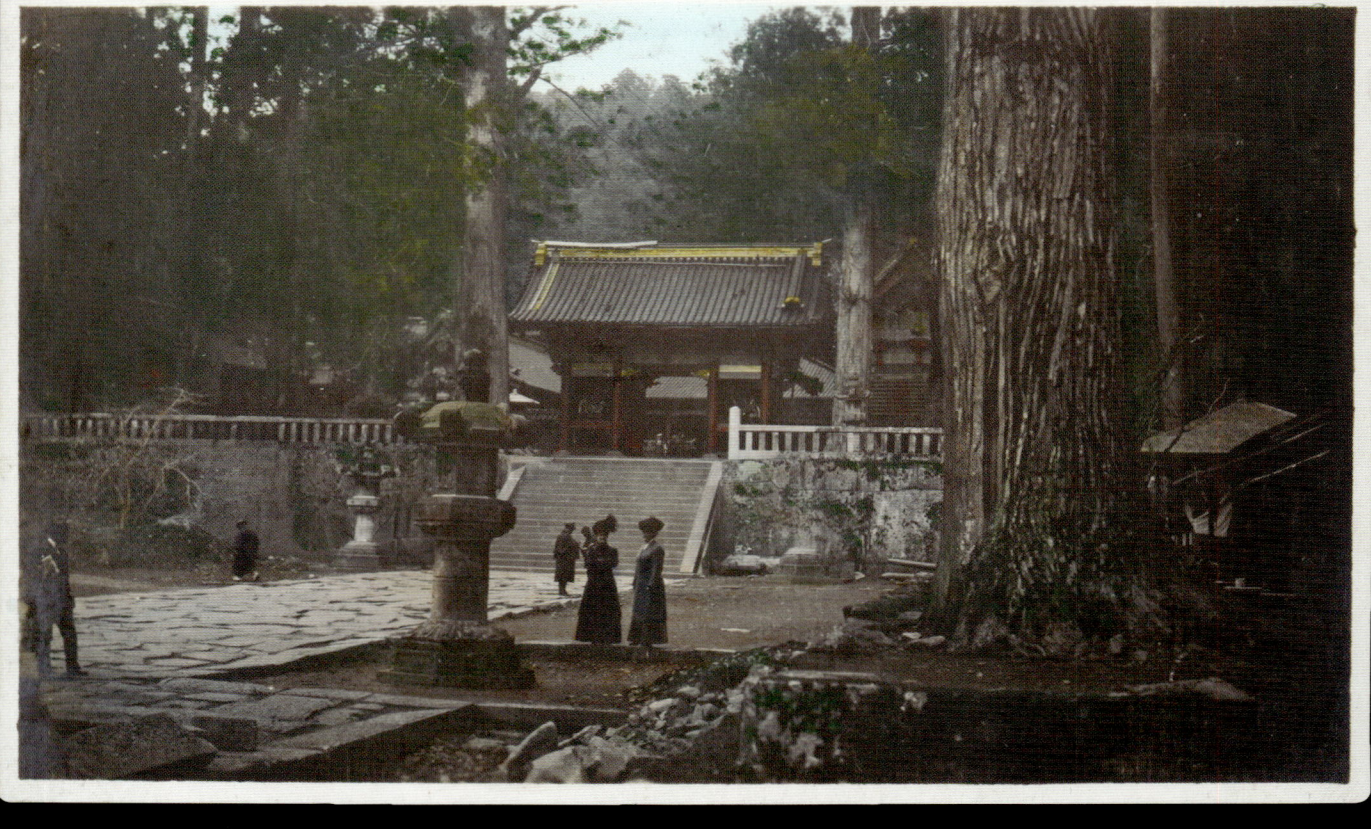

The cedar grove at the Nikko Temples.

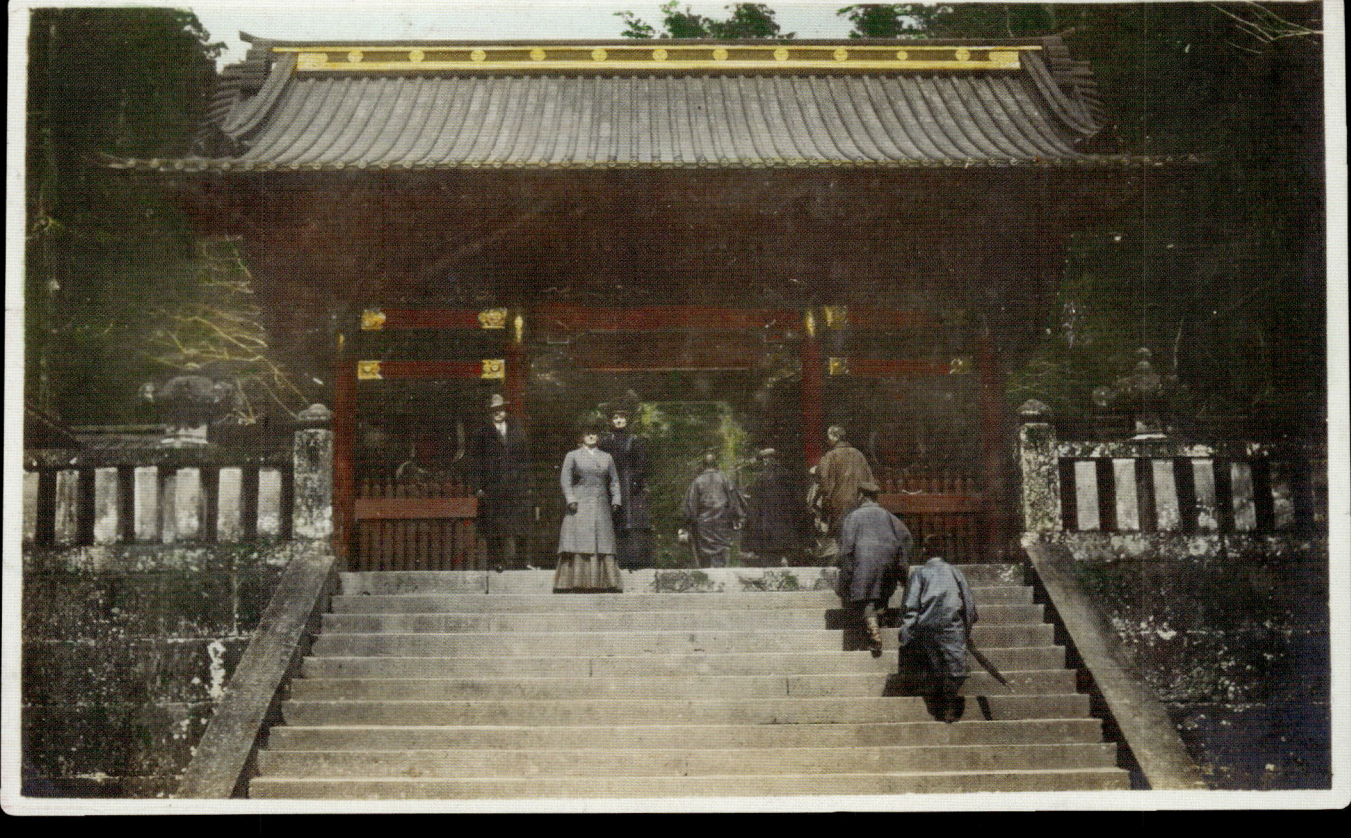

At the entrance to the Nikko Temples.

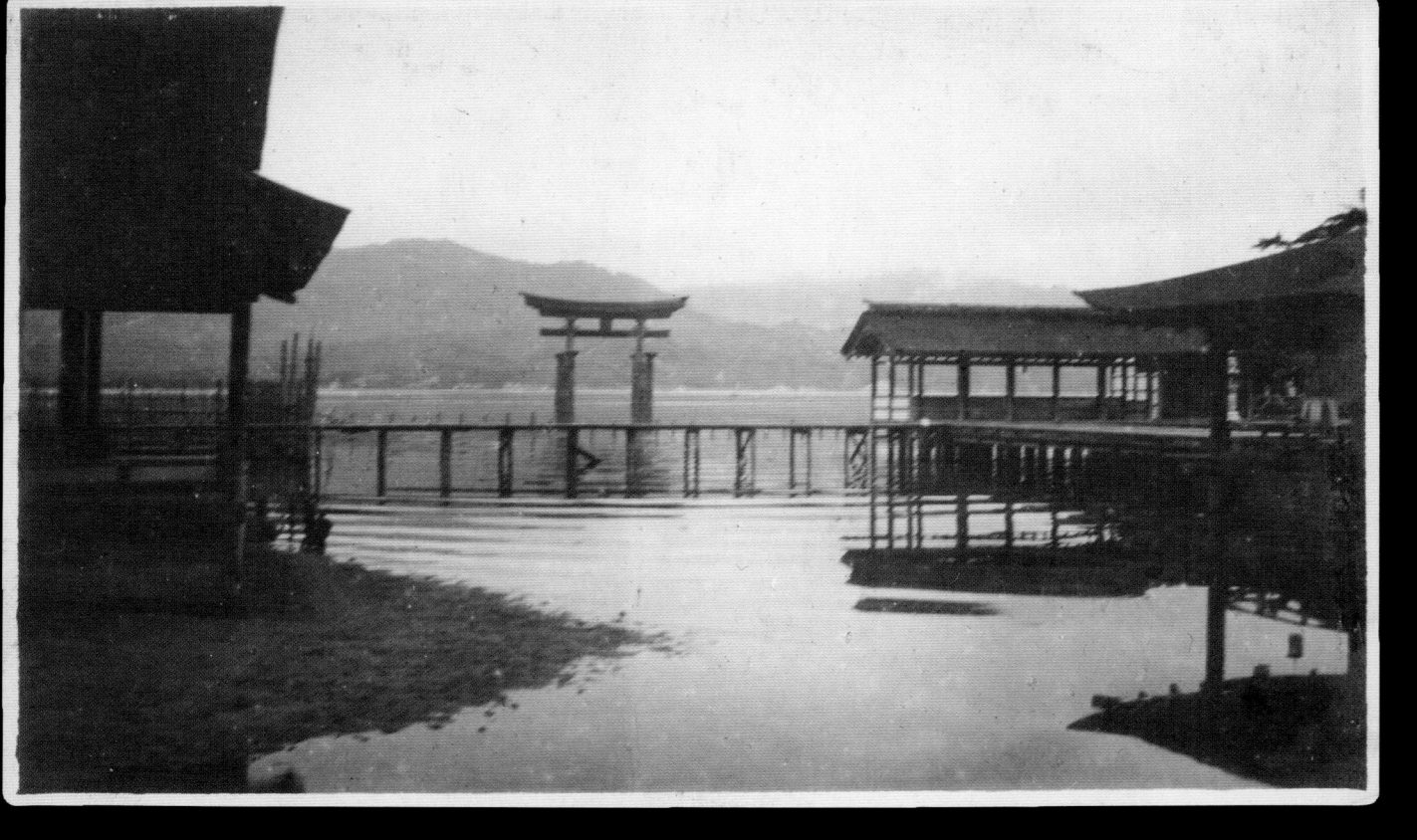

Torii gate at Miyajima—the scene was as pretty as a watercolor painting.

A tea house waitress could have stepped out of a wood block print.

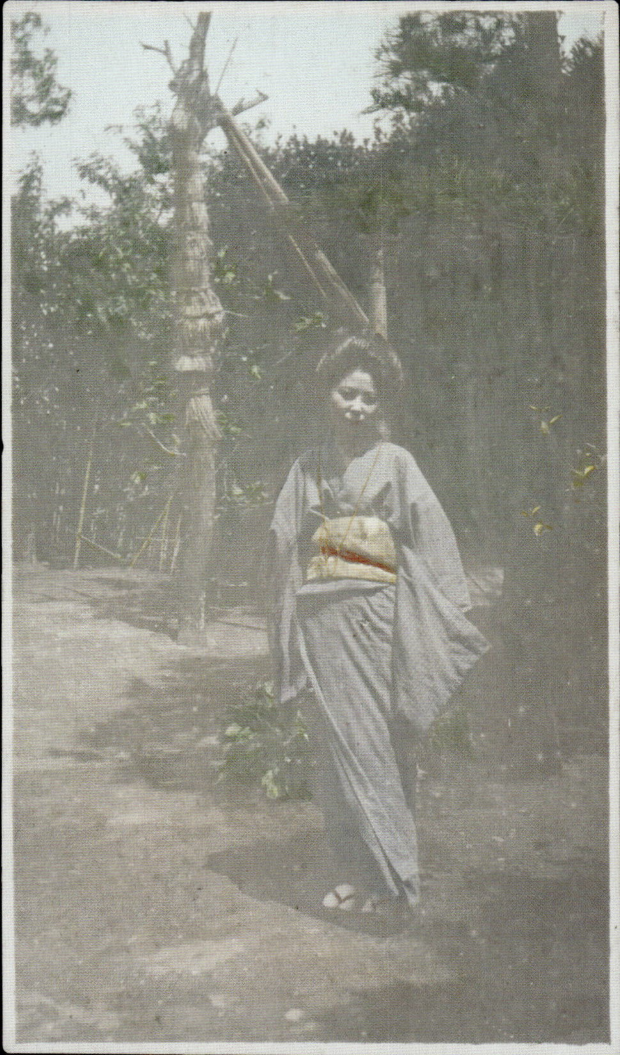

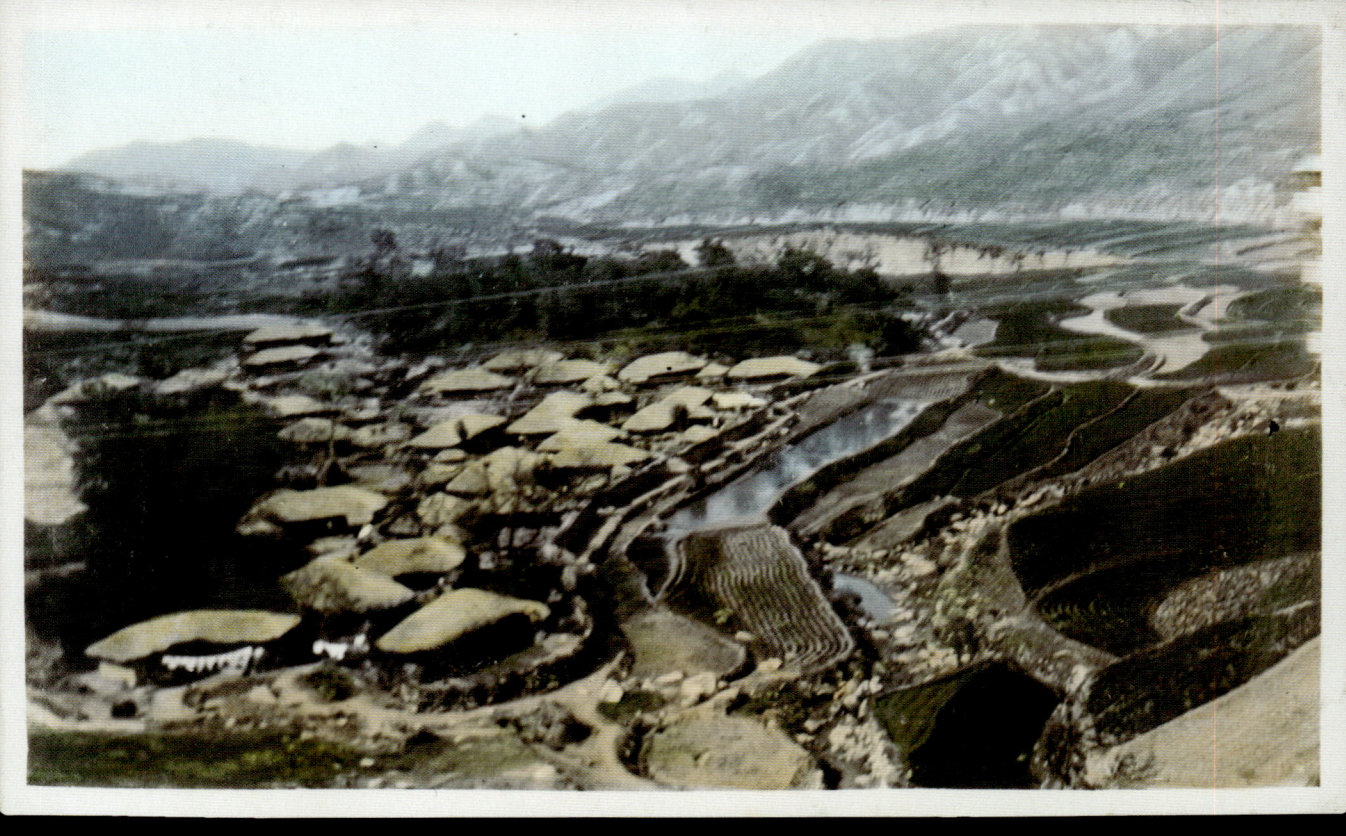

Korea May 1st — May 9th 1910

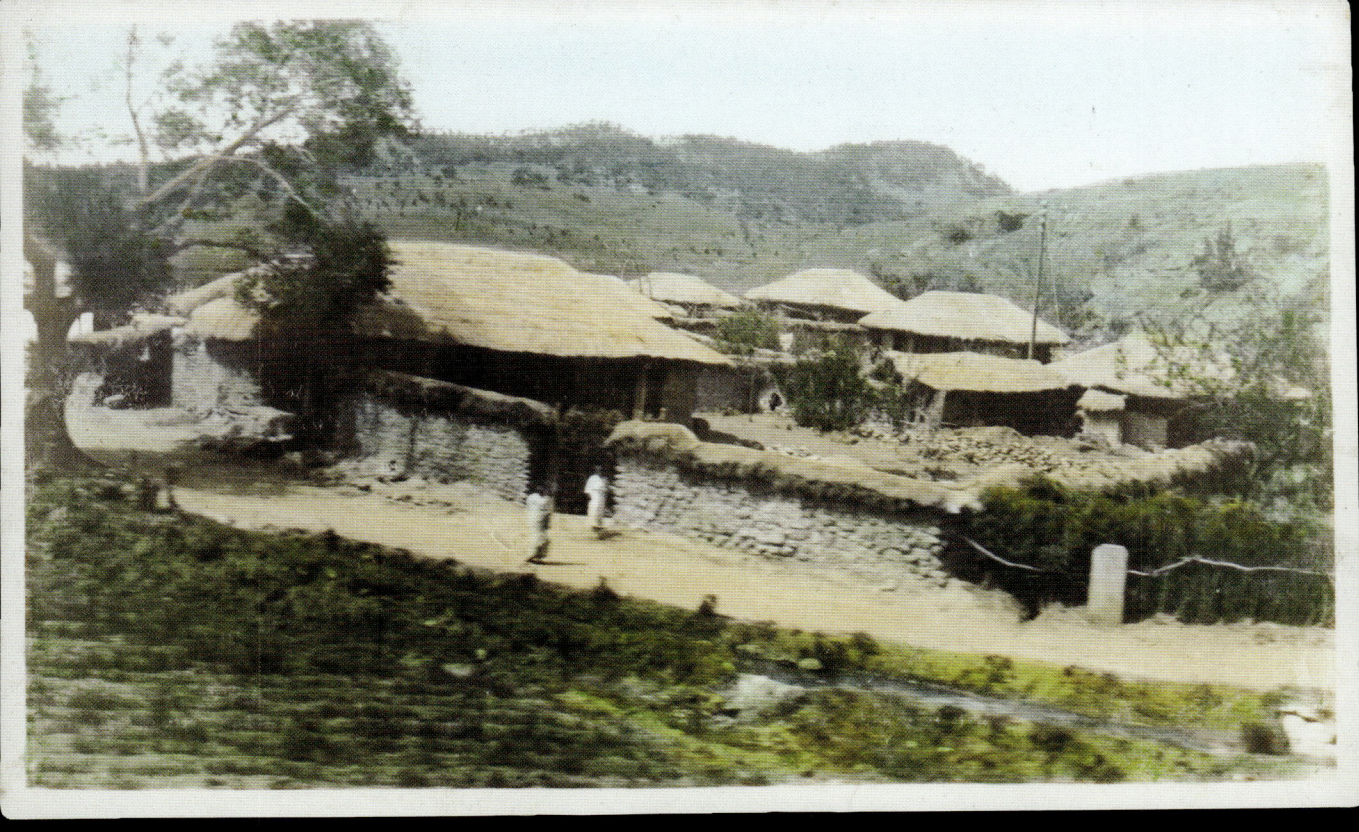

A farm compound from the train.

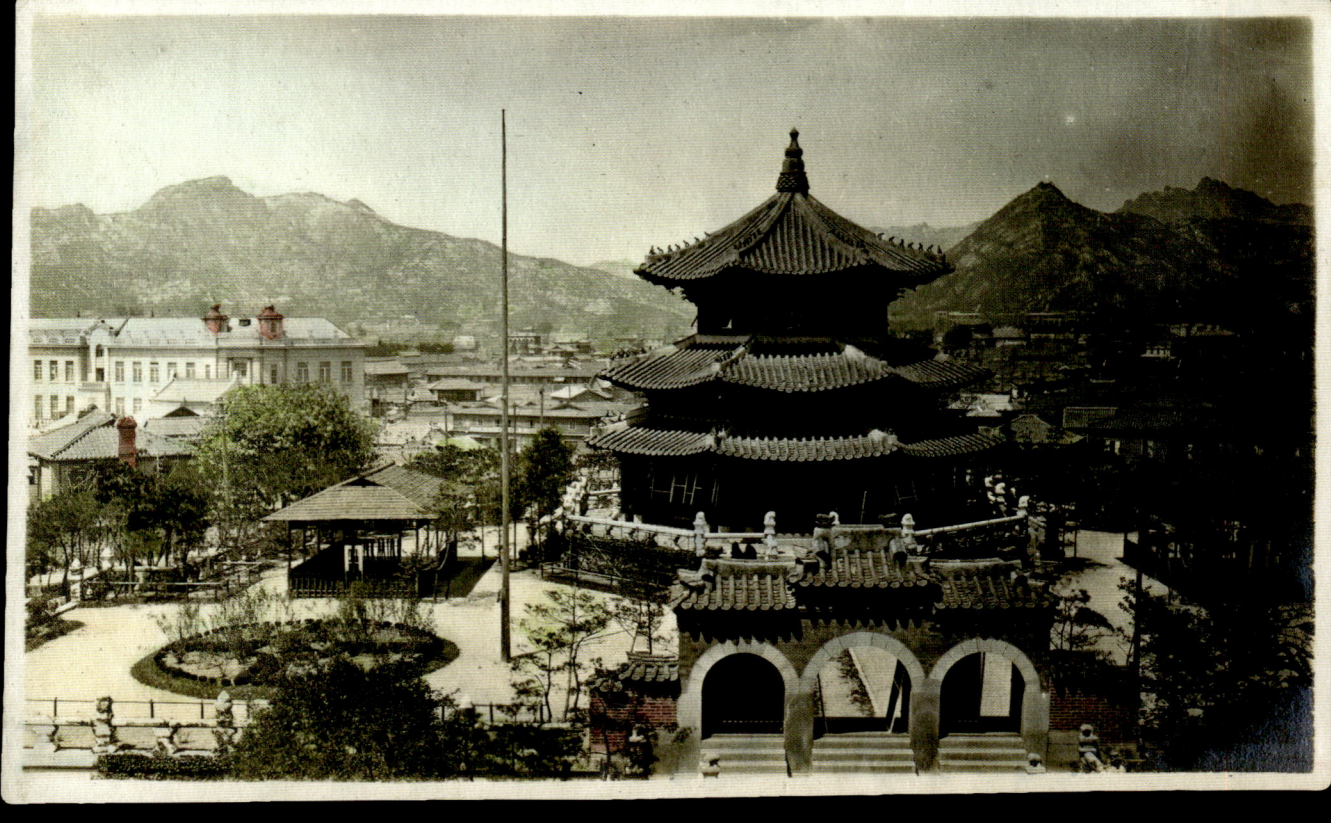

Temple of Heaven — Seoul

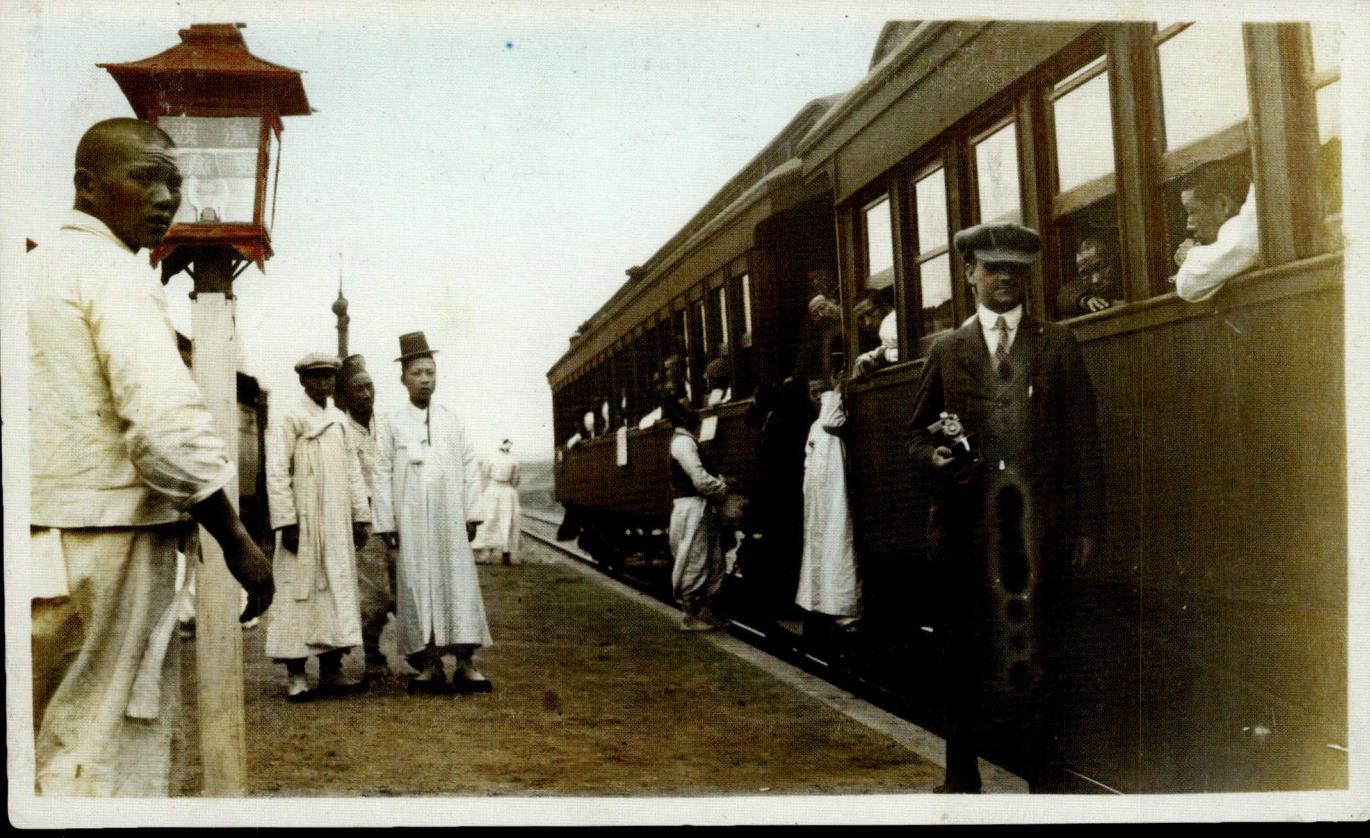

Train station—on to China!

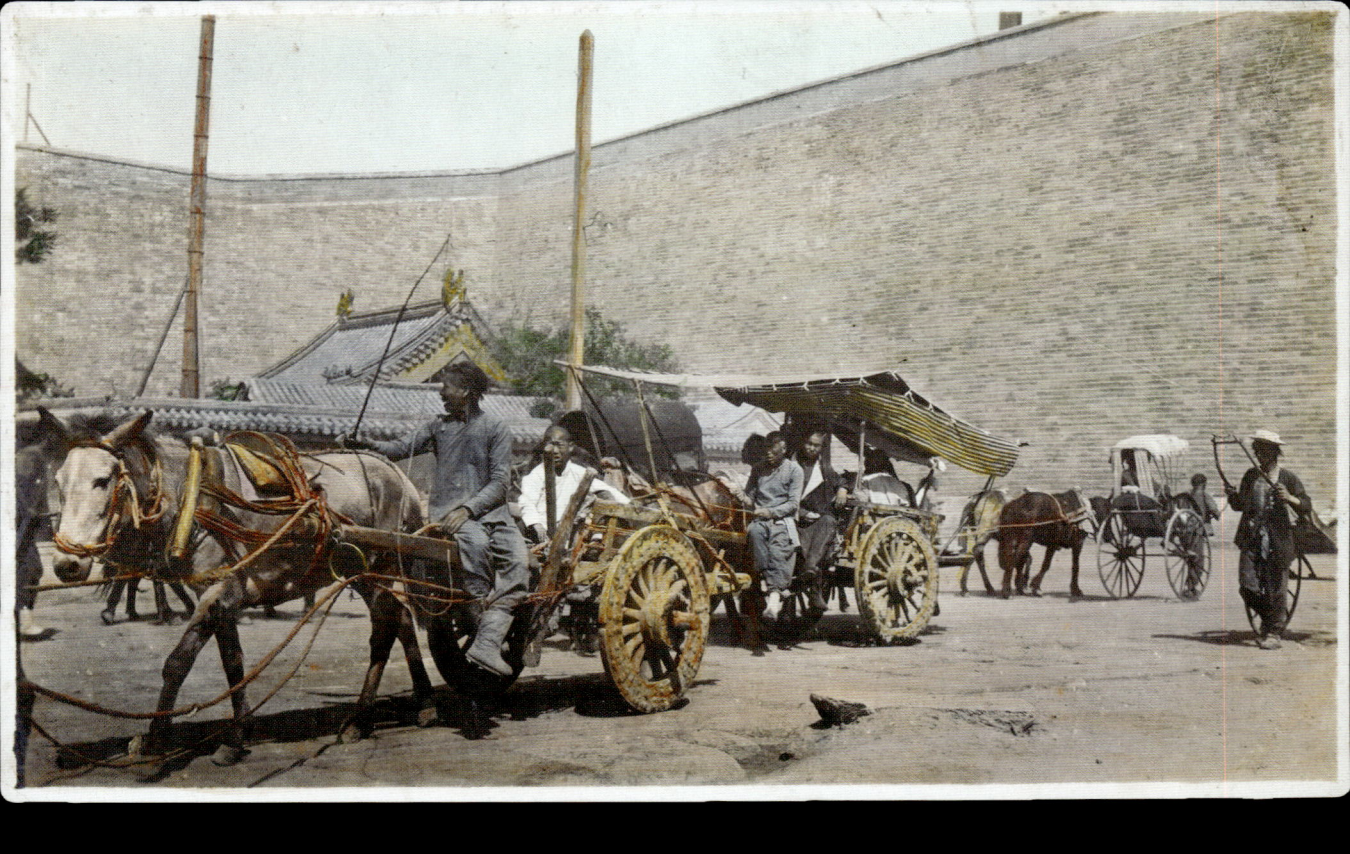

China May 12th — June 18th 1910

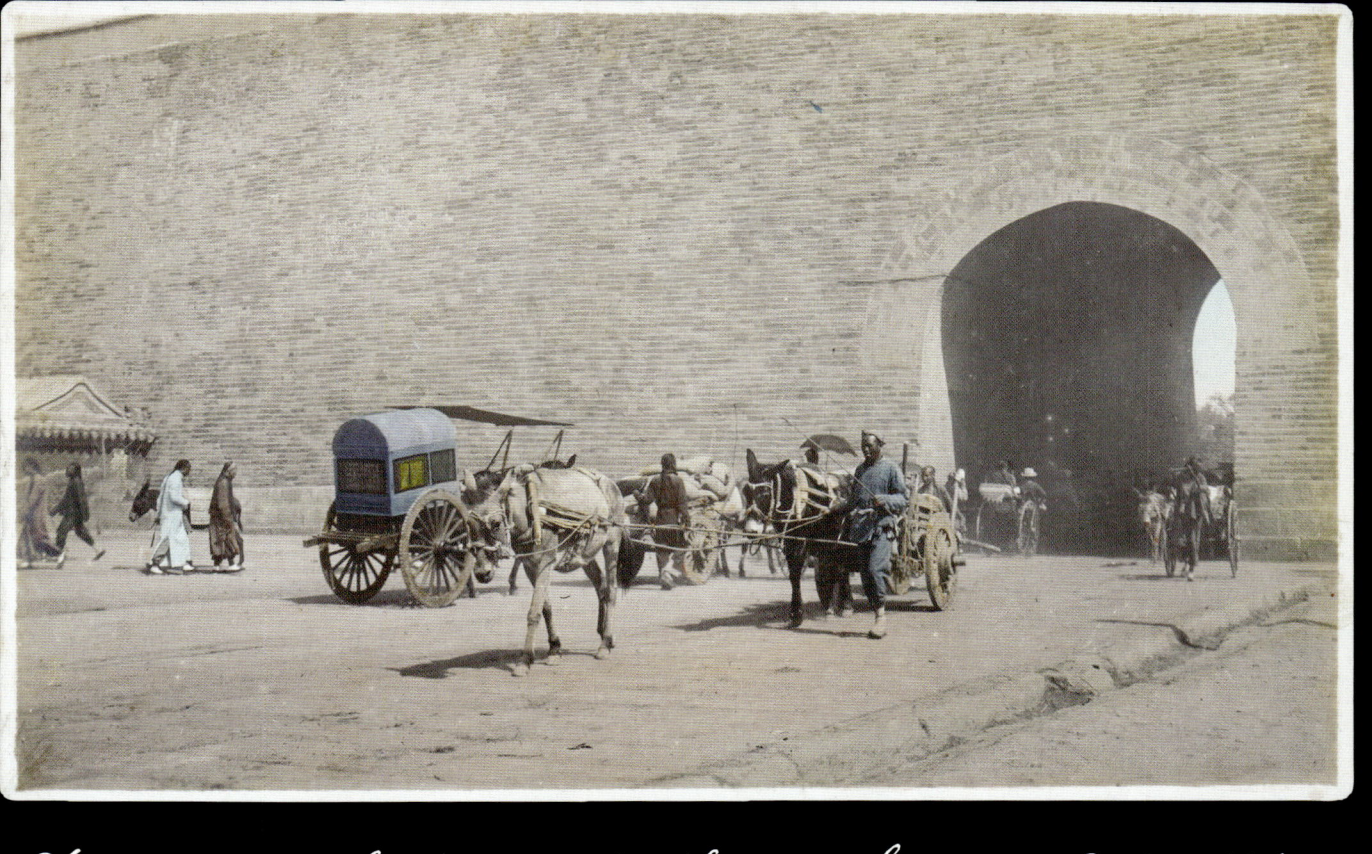

Chien Men Gateway to the Forbidden City. Blue covered vehicle is a Peking cart. It has no springs and is terribly uncomfortable.

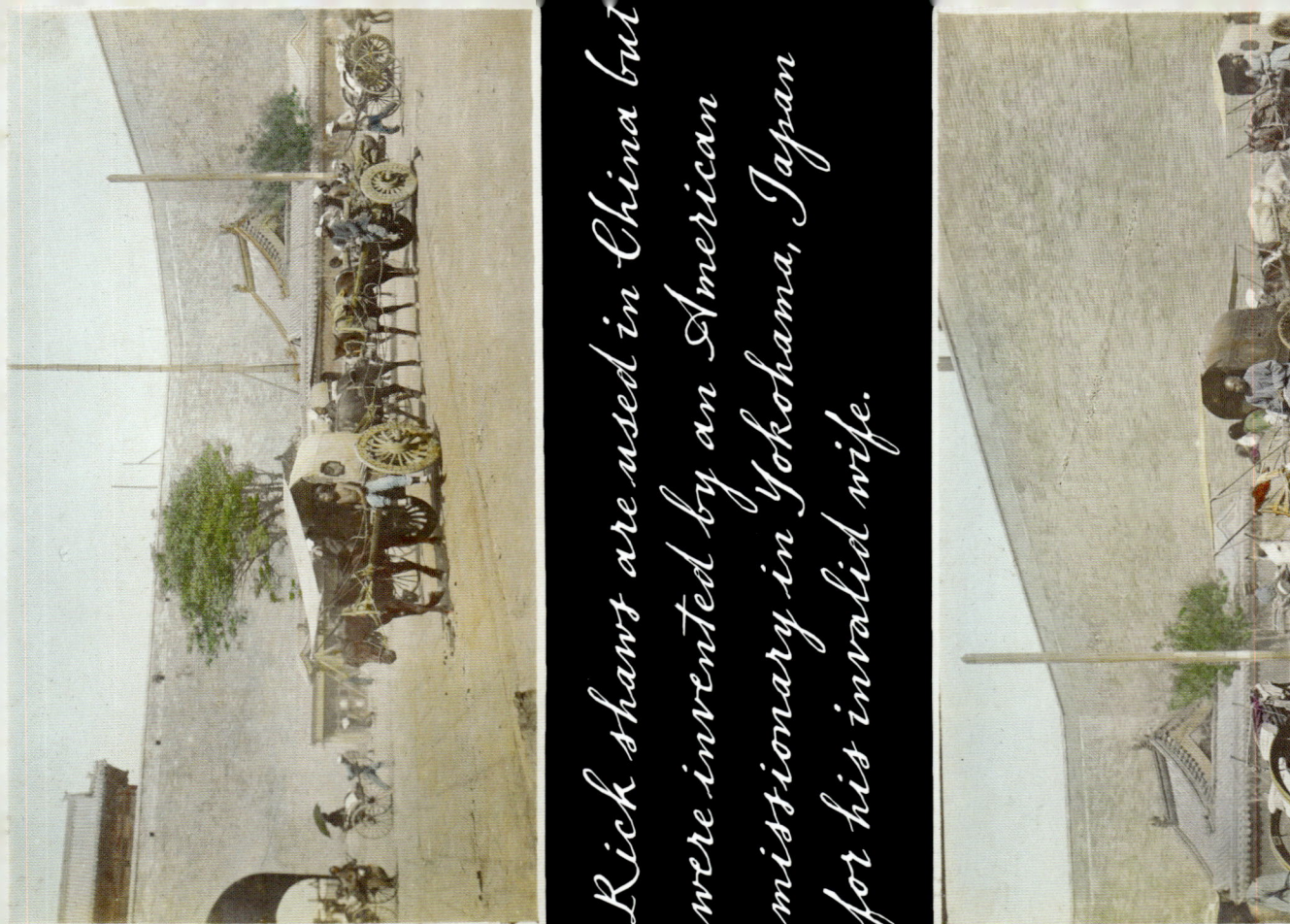

Rich shaws are used in China but were invented by an American missionary in Yokohama, Japan for his invalid wife.

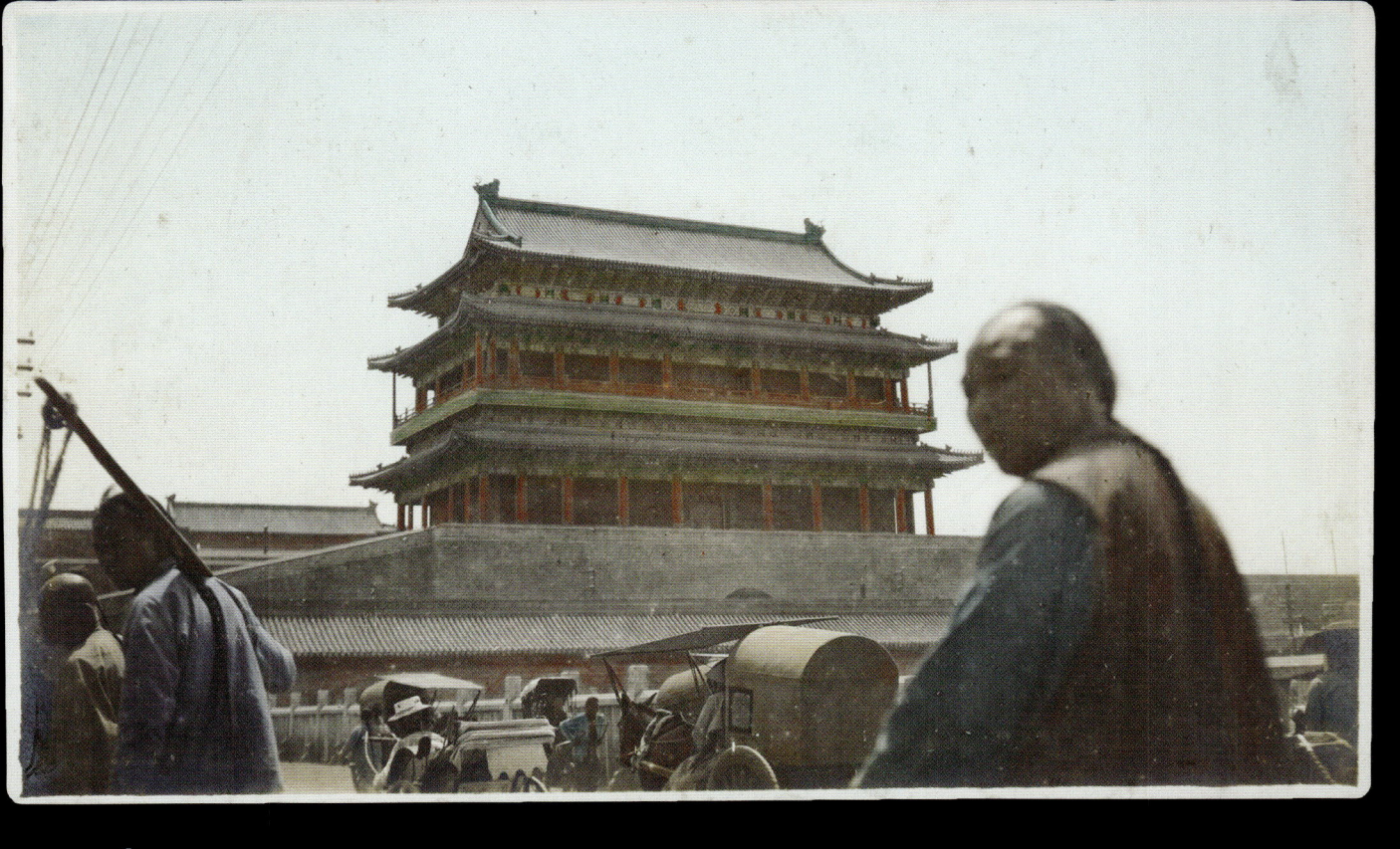

Like most Chinese, this man wore his hair in a long braid called a queue. Chien Men Gate—Peking

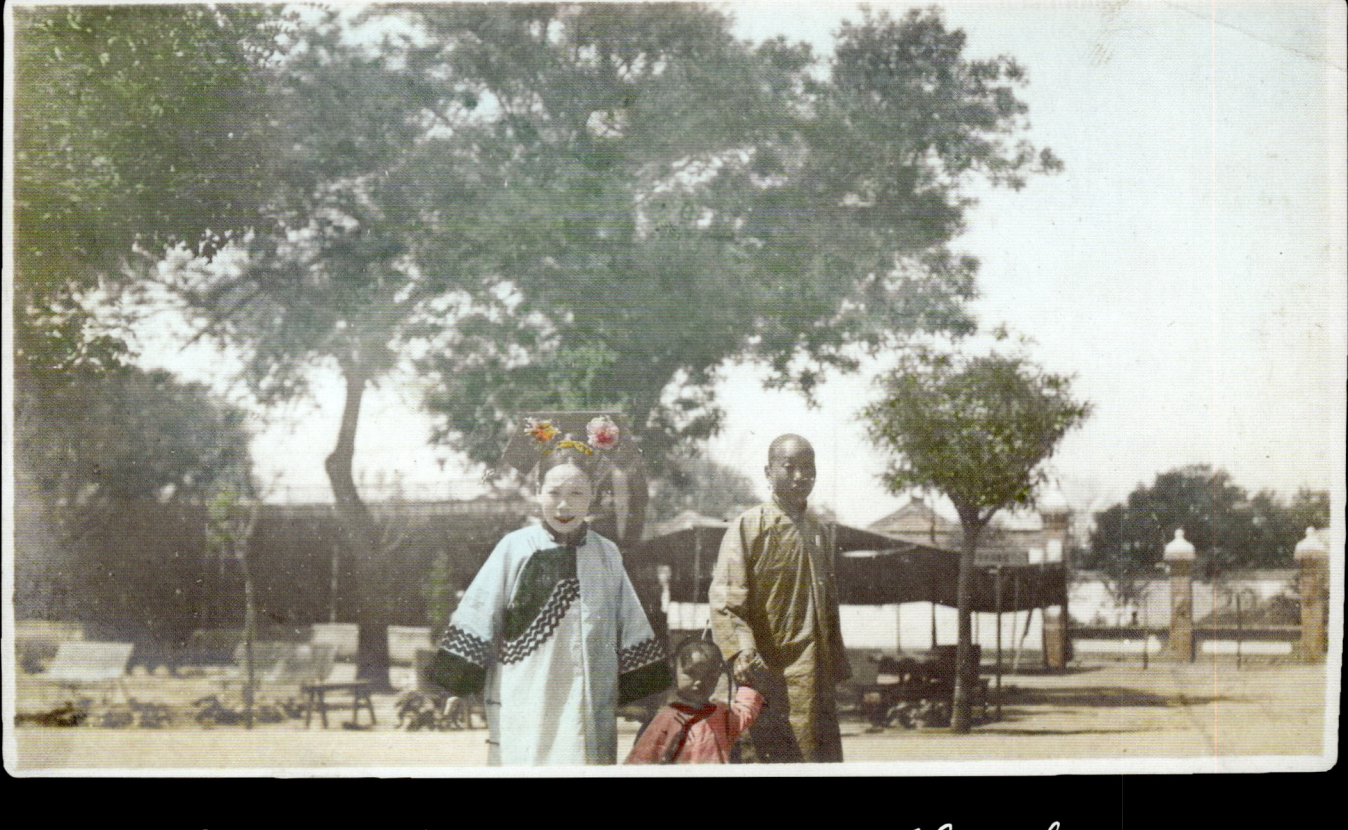

Manchu family wearing fine silk robes for a special occasion.

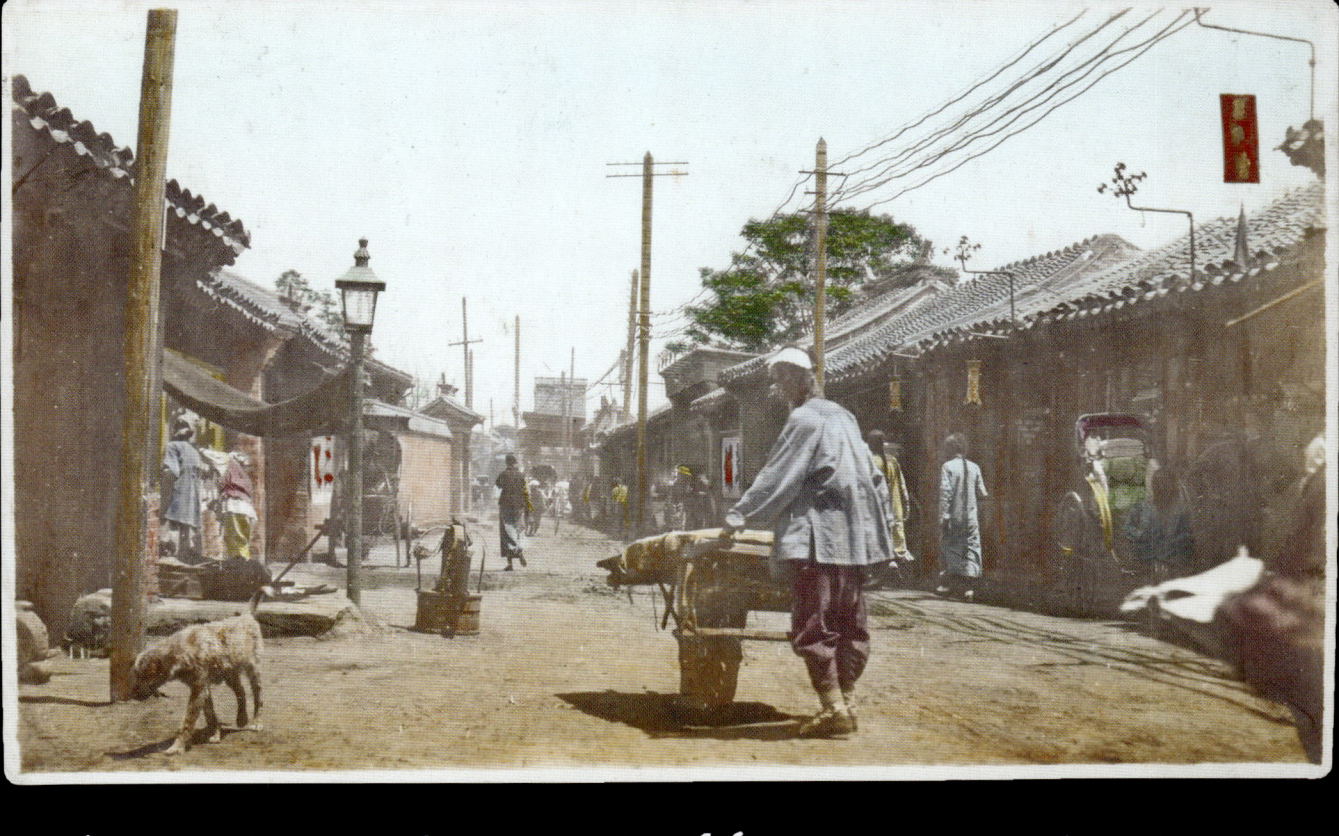

A peddler with his wheel barrow on a dusty Peking street.

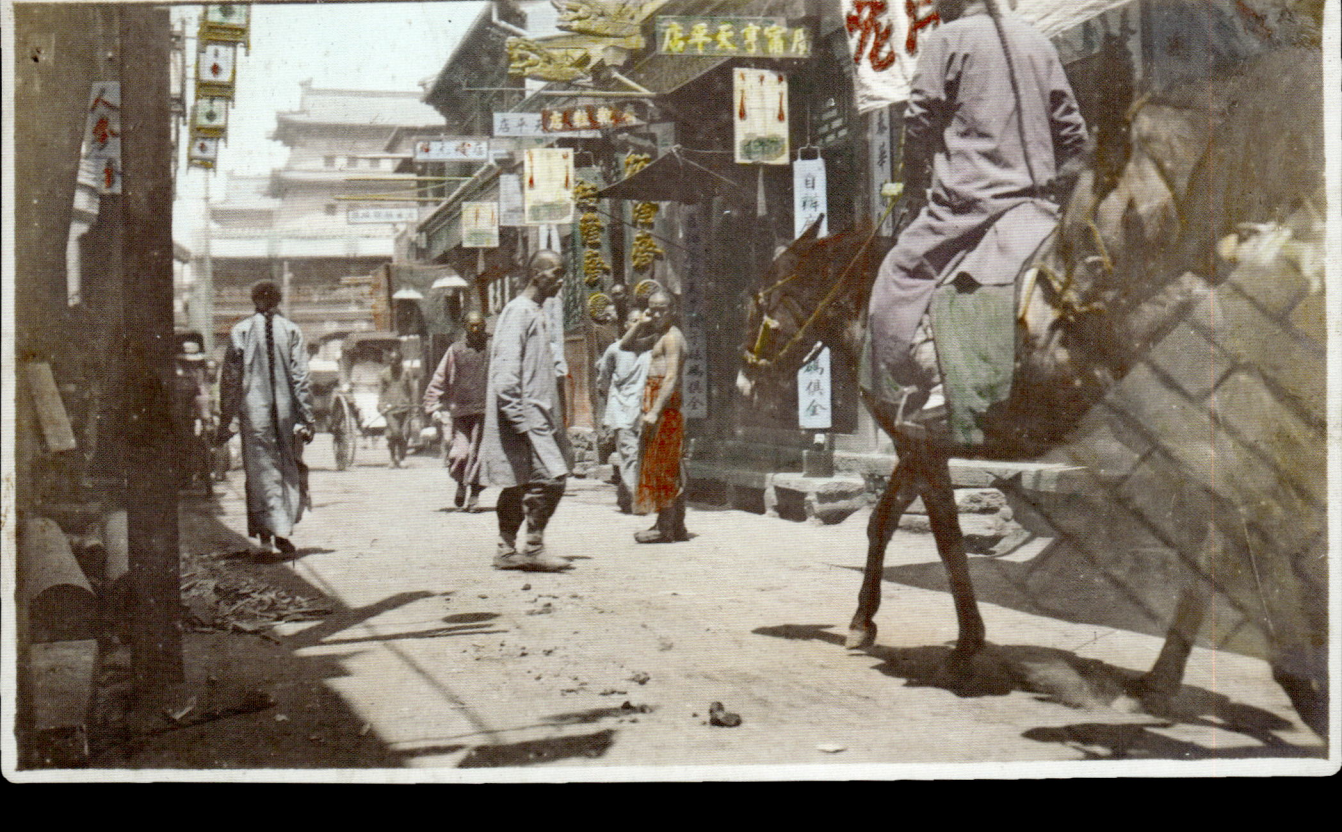

We were eager to explore the shops that lined the narrow streets.

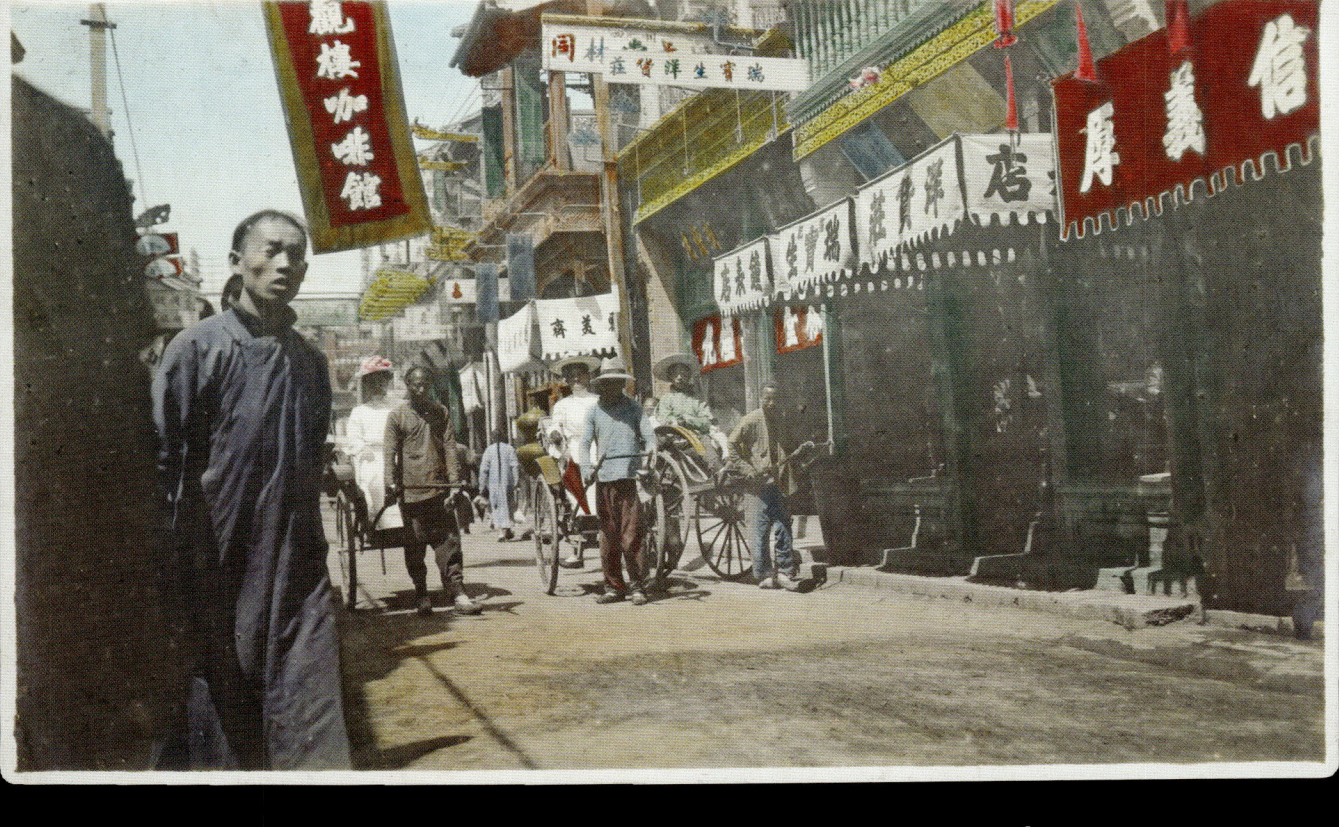

The weather was finally warm enough to wear our summer whites.

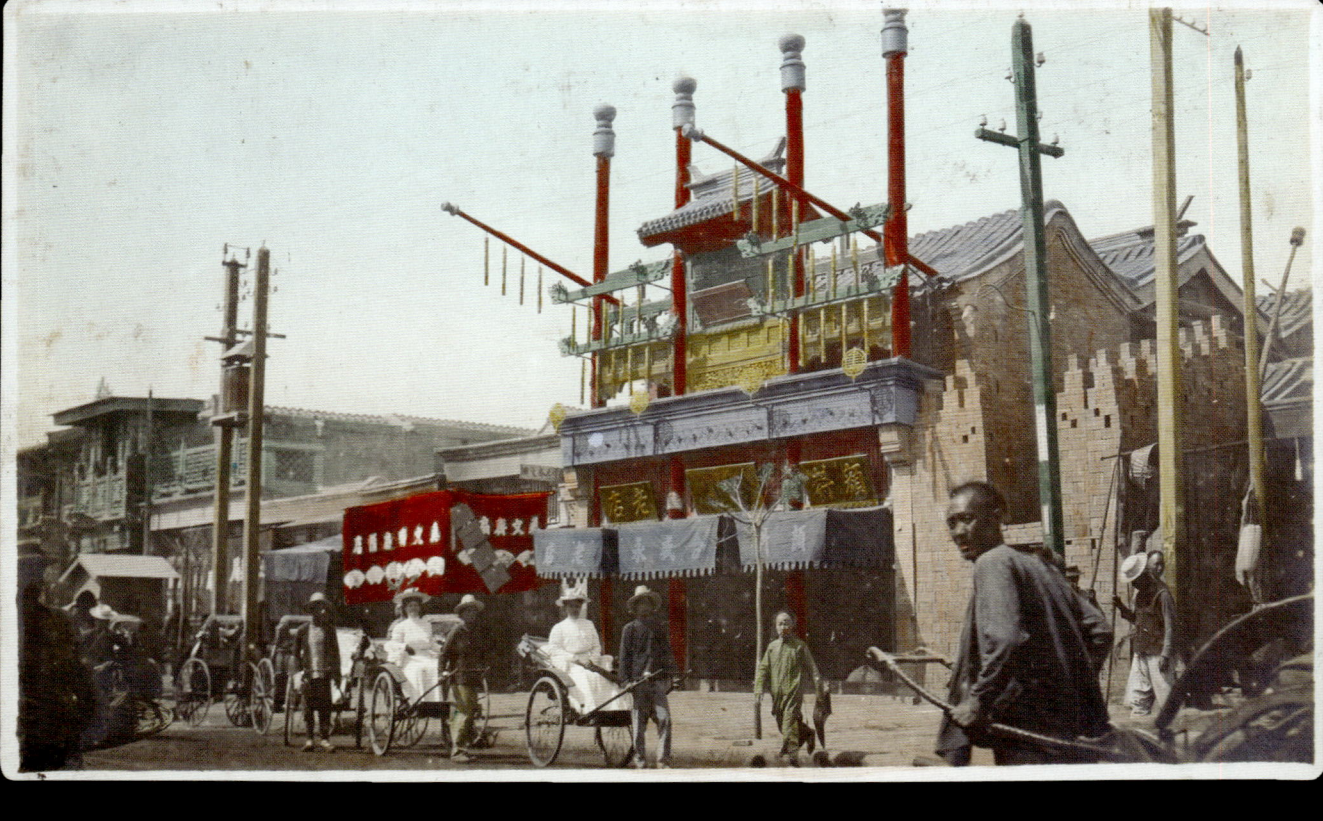

Dining out at a restaurant was an adventure where the only choice was to use chop sticks.

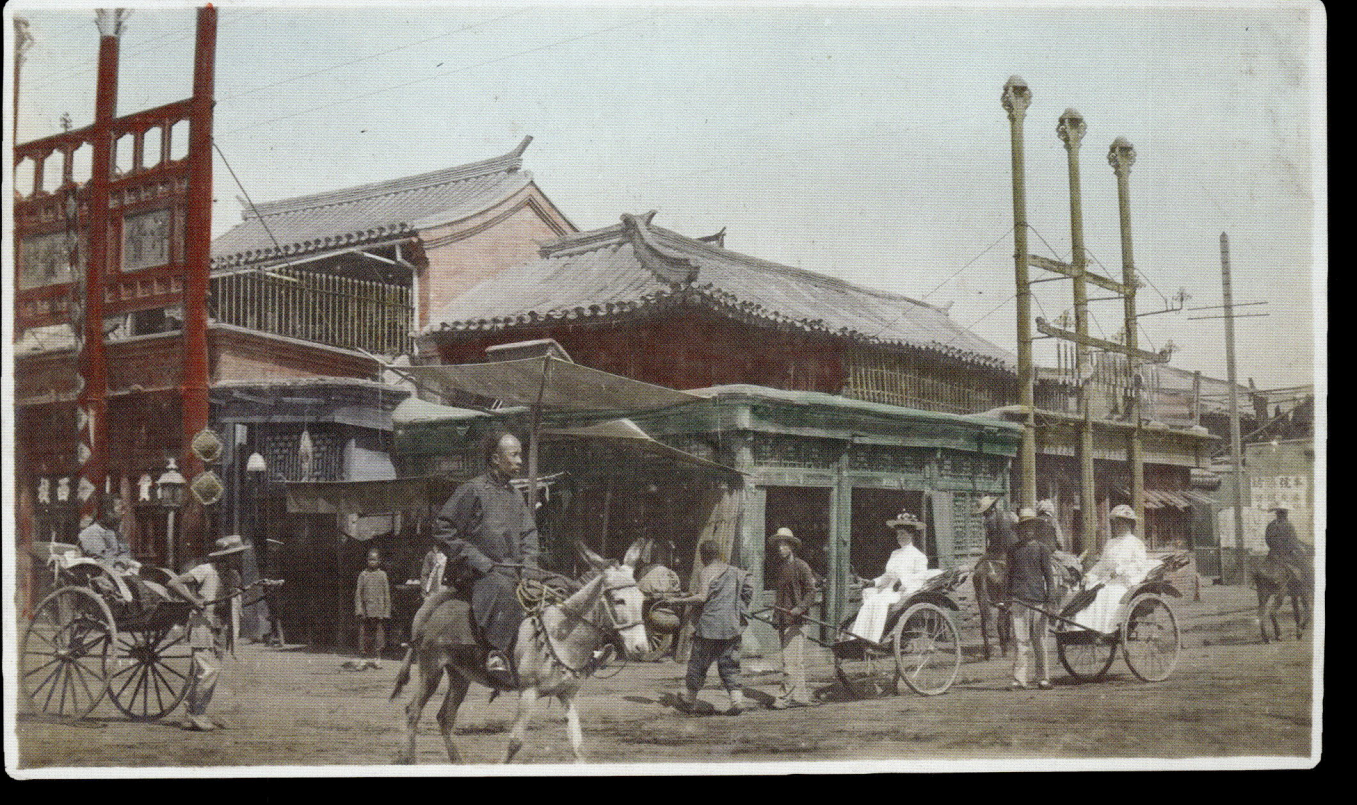

Luncheon was most satisfactory, although identifying the content of the meal was a challenge.

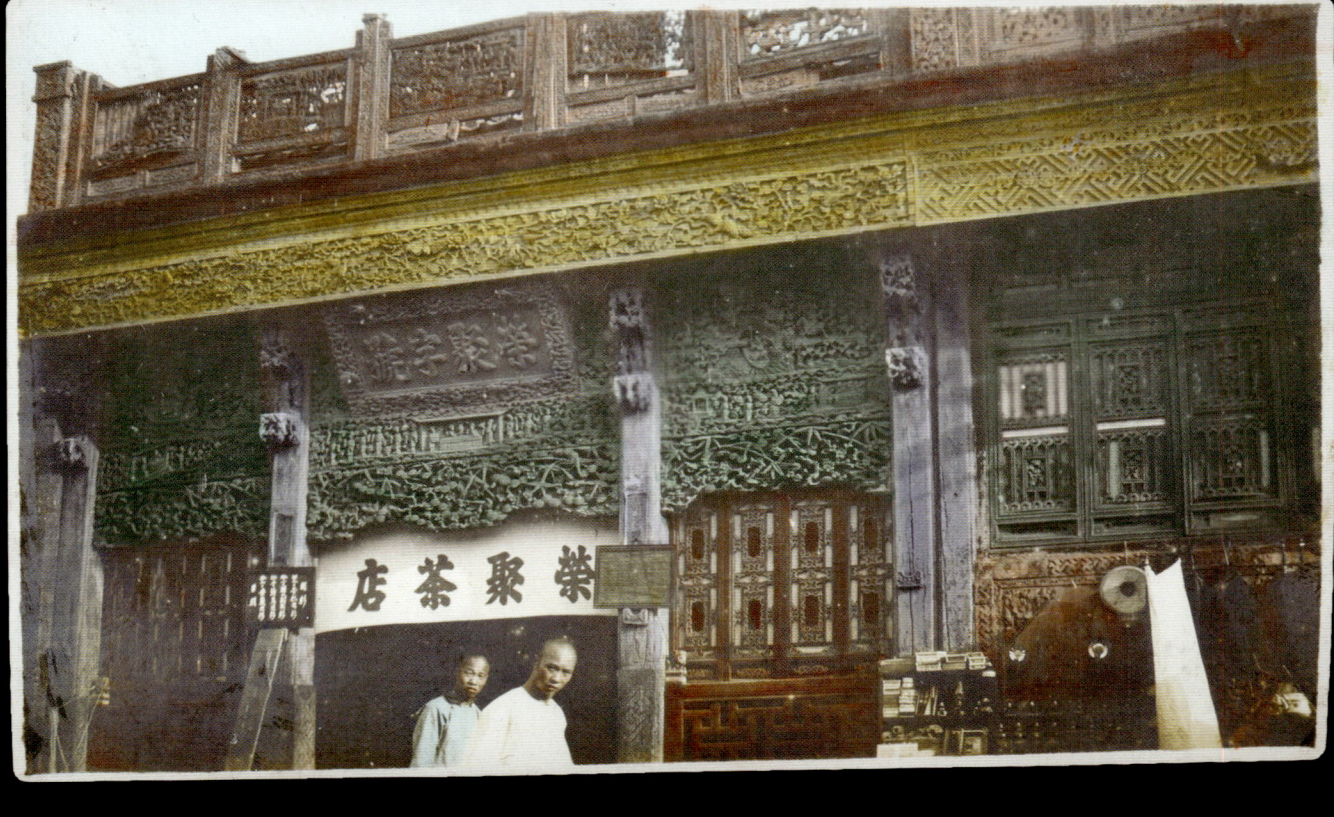

Windows covered with carved lattice are lined in parchment to keep the interiors cool in summer and warm in winter.

We hoped for an opportunity to go to the theatre and watch a performance of the famous and popular Peking Opera.

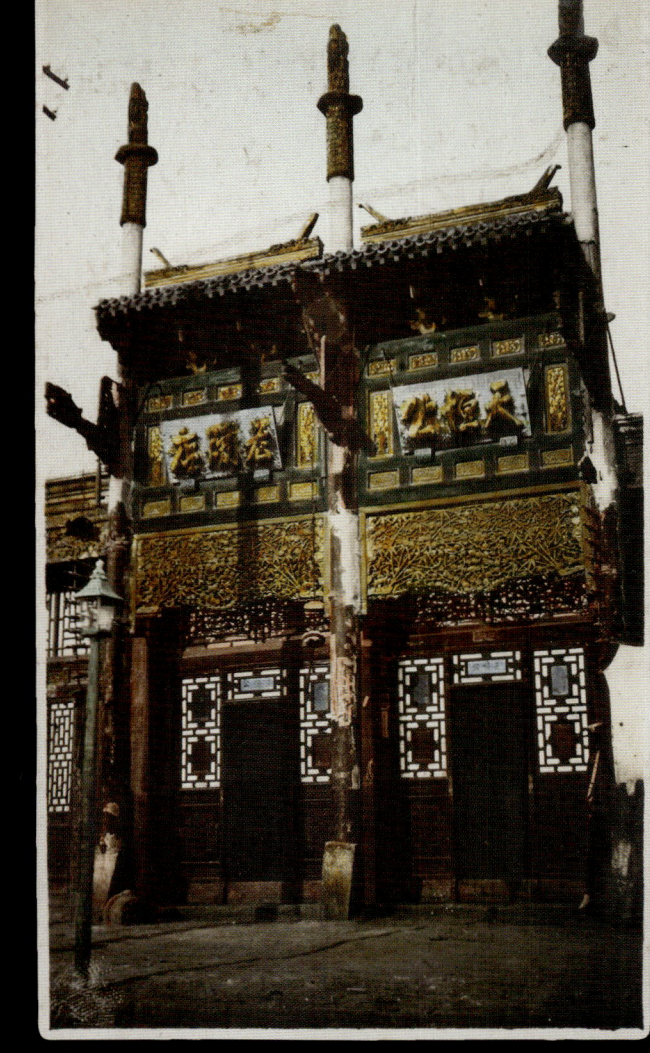

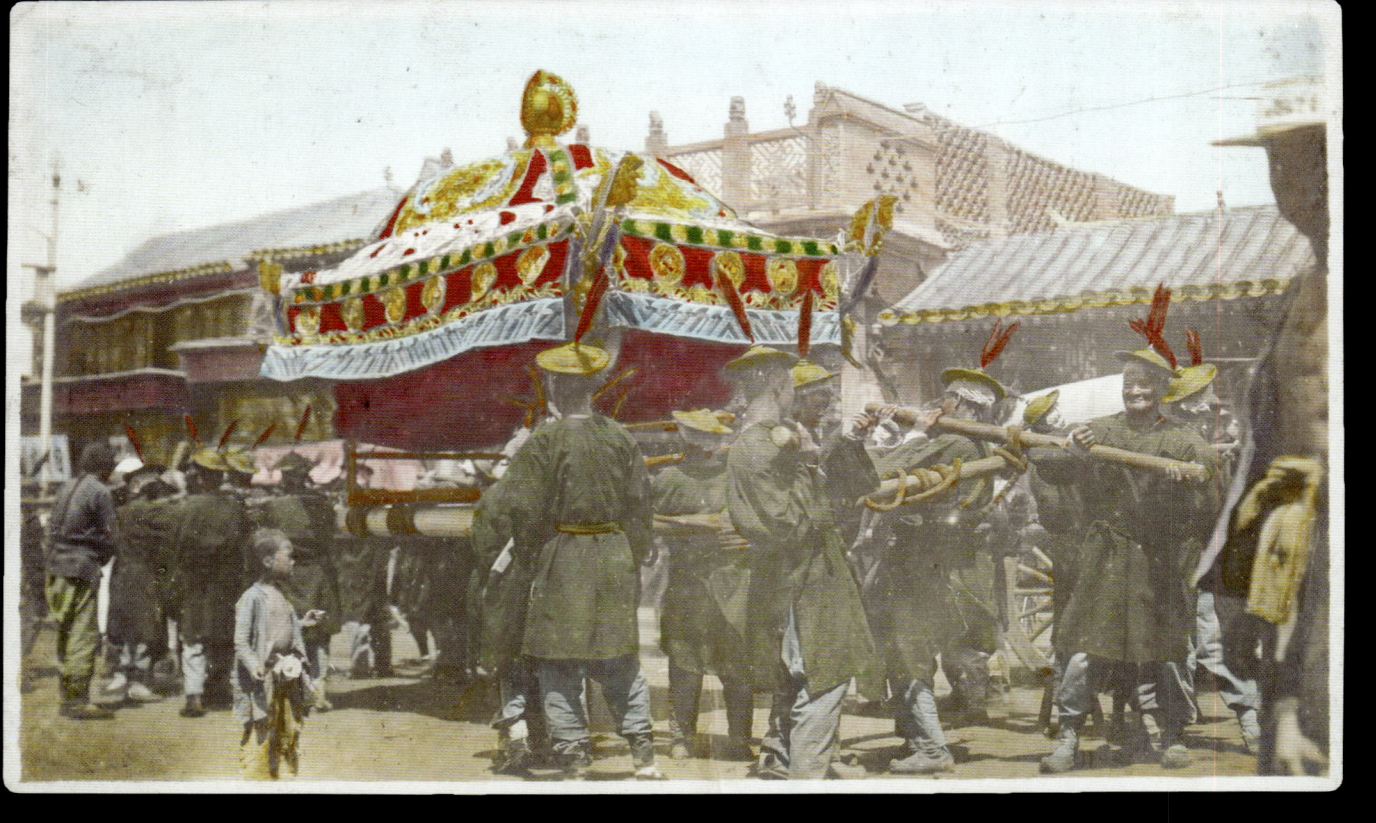

Chinese funerals are colorful and noisy celebrations and bear no resemblance to our somber processionals

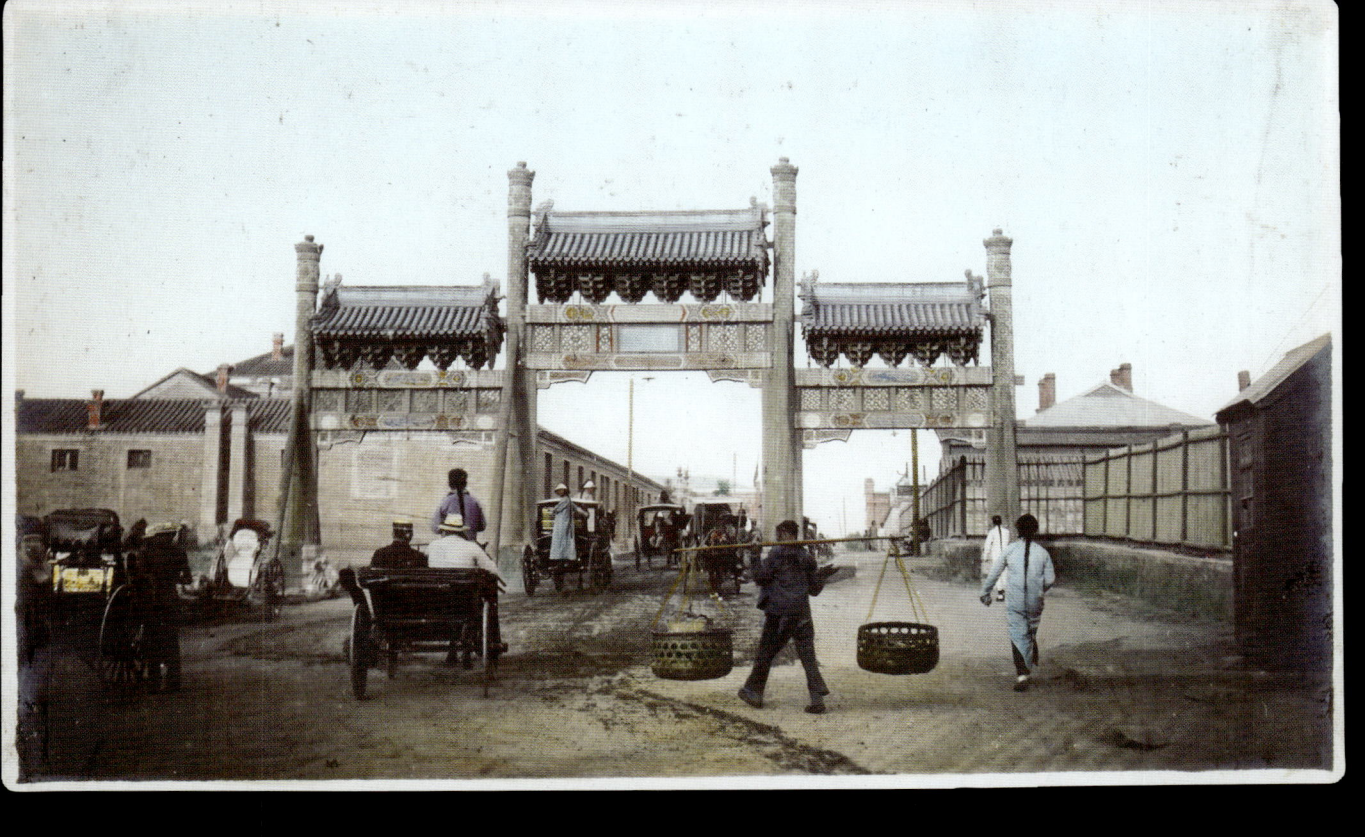

Legation Street—where foreign residents live in a separate area of the city behind high walls.

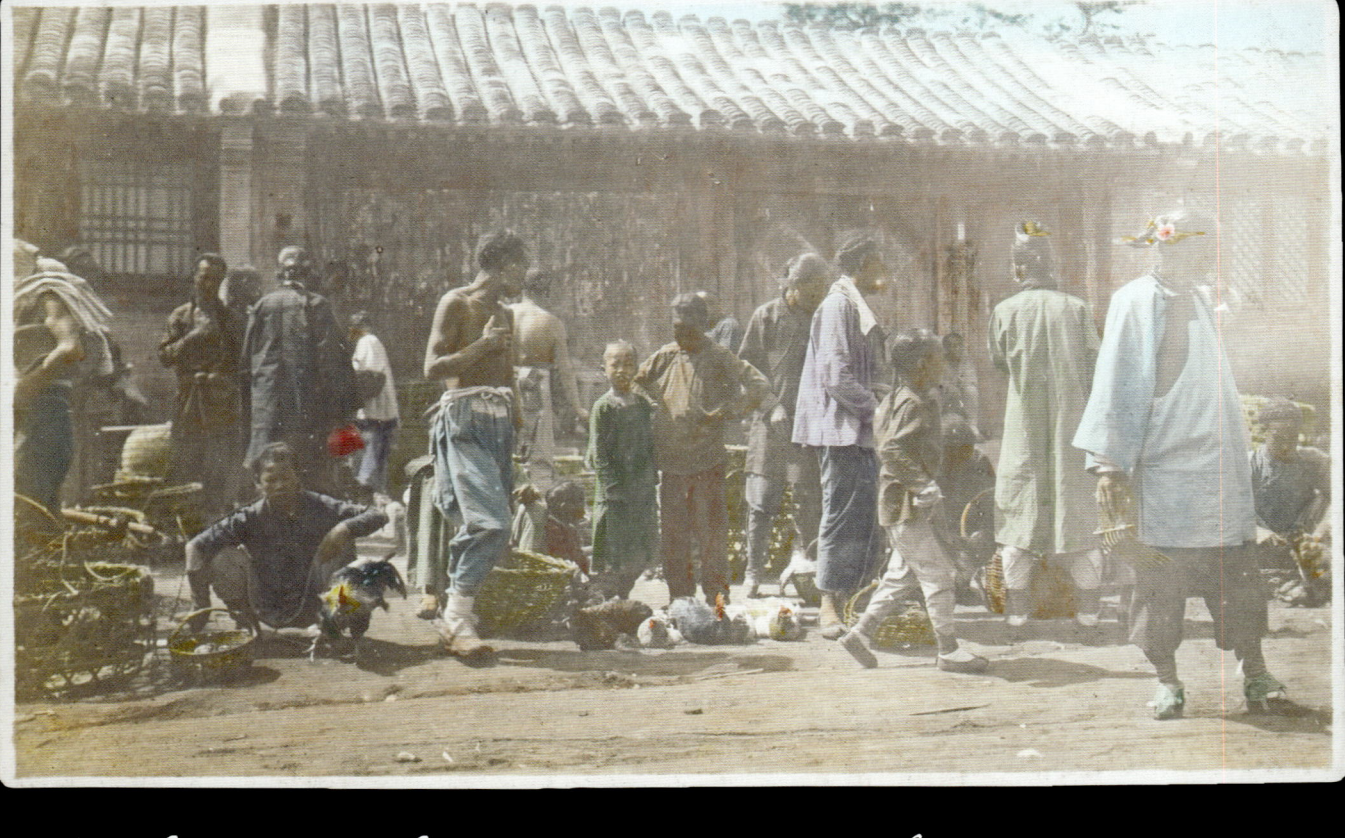

Chicken Market — the lady in blue stood in the crowded market place on tiny bound feet.

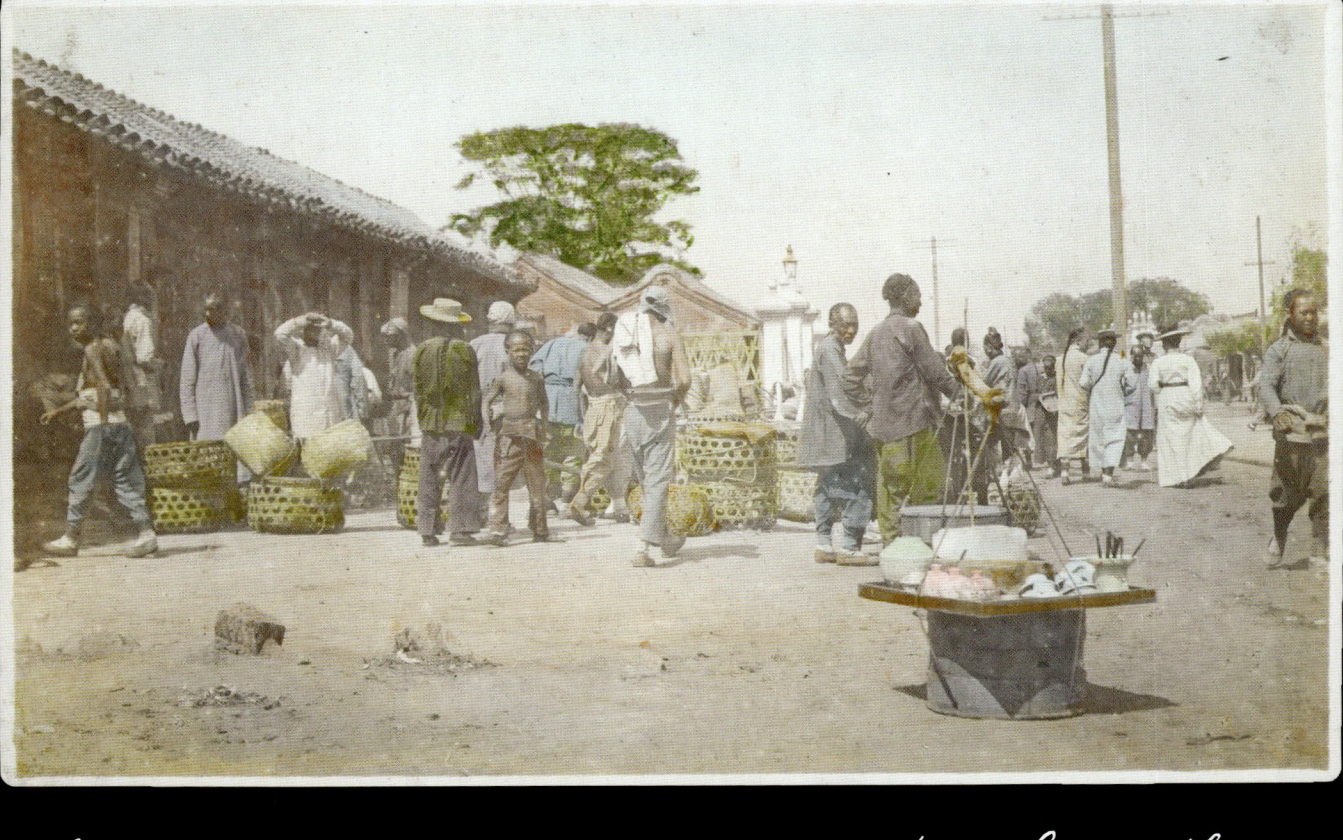

Chinese women wear trousers and jackets, thus we attracted many stares in our long dresses.

Is this a lion symbolizing Imperial Might? Or is it a watch dog guarding the Palace gate?

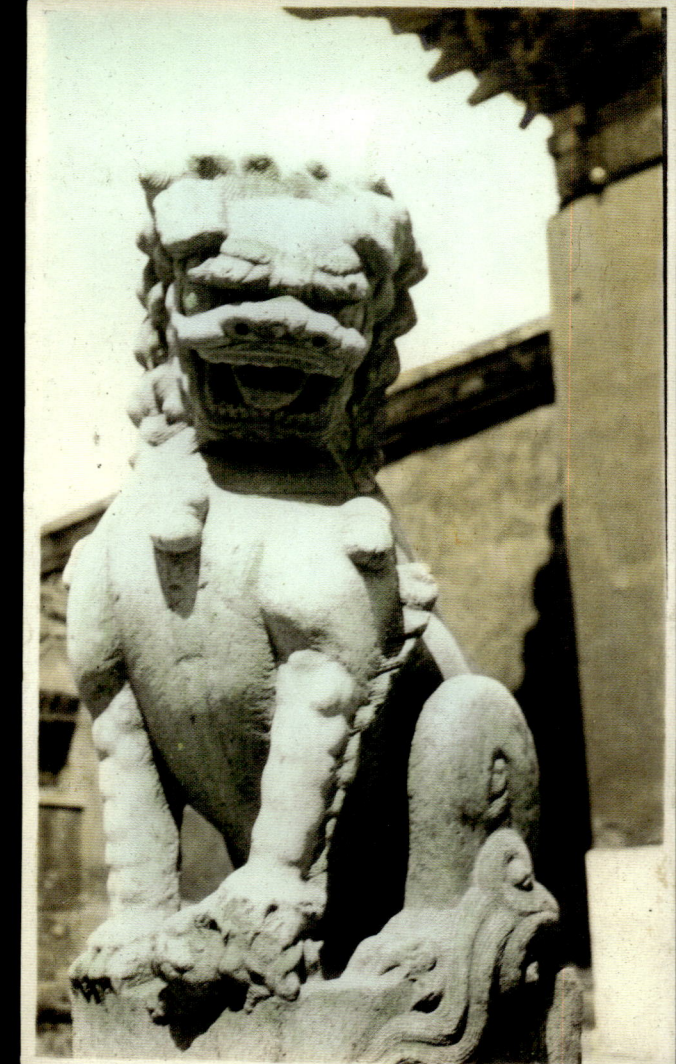

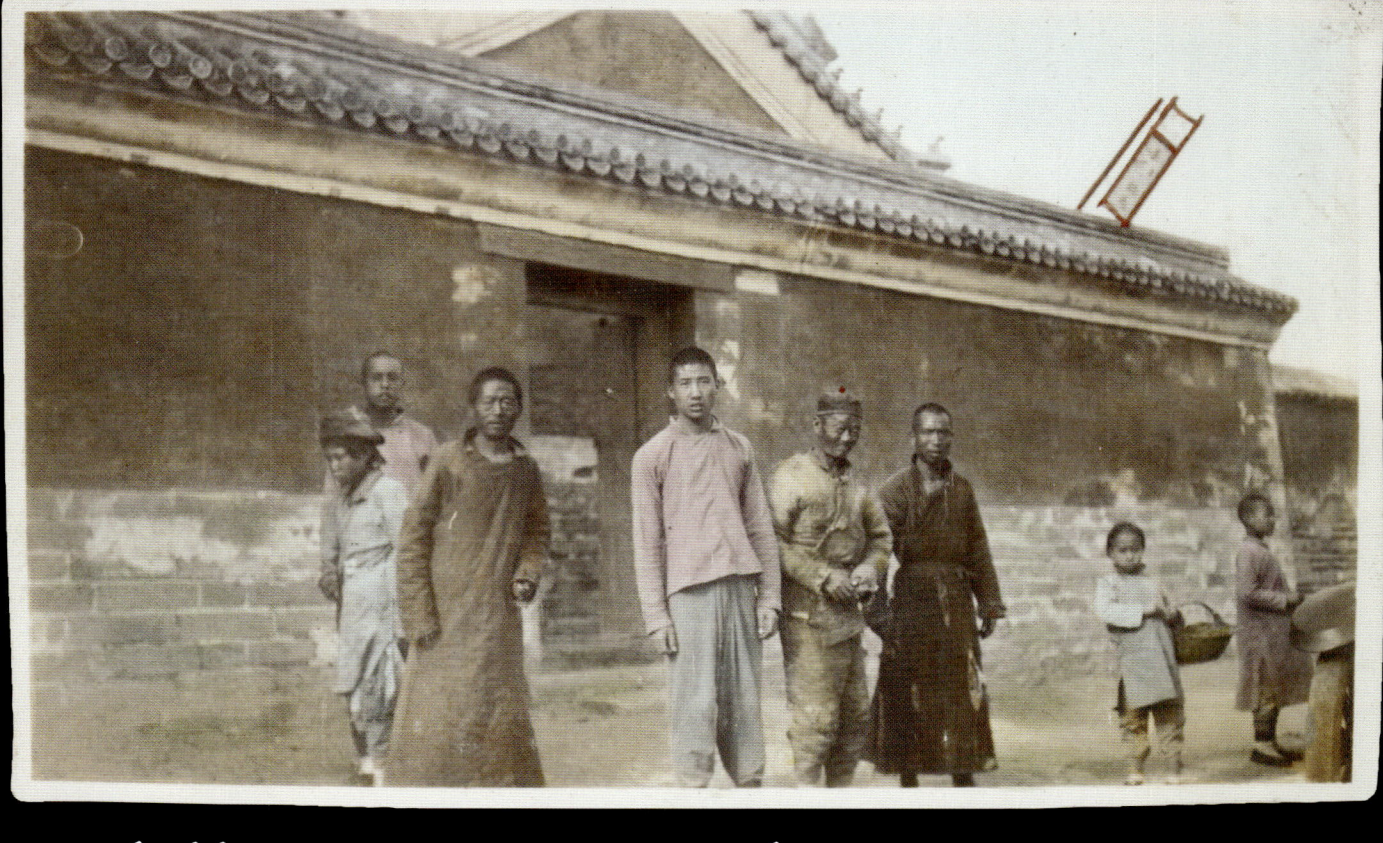

We bobbed past a group of boys in front of the Lama Morgue.

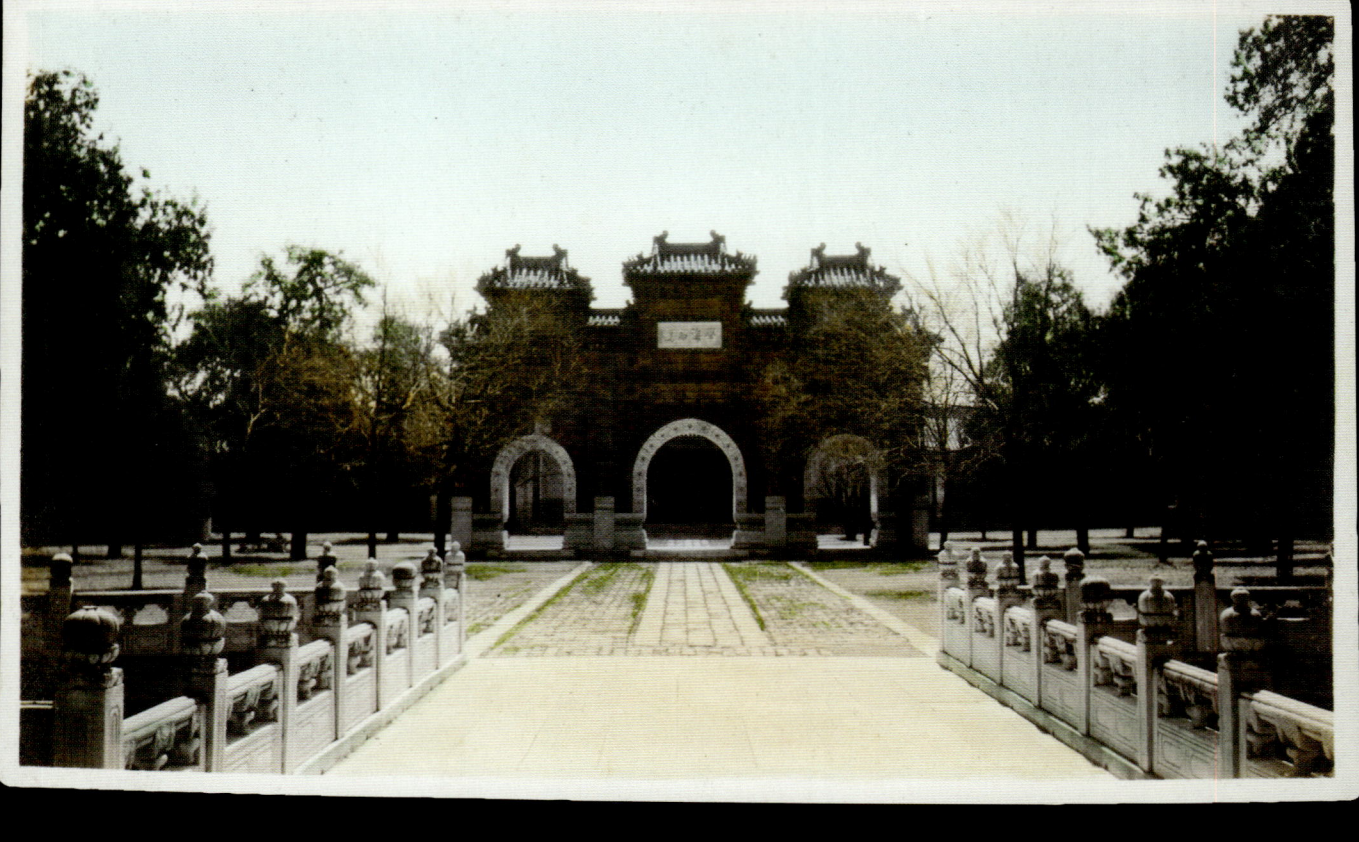

Tomb of the Banjin Lama—a stately approach to an historic monument.

Two Pagoda Temple—
on this occasion we
were accompanied by
acquaintances from the
American Legation.

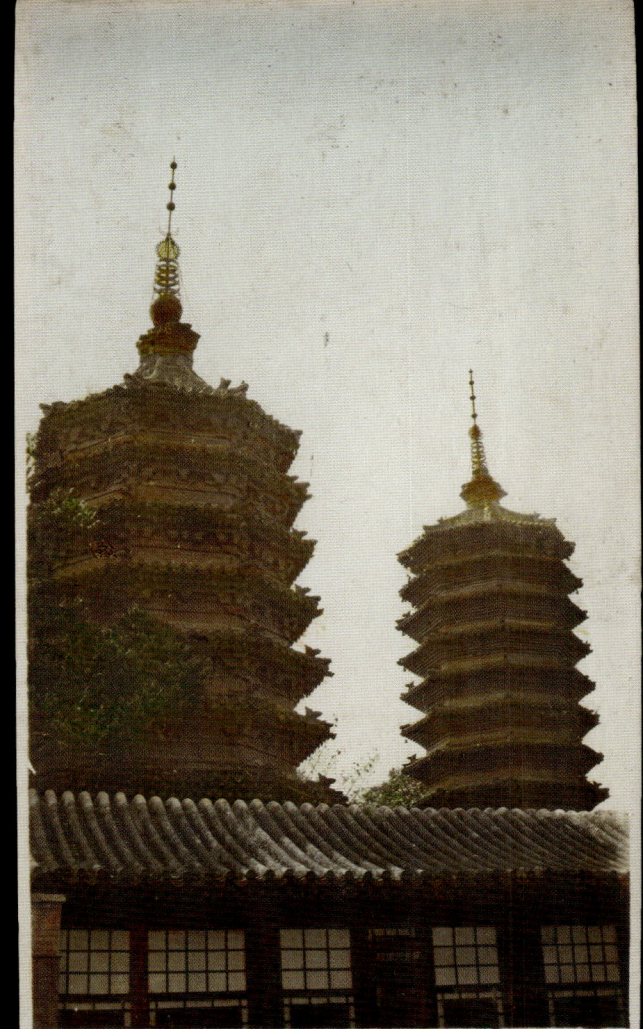

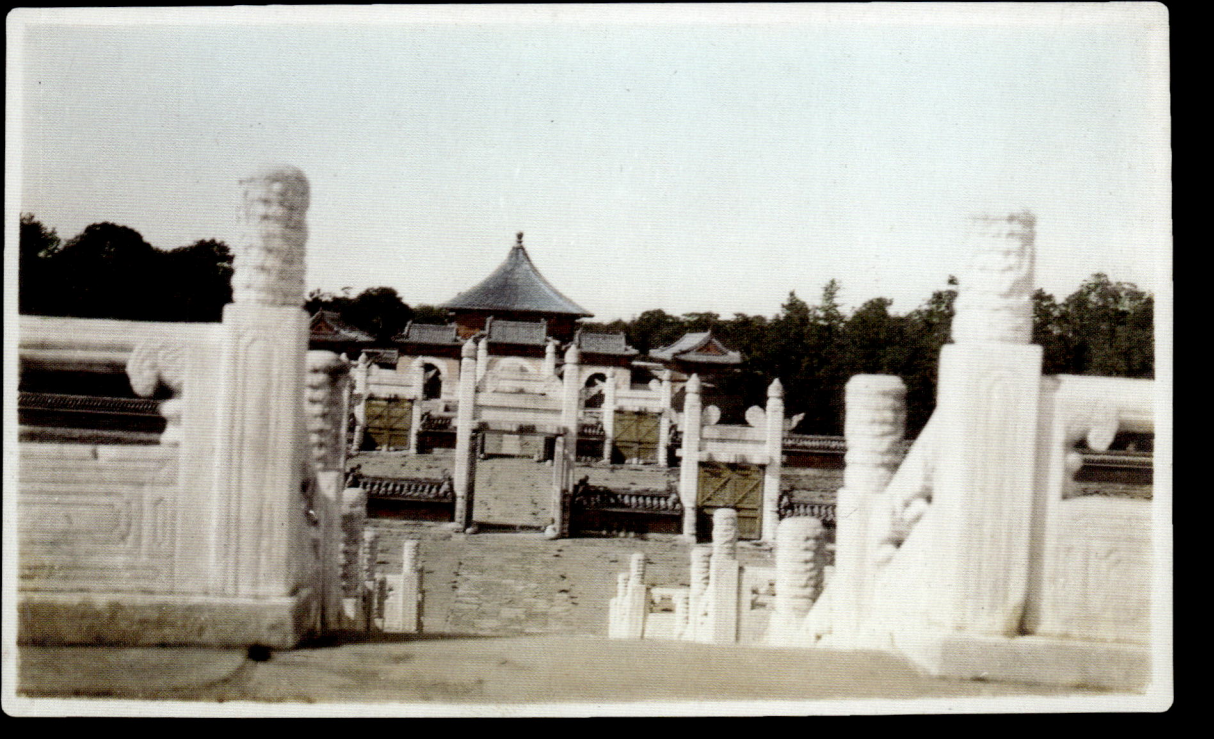

The Temple of Heaven and the famous Whispering Stadium. I stood at one end and whispered a message to a companion at the other end. She heard it as clearly as if I had been next to her. Amazing!

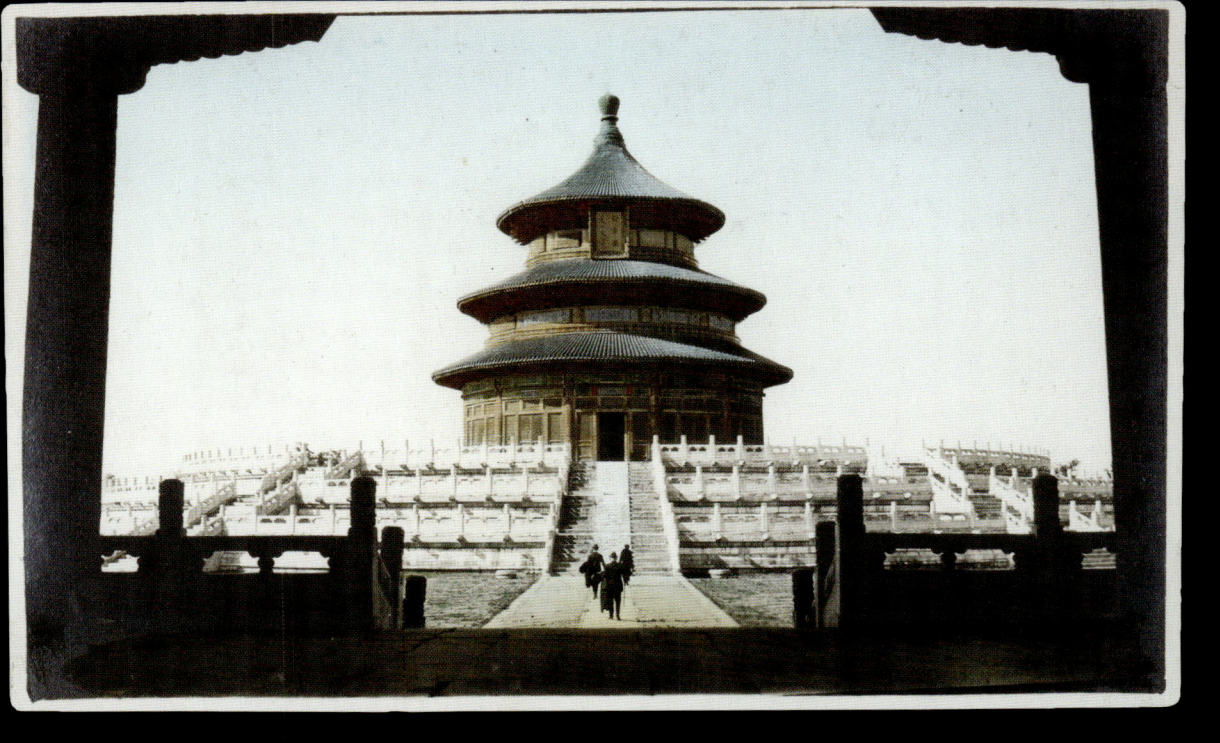

The Temple of Heaven is among the most famous and sacred buildings in Peking. The distinctive roof is somewhat reminiscent of the marvelous hats worn by Mandarin gentlemen.

Thousand year old temple—Peking. We found these statues a bit alarming with their bulging eyes and frightening stance.

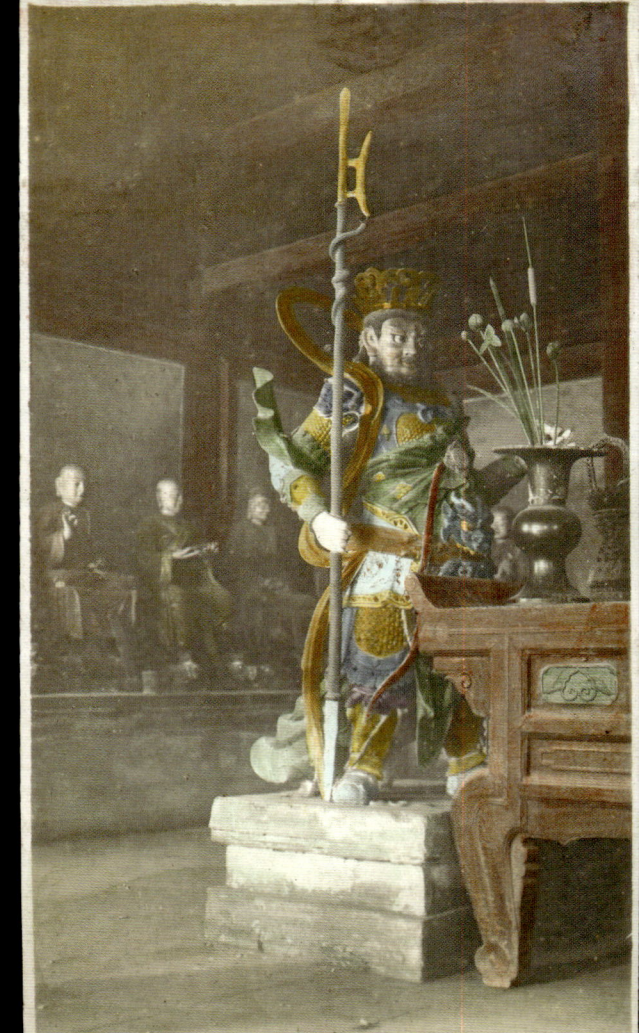

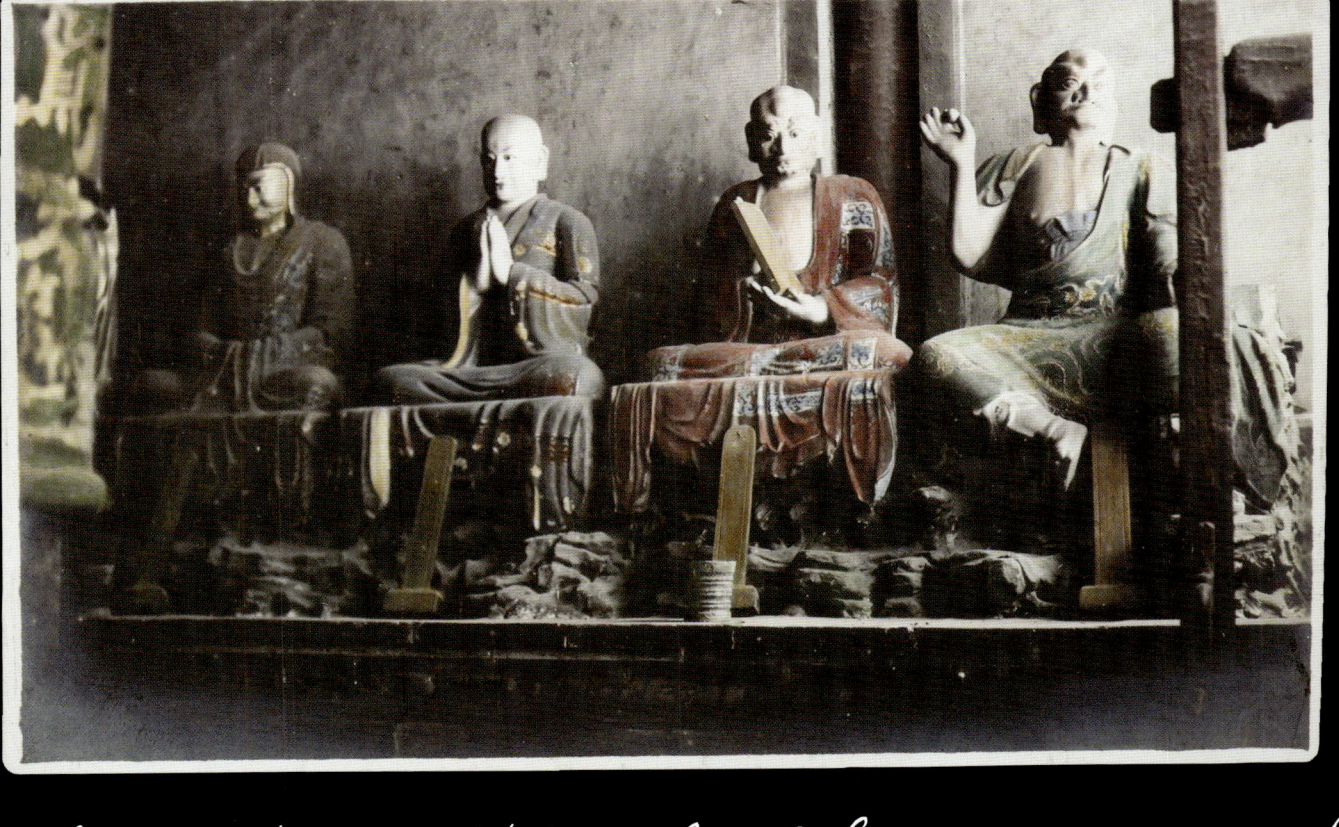

Thousand year old temple—Peking. More carved wooden statues, but these had a friendly and benevolent demeanor.

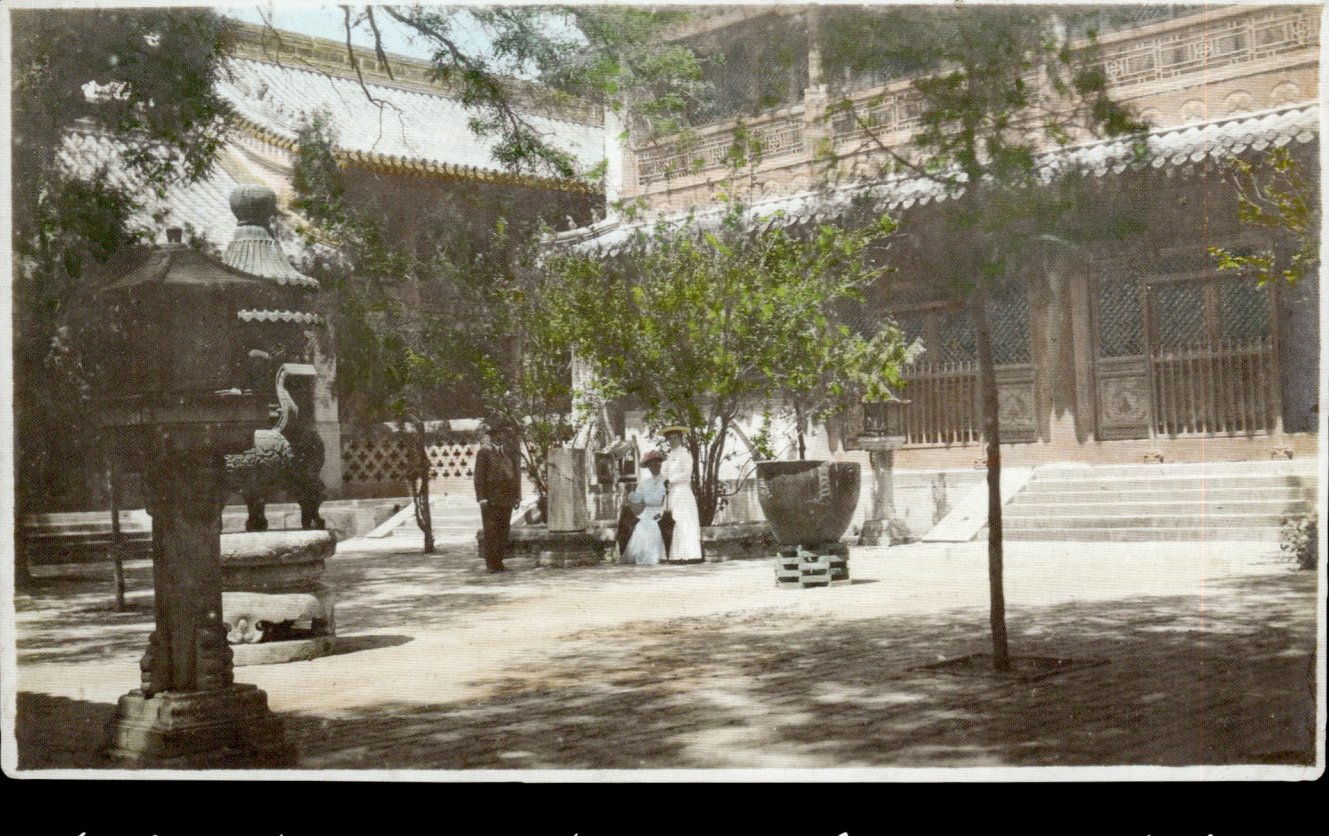

A shaded courtyard was a welcome respite from the midday sun.

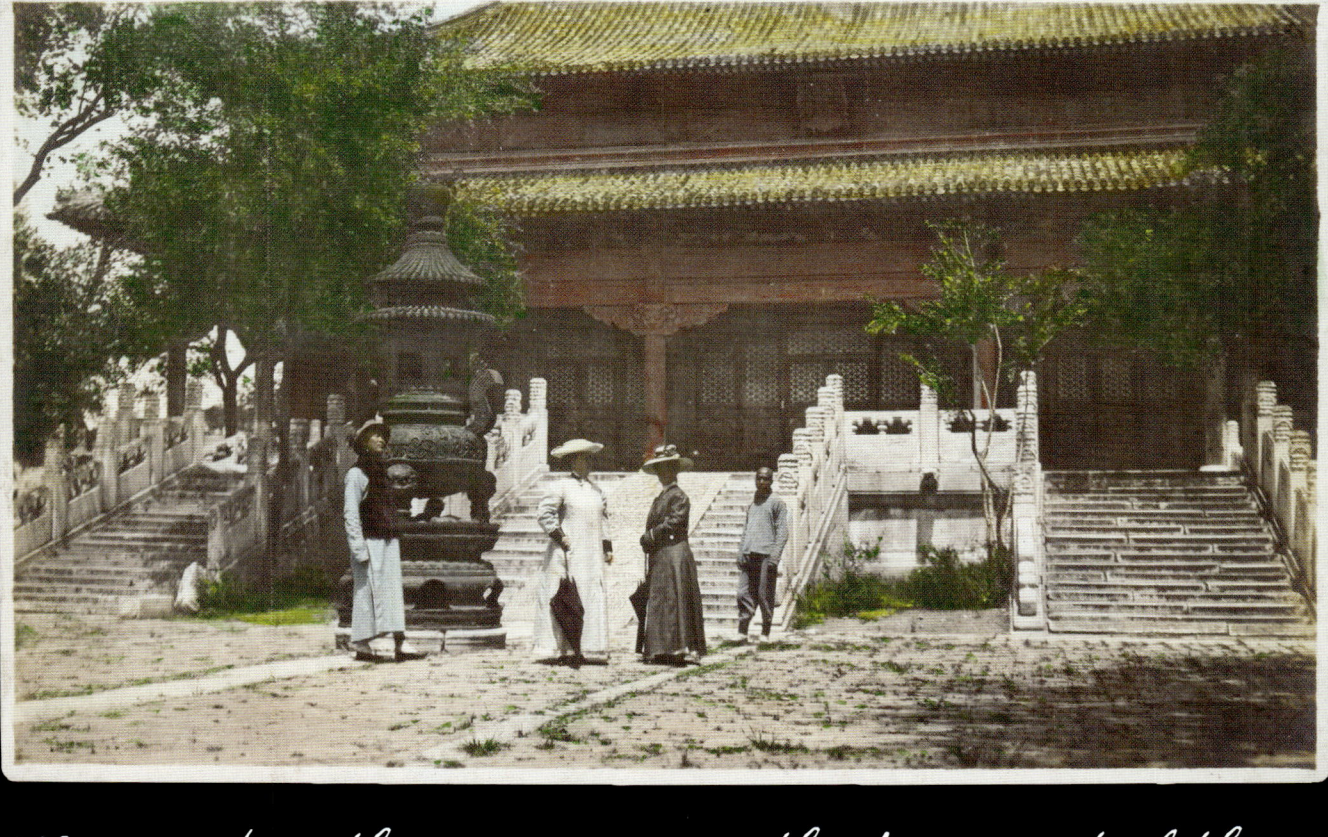

We posed with our guide in the forecourt of the Yellow Temple.

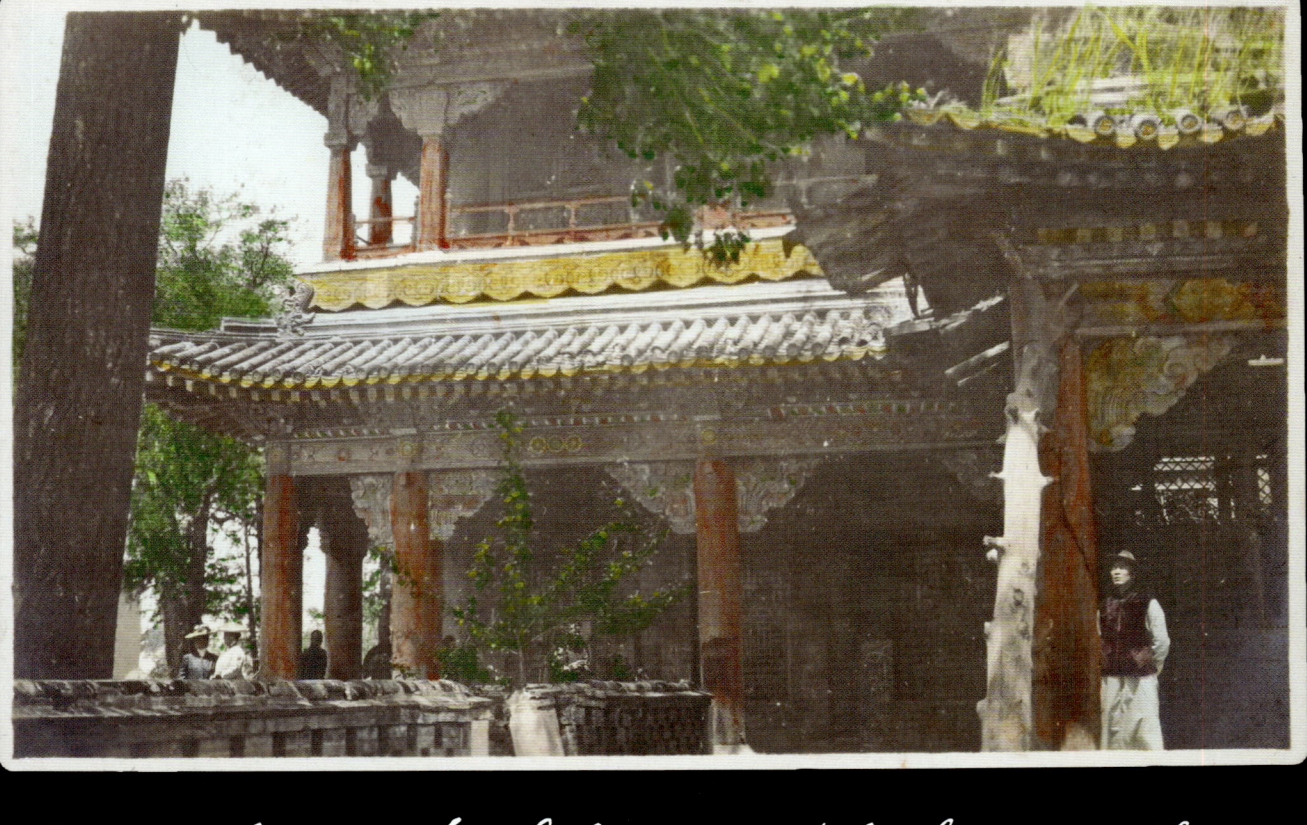

Not until I was back home and looking with a magnifying glass did I notice an unidentified man in the shadows behind me.

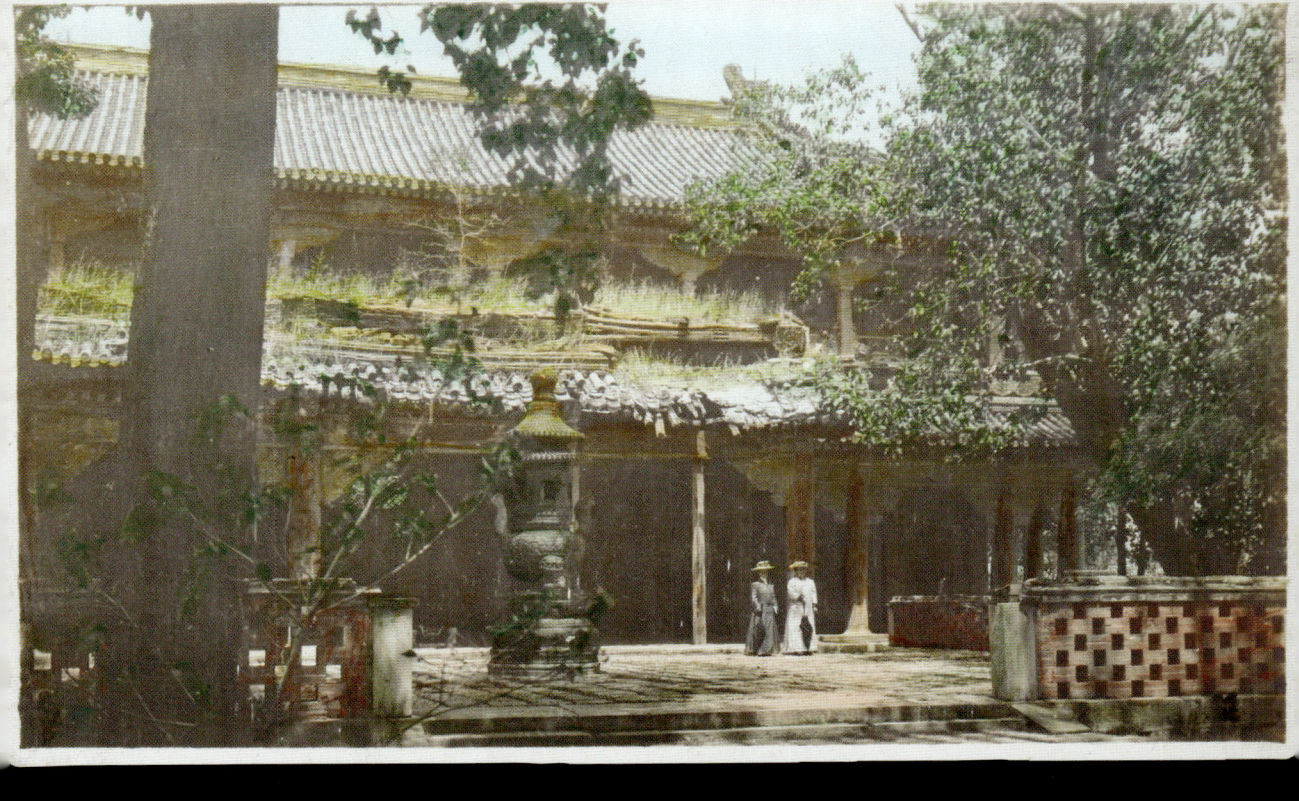

We were not able to enter this building in the
compound. I shall always be curious to know
what slumbered within its walls.

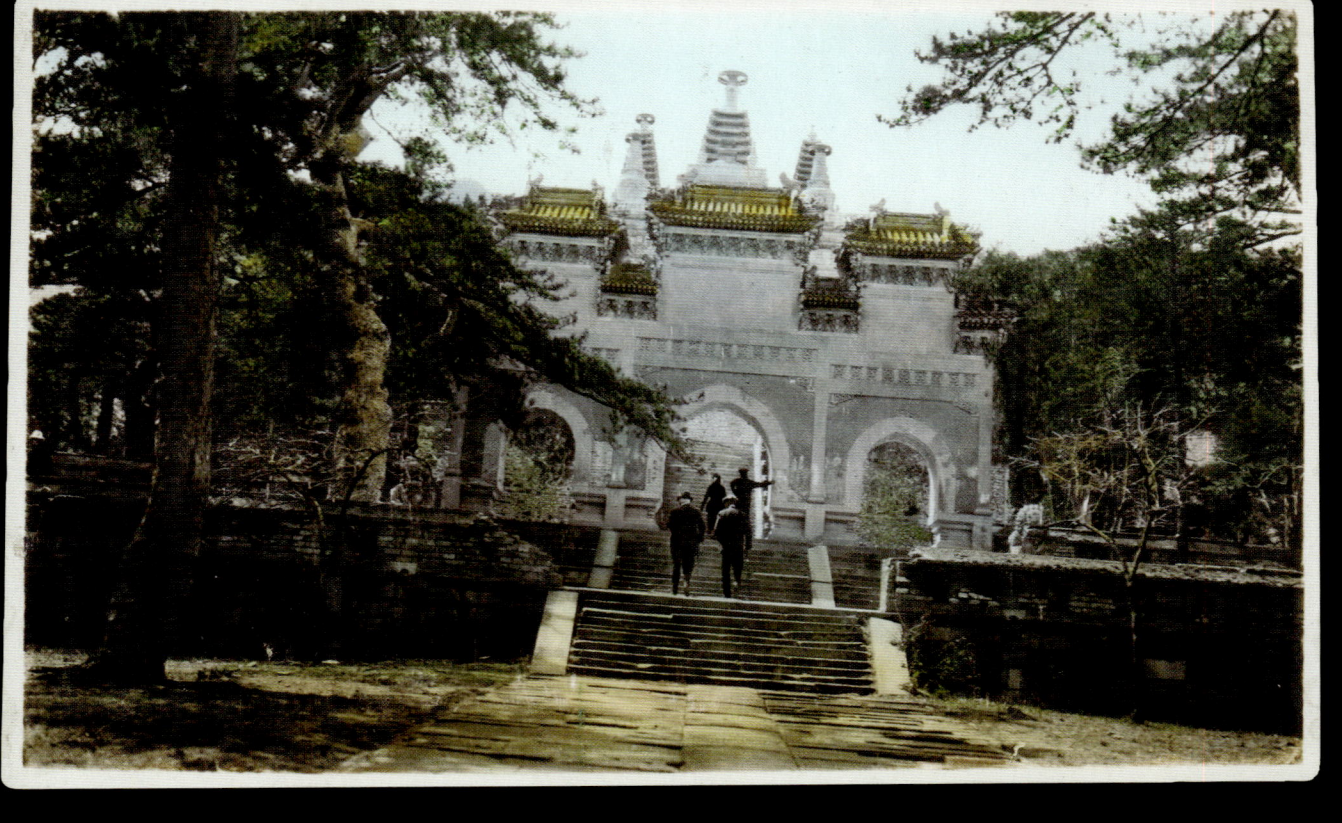

Staircase and gateway leading to the White Cloud Temple—Peking

White Cloud Temple—
built in 1227 at the
end of the reign of
Genghis Khan.

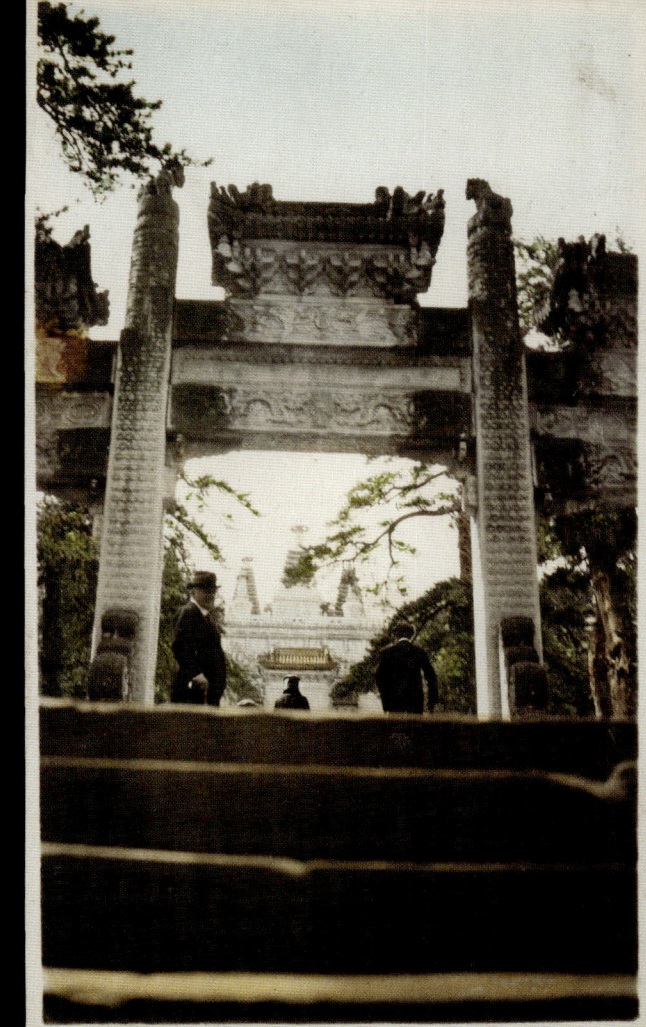

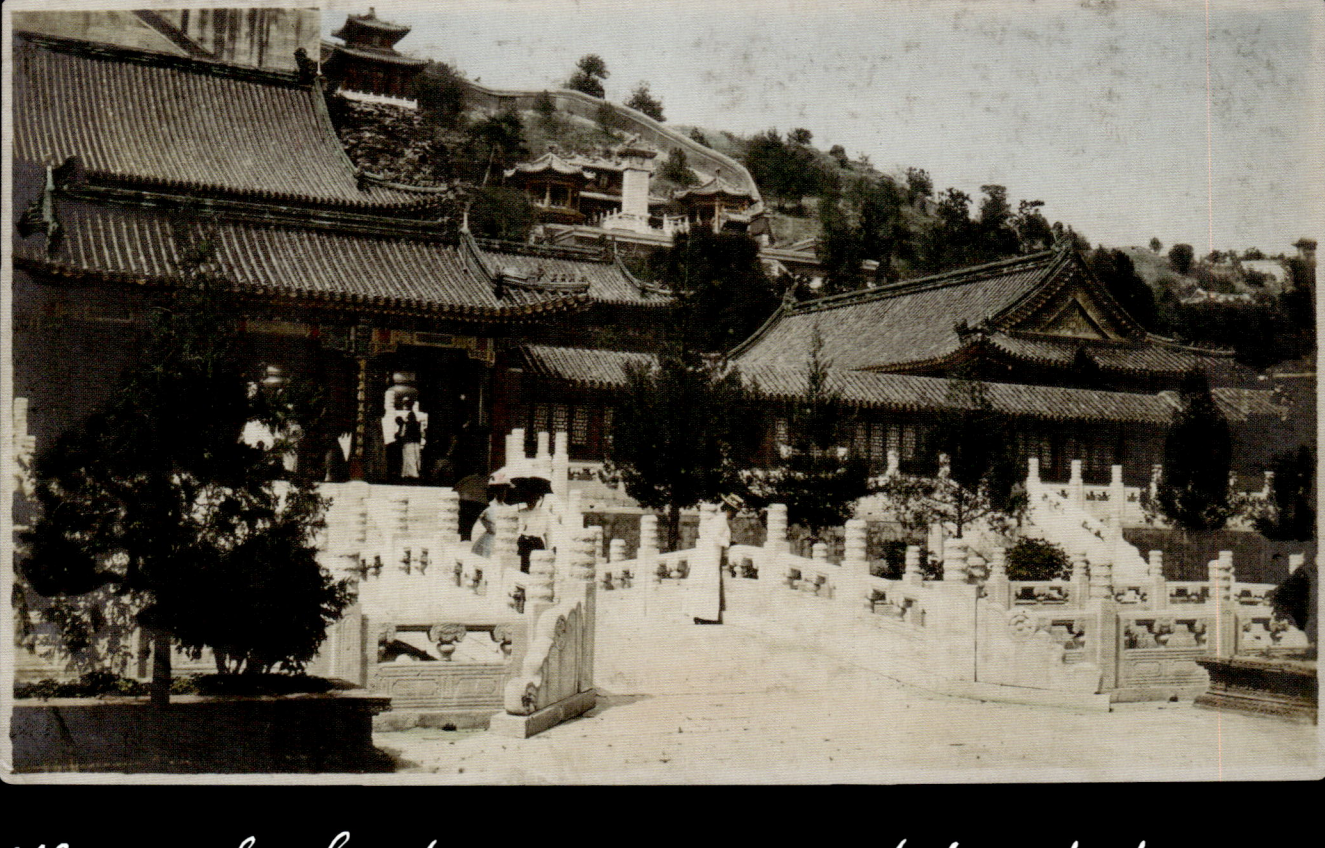

We were lucky to receive an invitation to tour
the Summer Palace, beloved residence of the late
Dowager Empress.

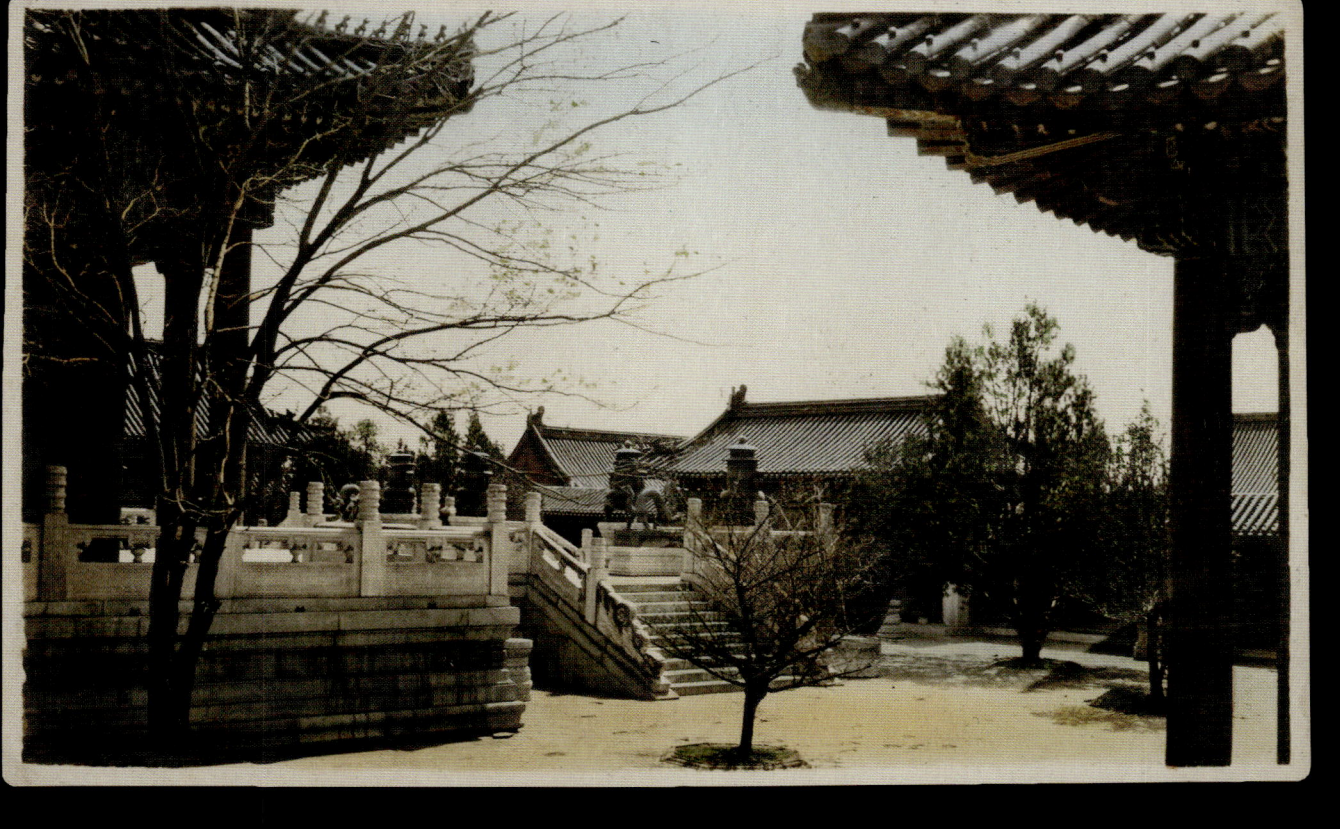

After near destruction 50 years ago, the Empress all but emptied the Treasury toward the restoration of the Palace.

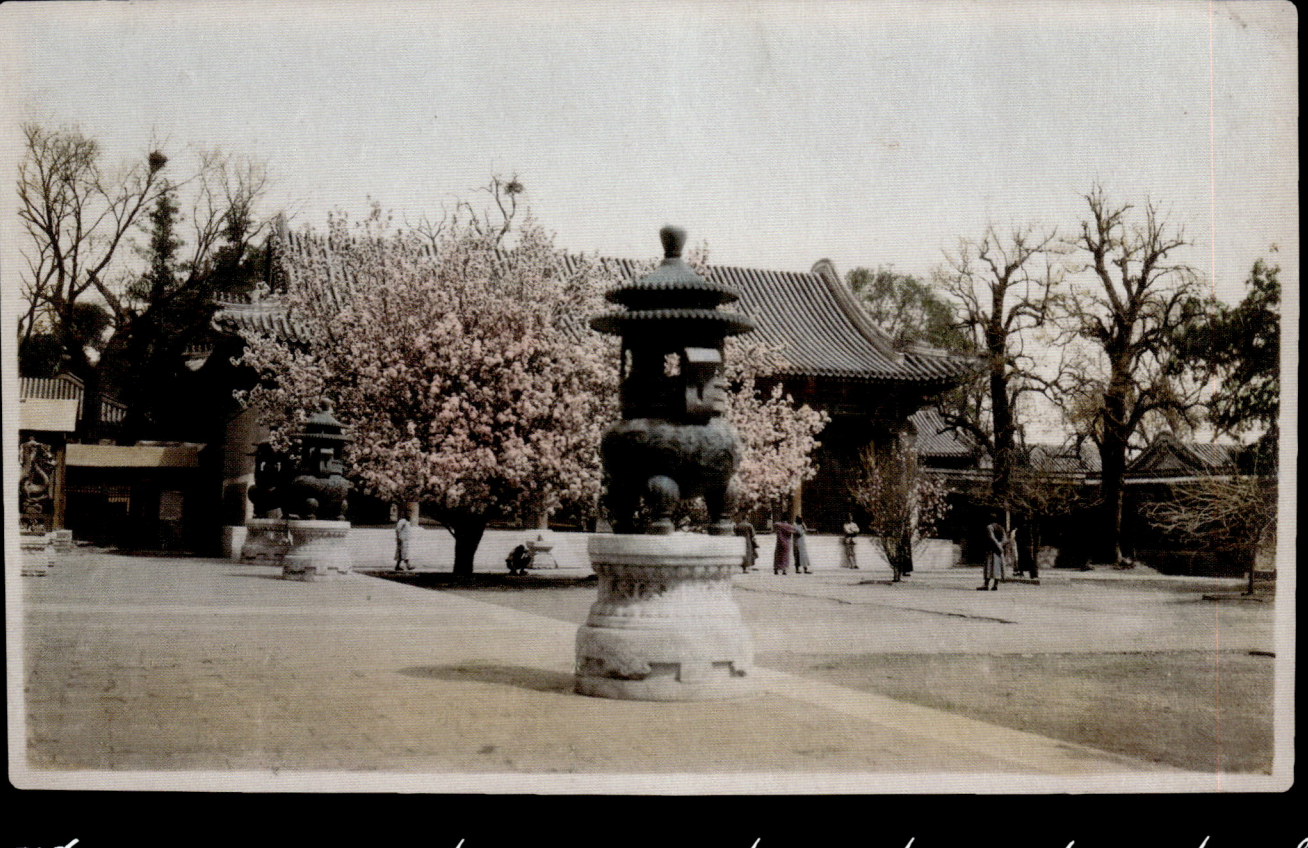

The gardens and compounds and courtyards of the Summer Palace attracted few visitors apart from we four Americans.

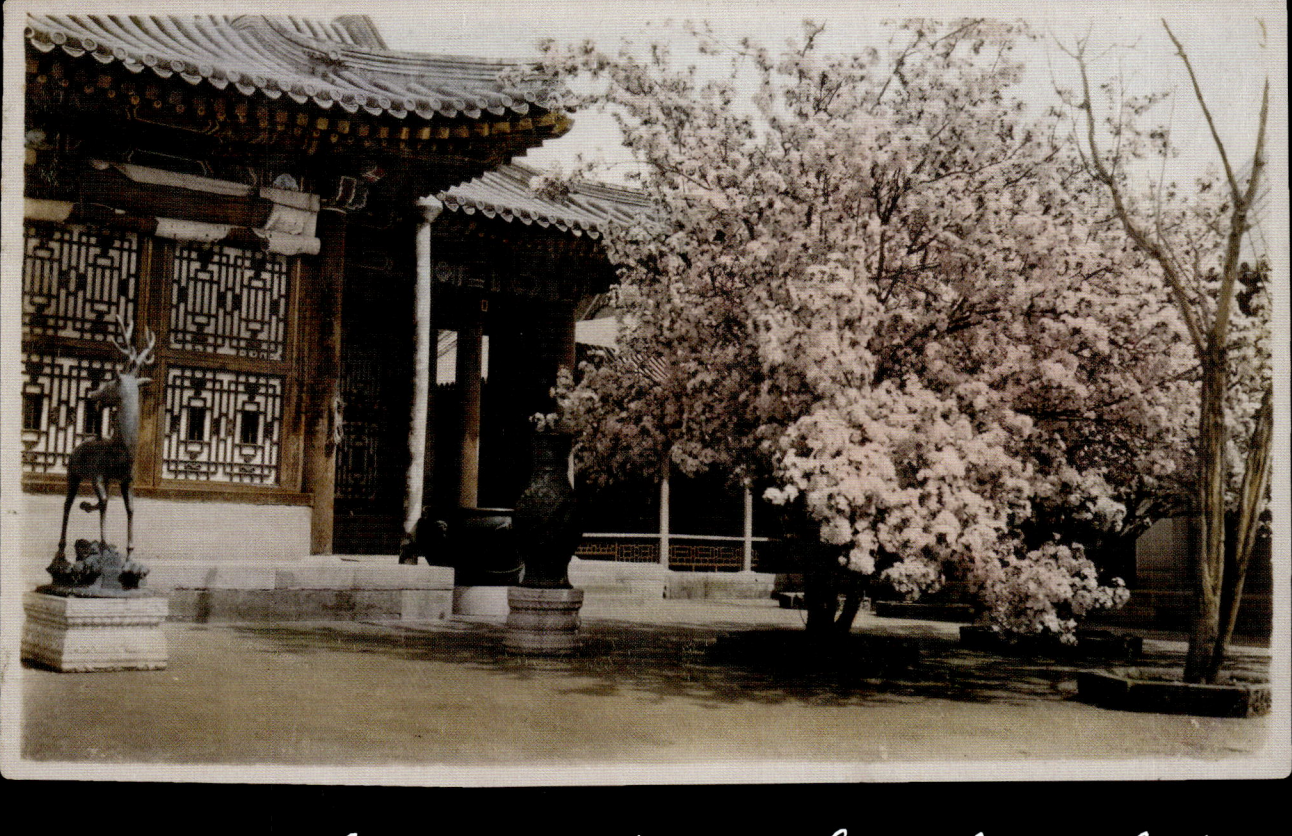

Bronze sculptures and a pink crab apple tree in front of a pavilion with blue roof tiles and a carved and painted facade.

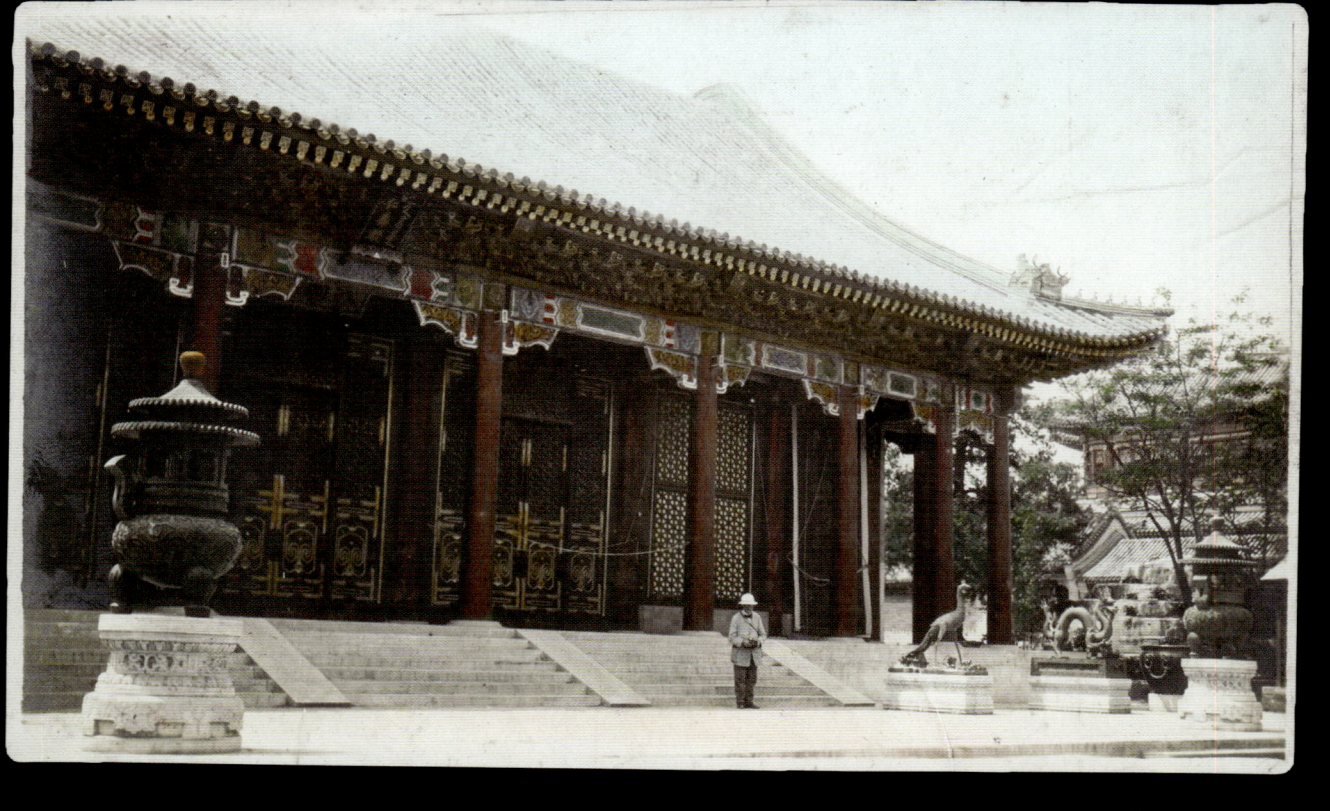

Who should have found us as we toured the Summer Palace? Byron L. Smith—a friend all the way from Chicago!

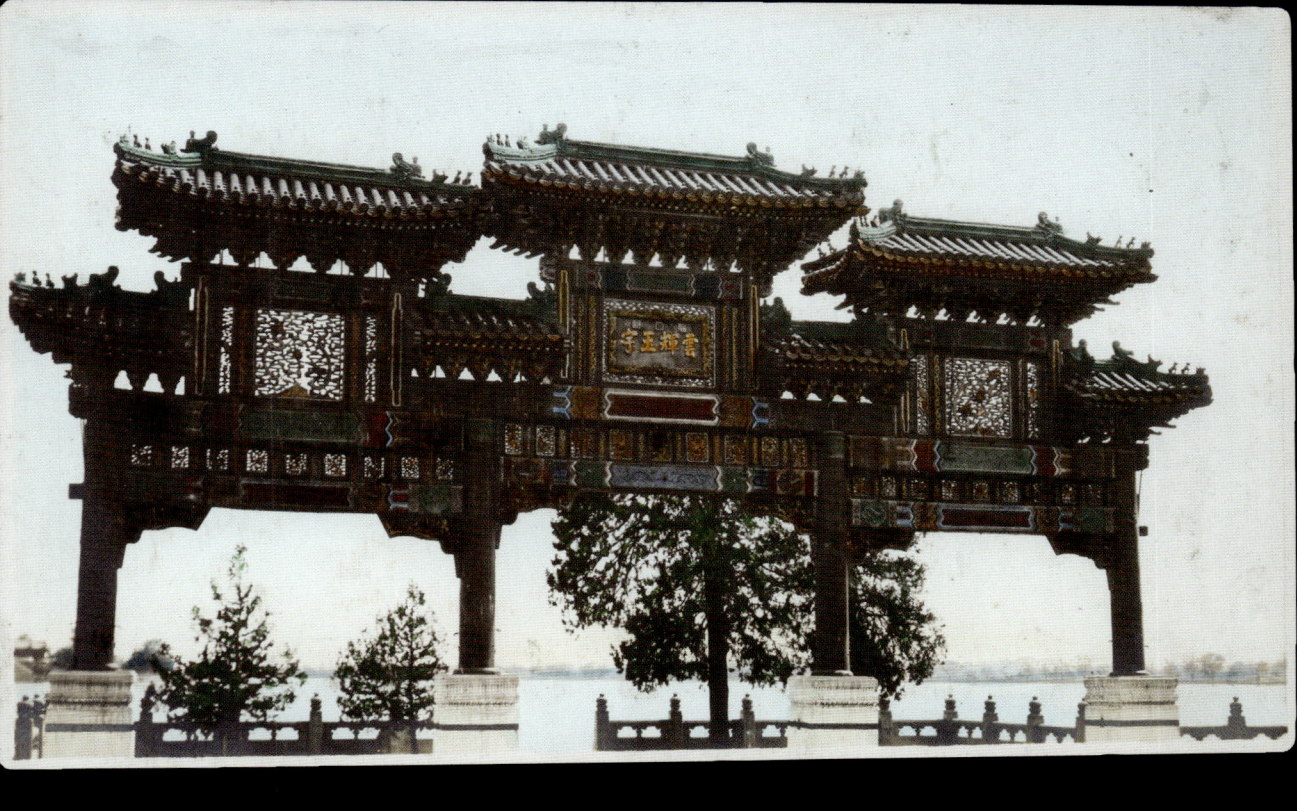

Ornamental gateway, called a pailou, seemed to float above a marble terrace overlooking the shimmering lake.

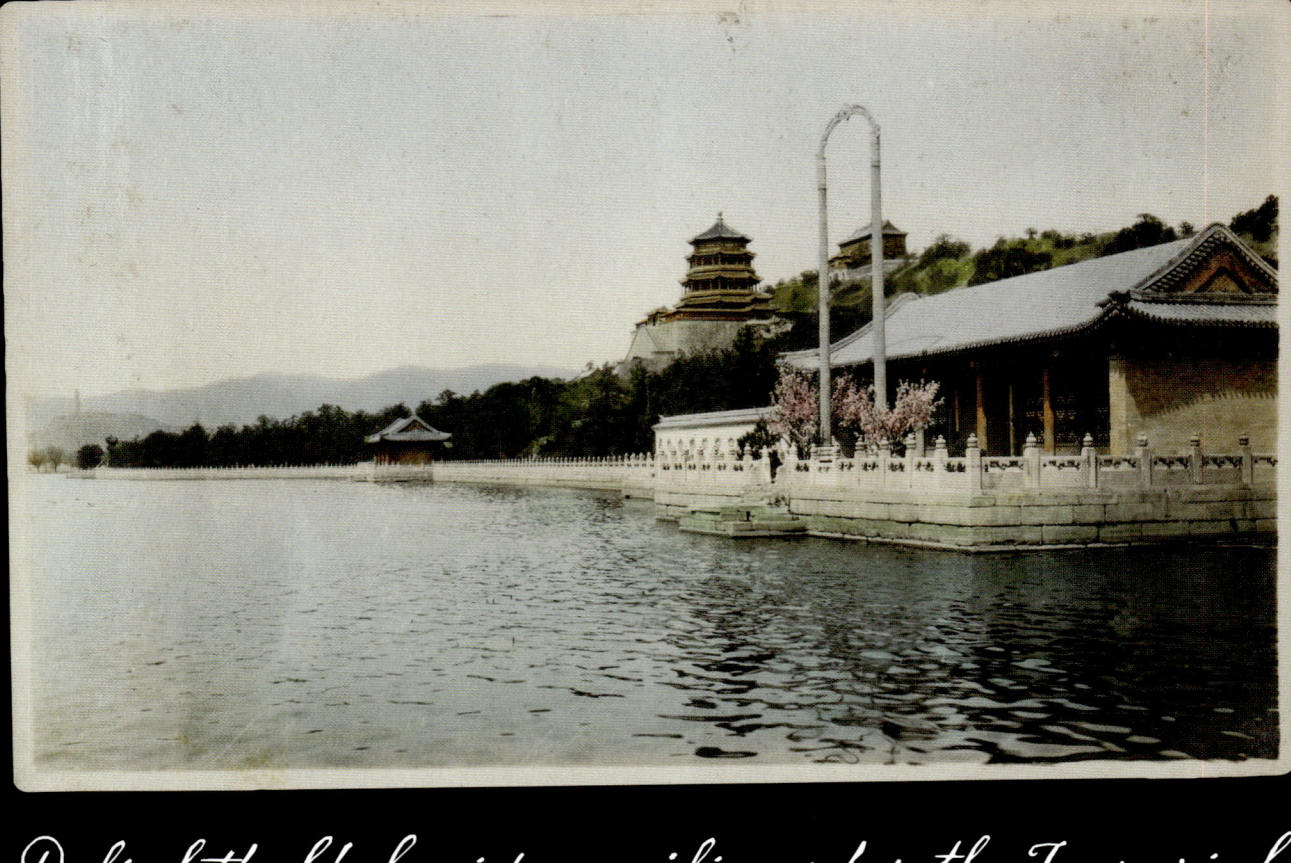

Delightful lakeside pavilions for the Imperial boating parties and other outdoor pleasures. — Summer Palace

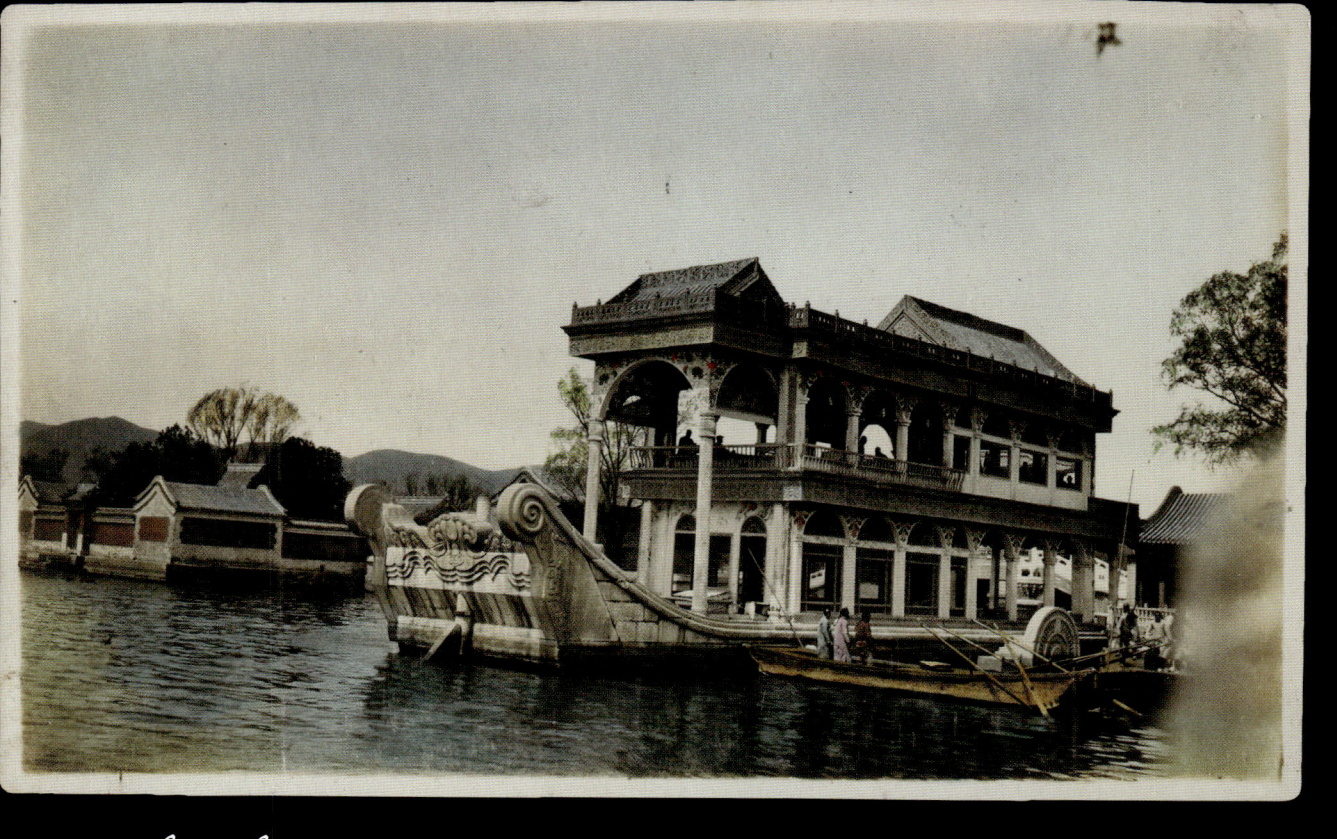

Marble boat was a favorite spot for Emperors and Empresses and their entourages to escape the heat. —Summer Palace

Upon returning home and studying this photograph more closely, I wondered if the retreating white figures were ghosts inhabiting the Painted Corridor of the Summer Palace.

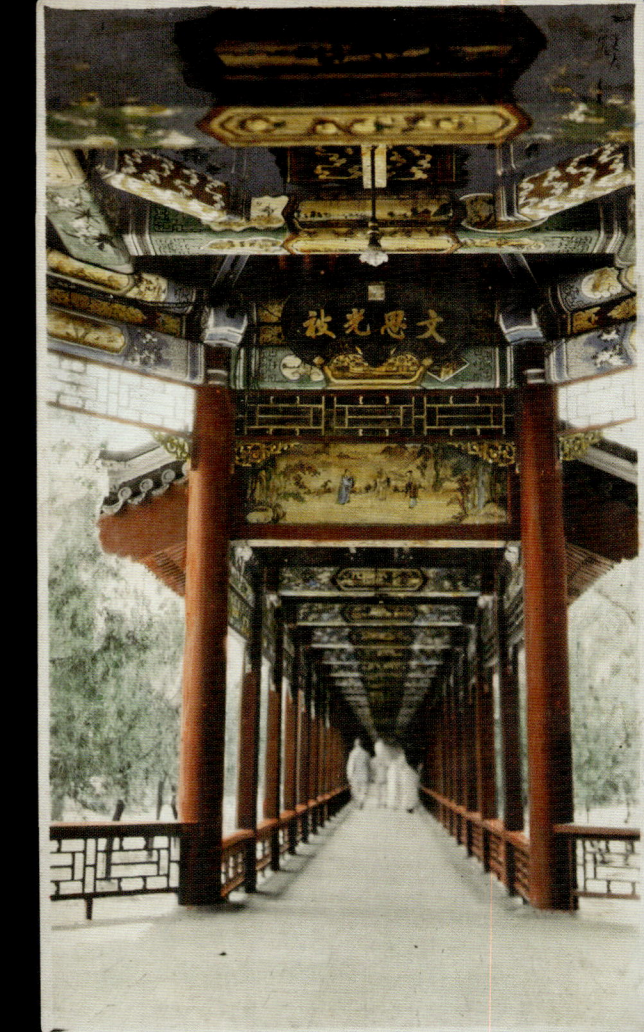

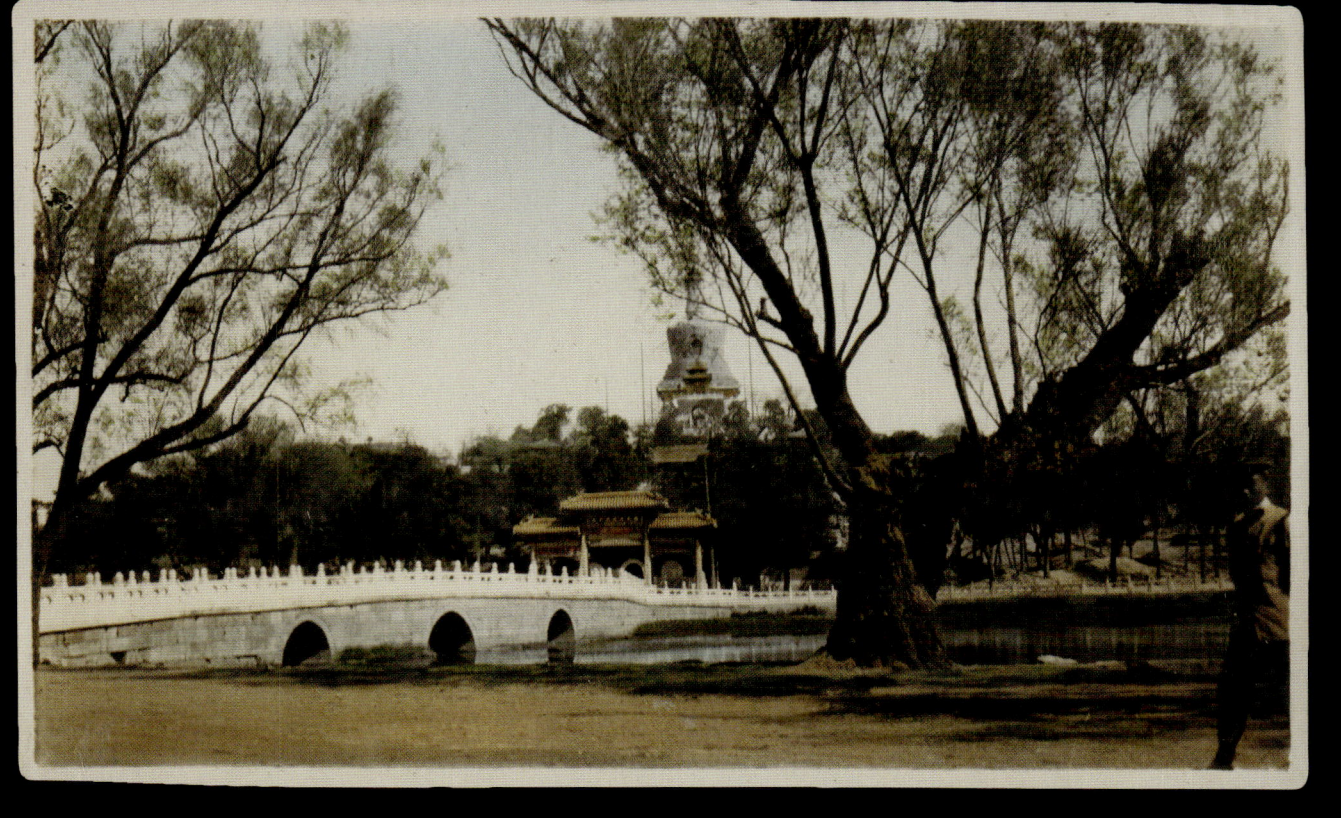

A graceful bridge terminates at another impressiv pailou gateway. The compounds of the Winter Palace lie beyond.

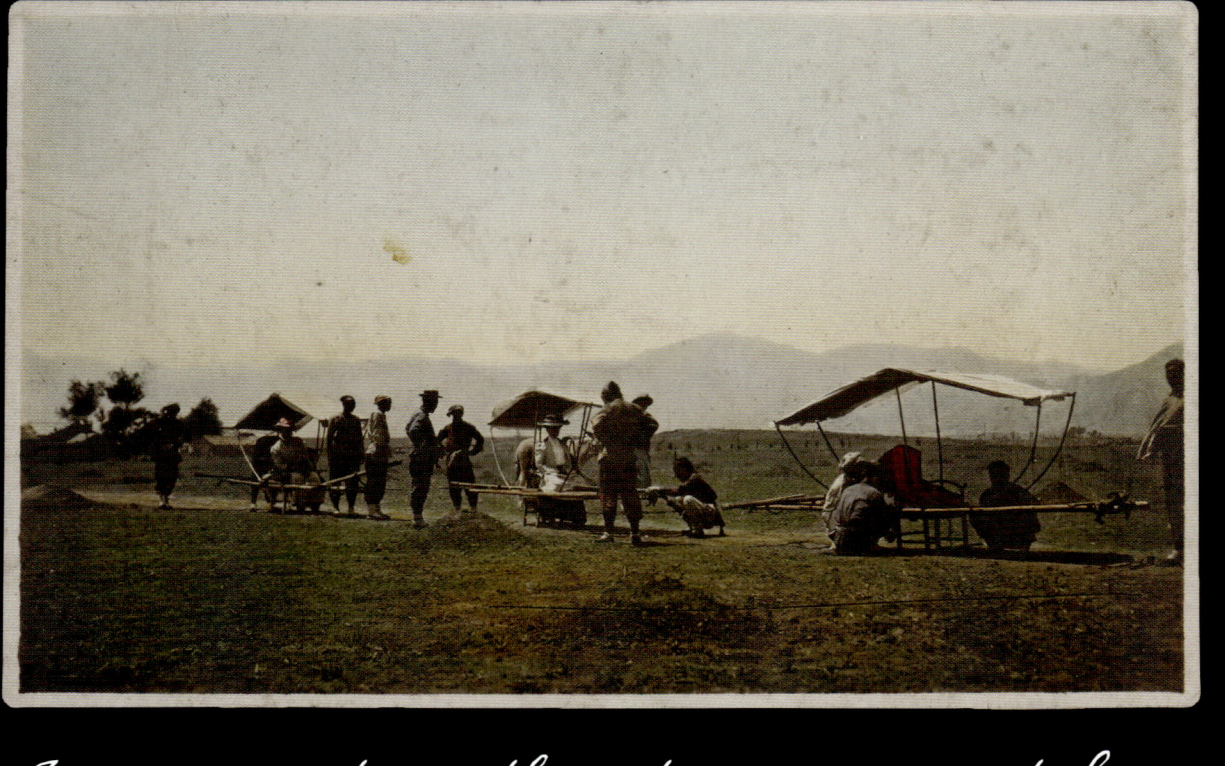

Journeys outside the city were undertaken in sedan chairs. Each of us was weighed before departure. Anyone tipping the scales over 150 pounds had three bearers.

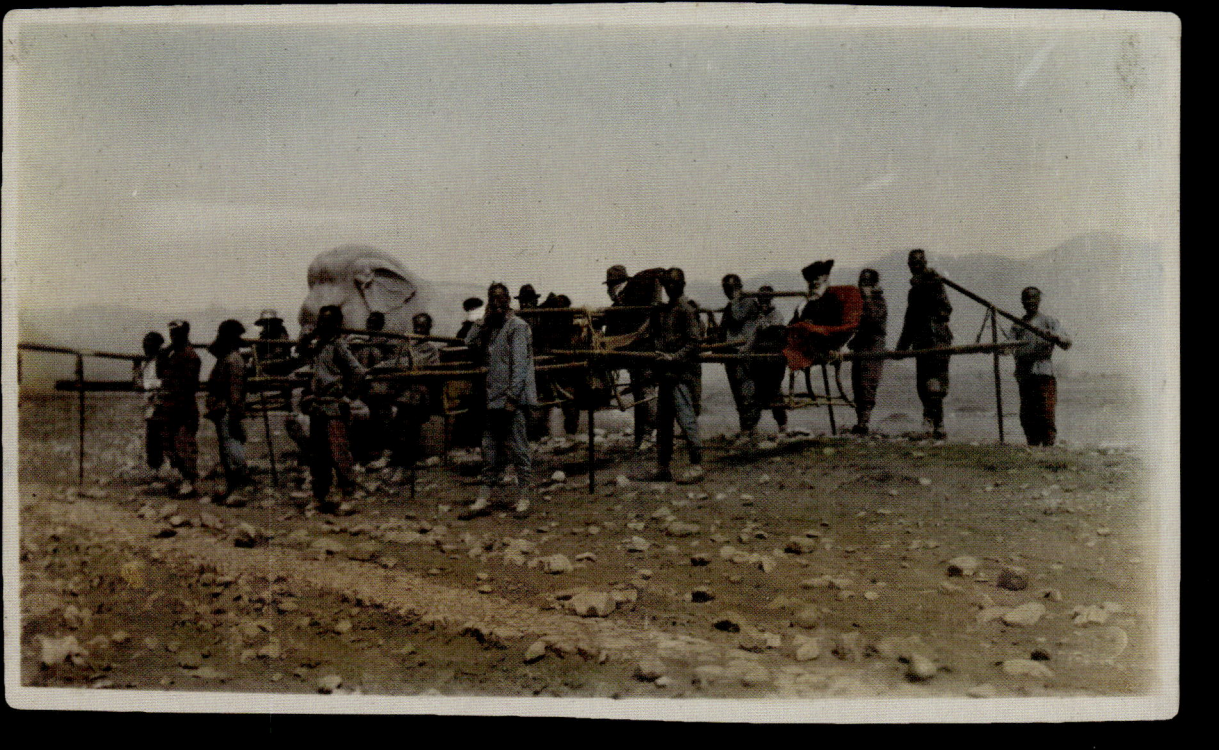

There is an art to riding in a sedan chair. We must sit very straight and still so as not to upset the balance and risk an ungainly tumble. Thus we shift and turn at our peril.

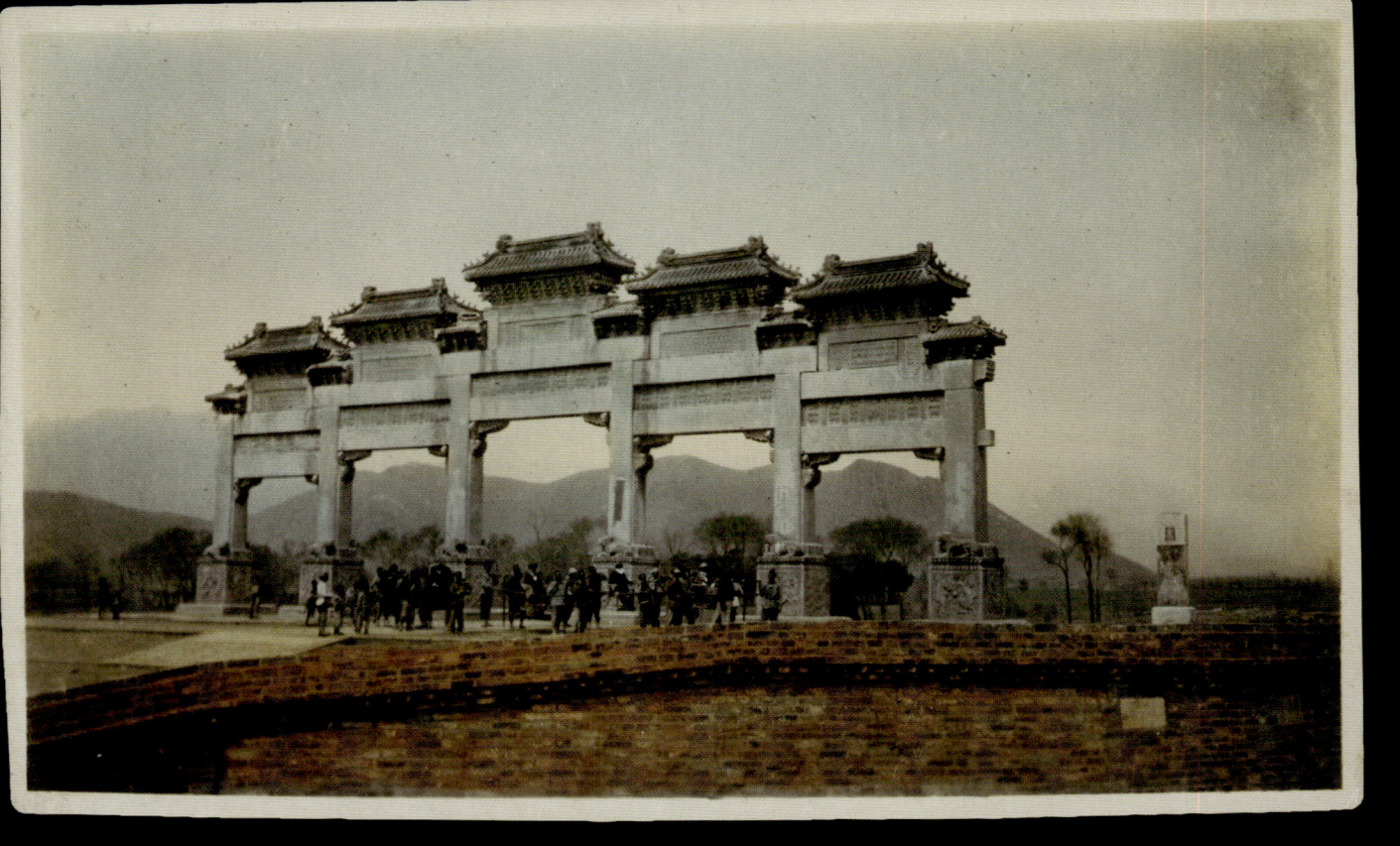

We left most of our retinue, which out numbered us by nearly four to one, at the 16th century pailou gate.

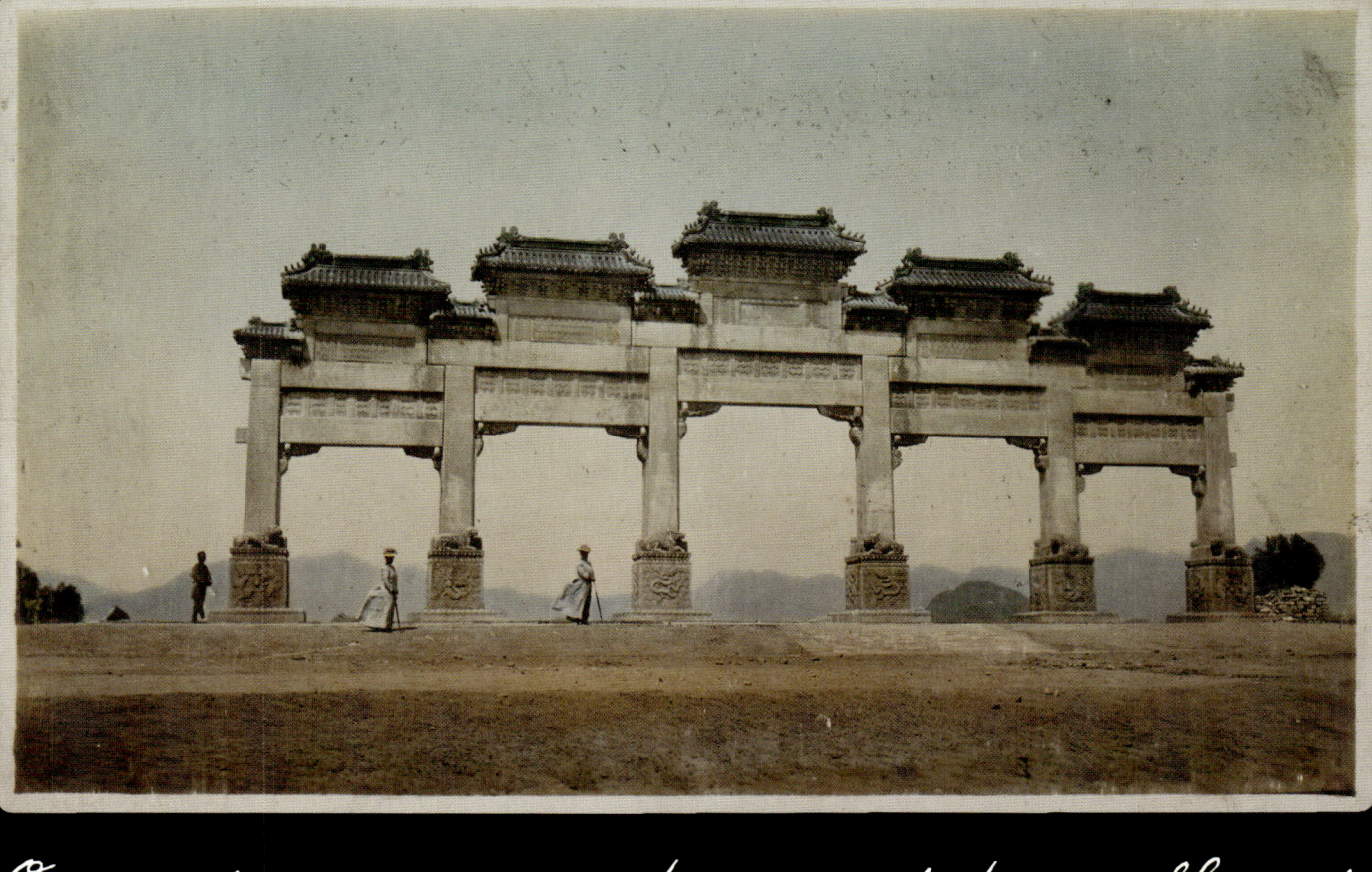

Our guide was surprised we insisted on walking to the Ming Tombs—5/ 19/ 1910

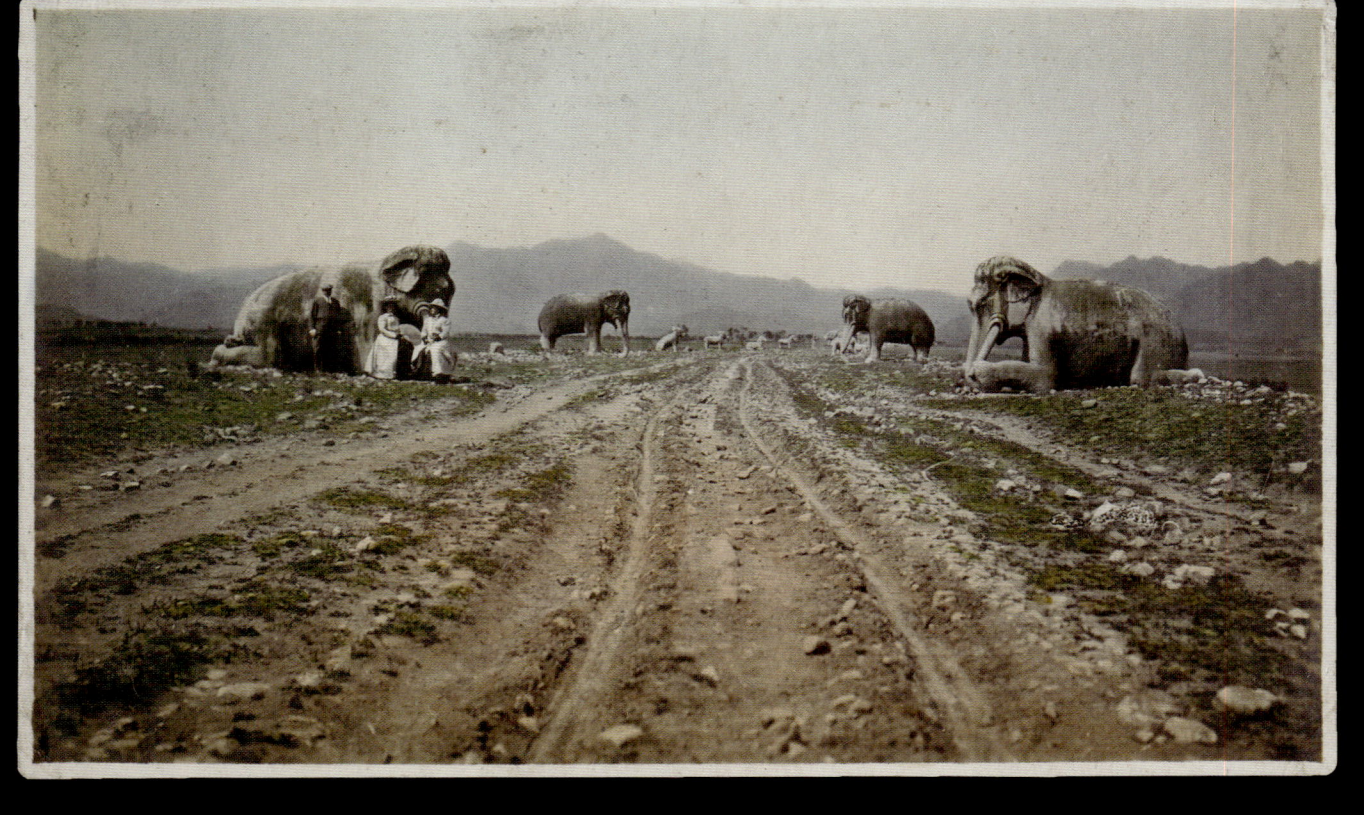

Road to the Thirteen Tombs of the Ming Emperors 30 miles northwest of Peking in the Western Hills.

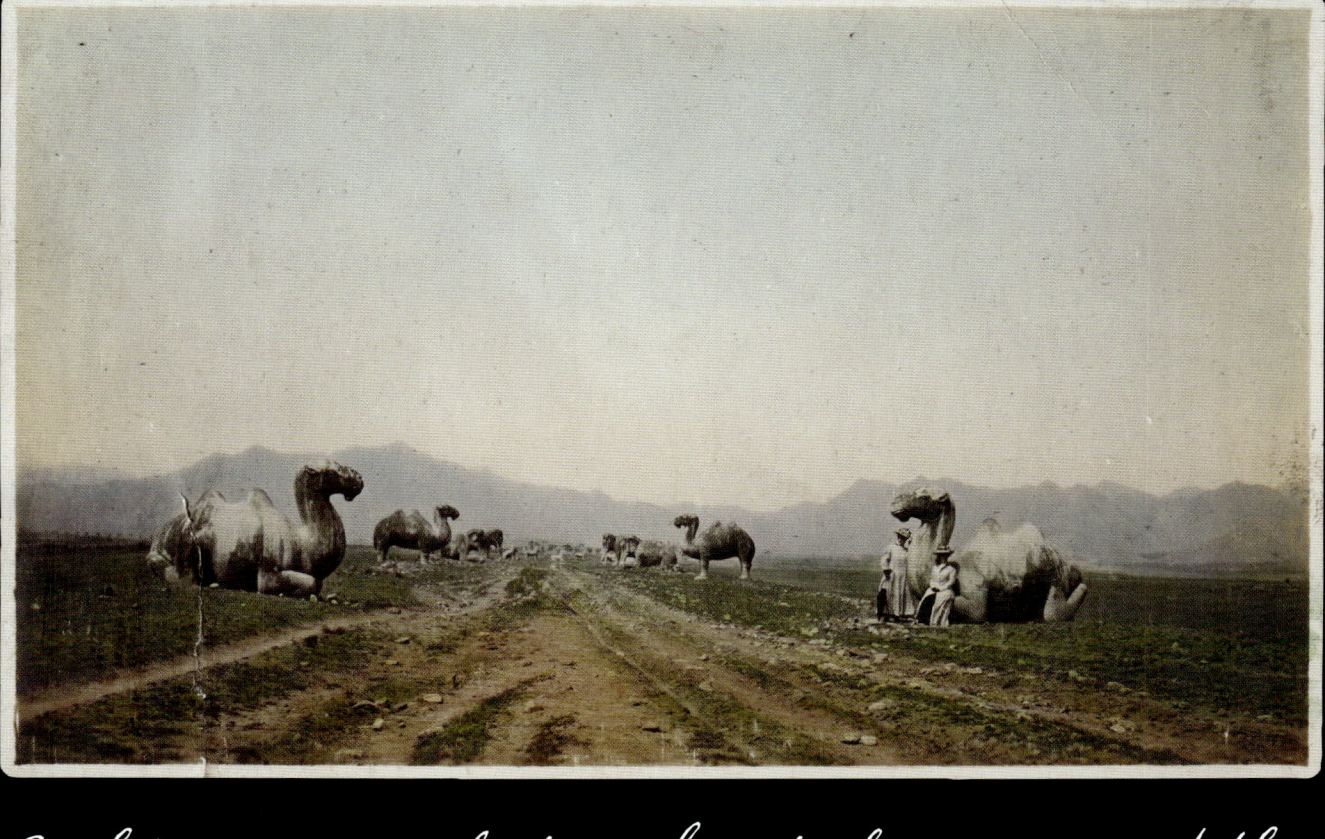

Eighteen pairs of stone beasts have guarded the Road to the Ming Tombs for 500 years.

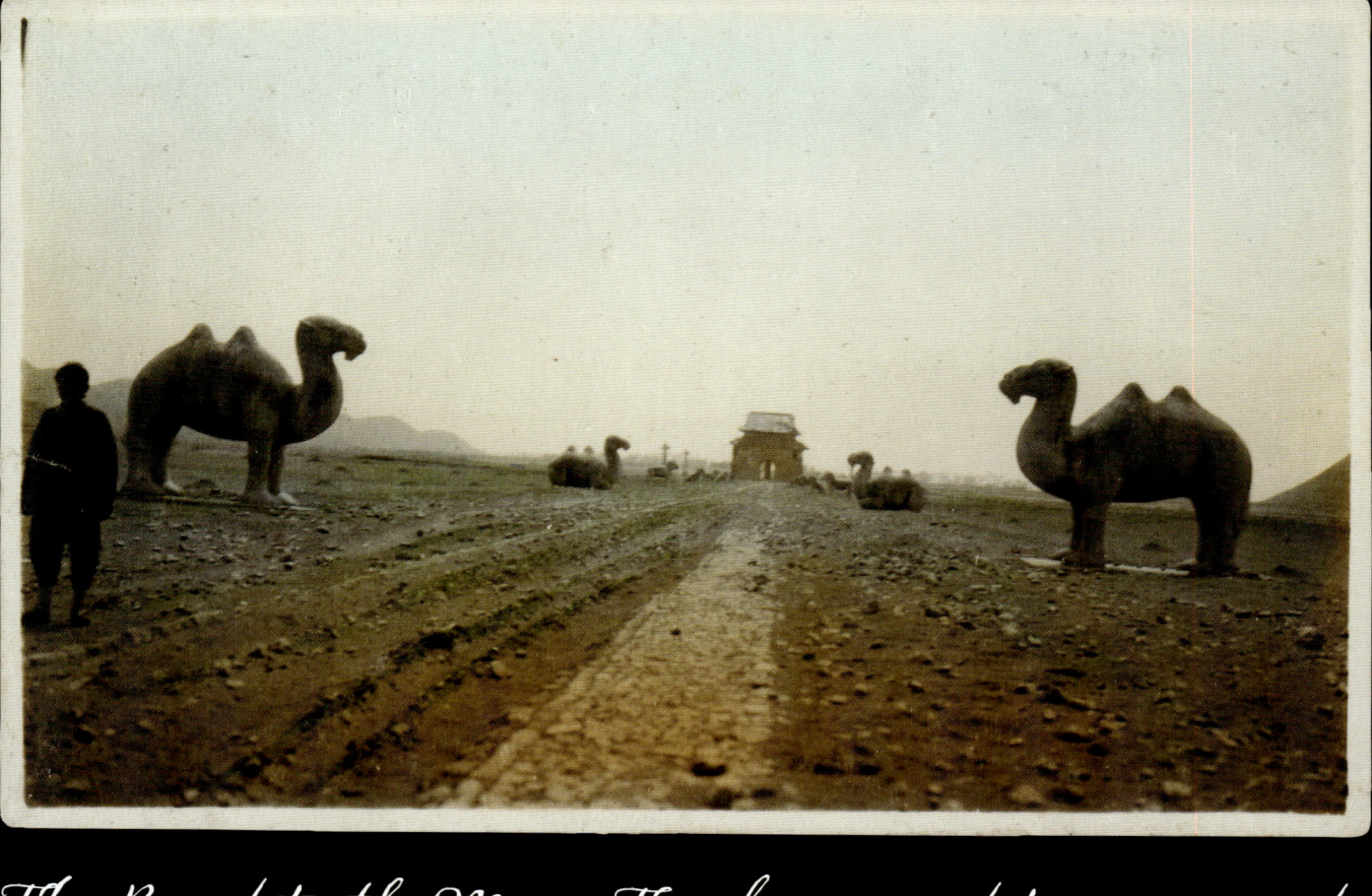

The Road to the Ming Tombs seemed to go on and on... until, at last, the end was in sight.

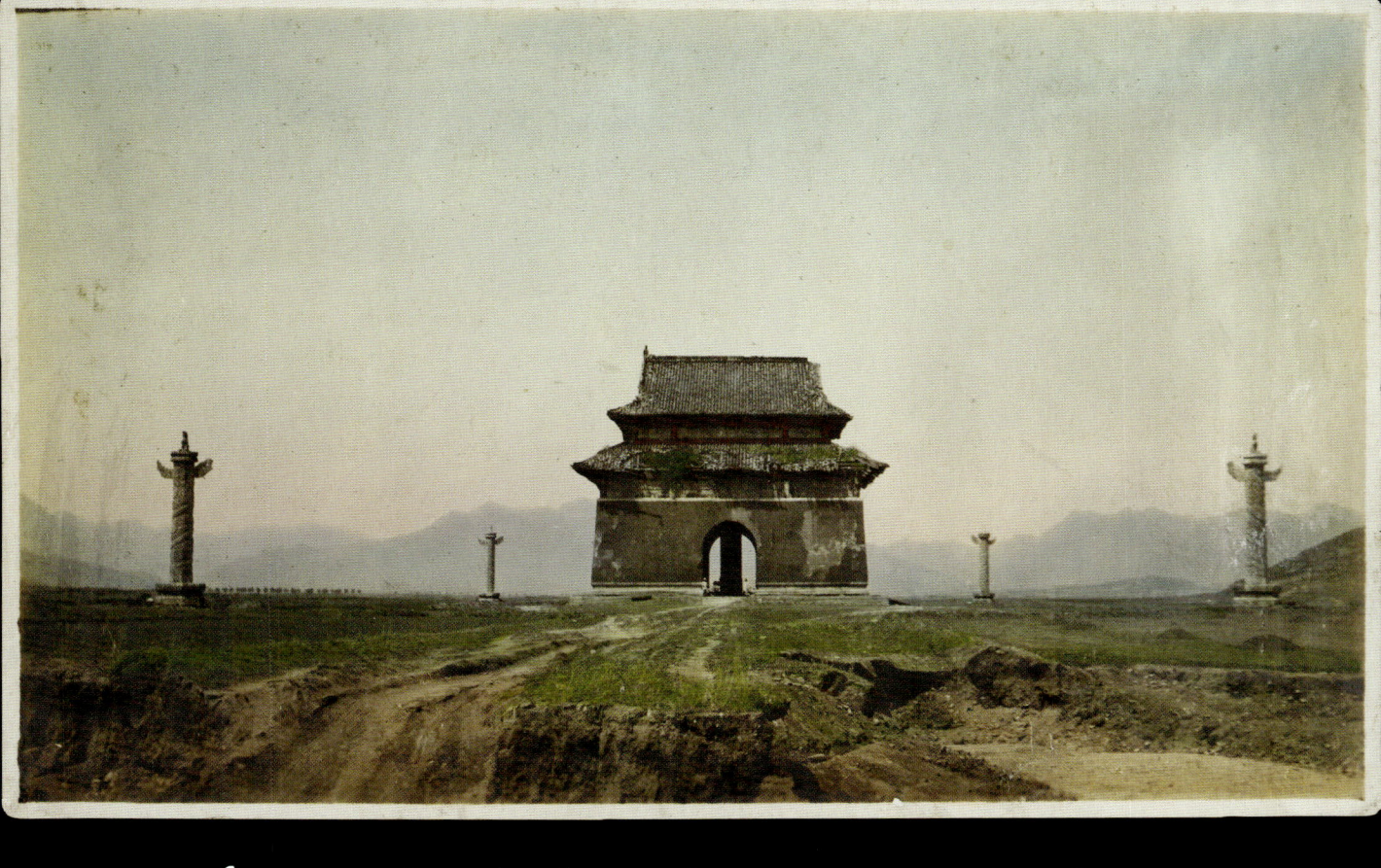

It is acknowledged that the Ming (which means brilliant) period was a Golden Age in China.

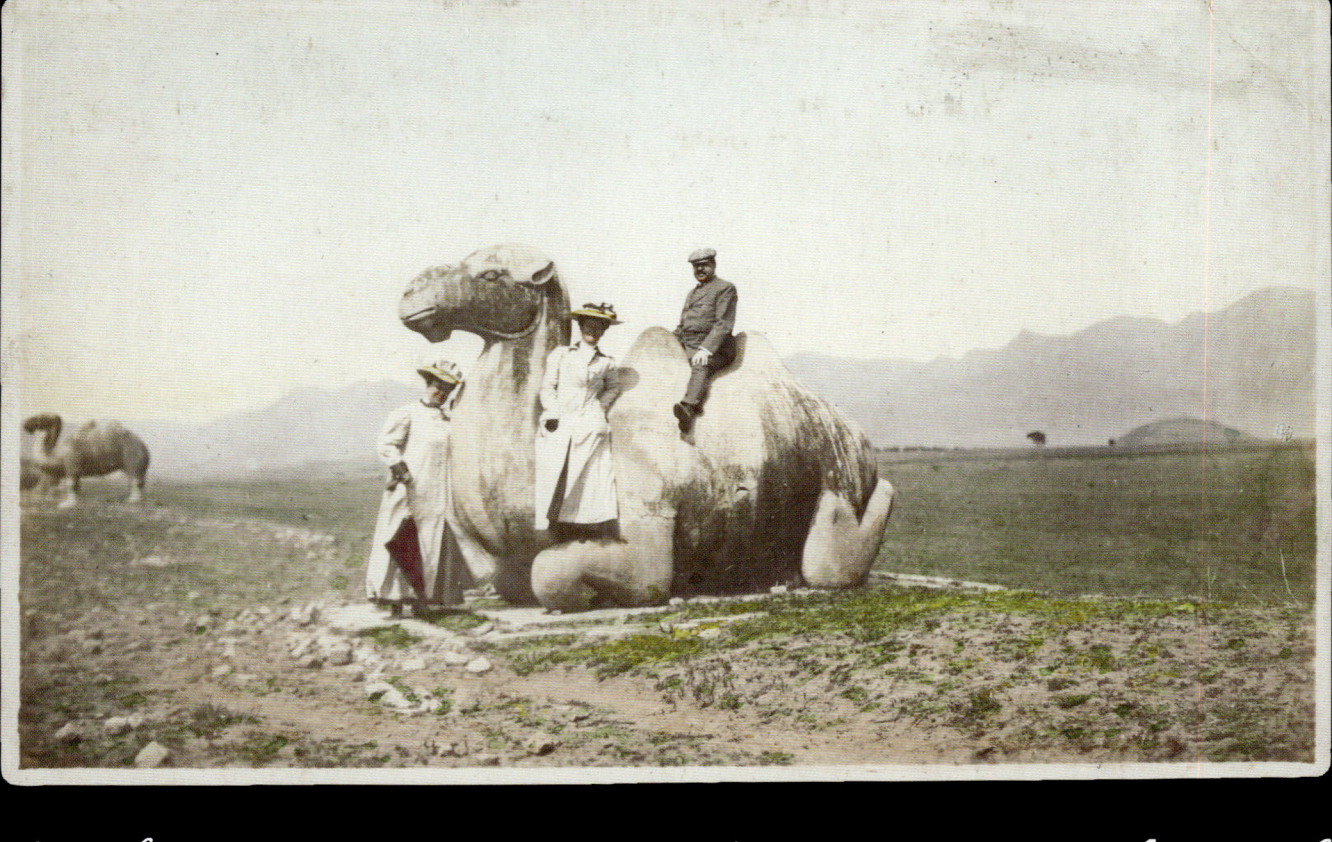

On the return journey we disported ourselves like children in the school yard.

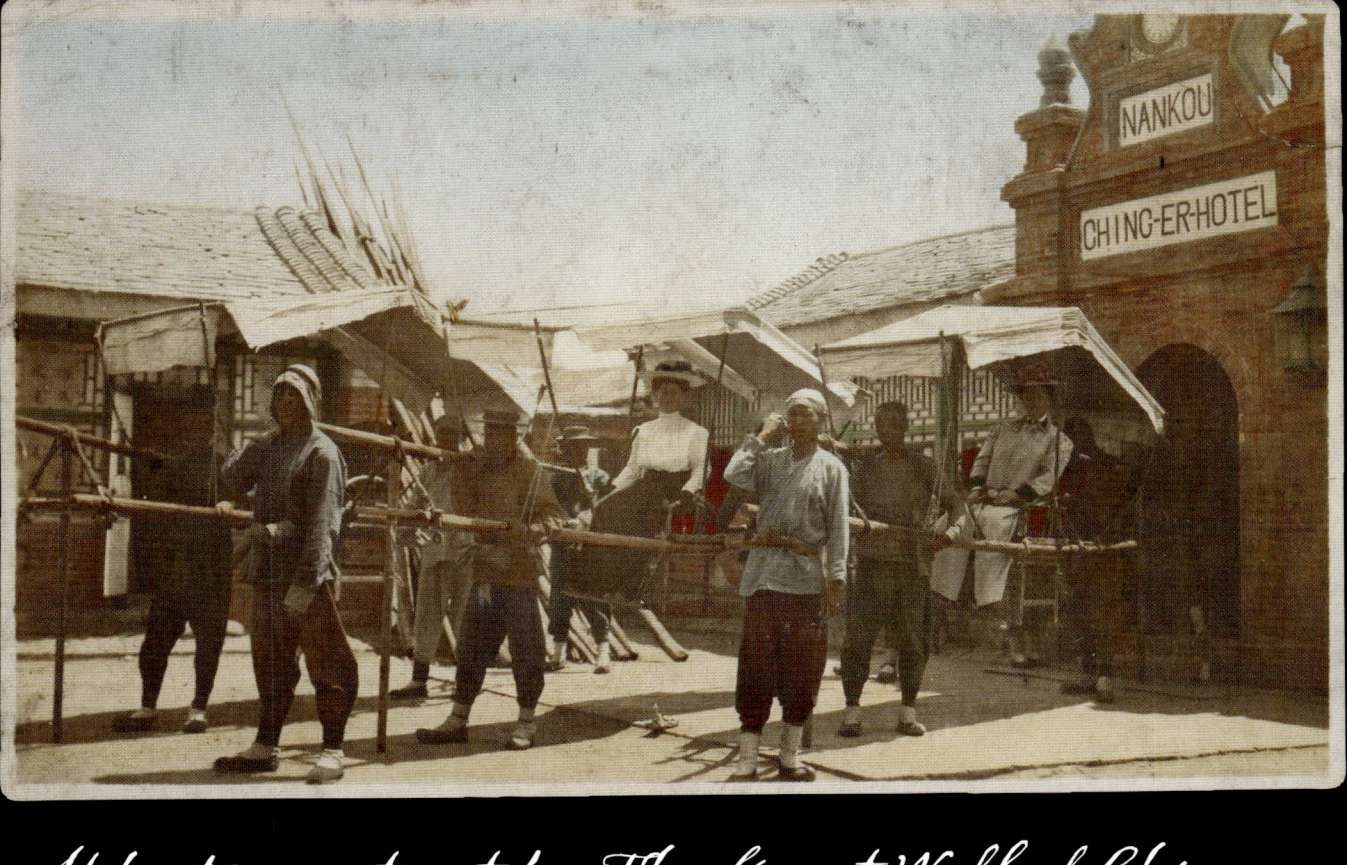

At last we set out for The Great Wall of China from Nankow Pass—5/22/1910

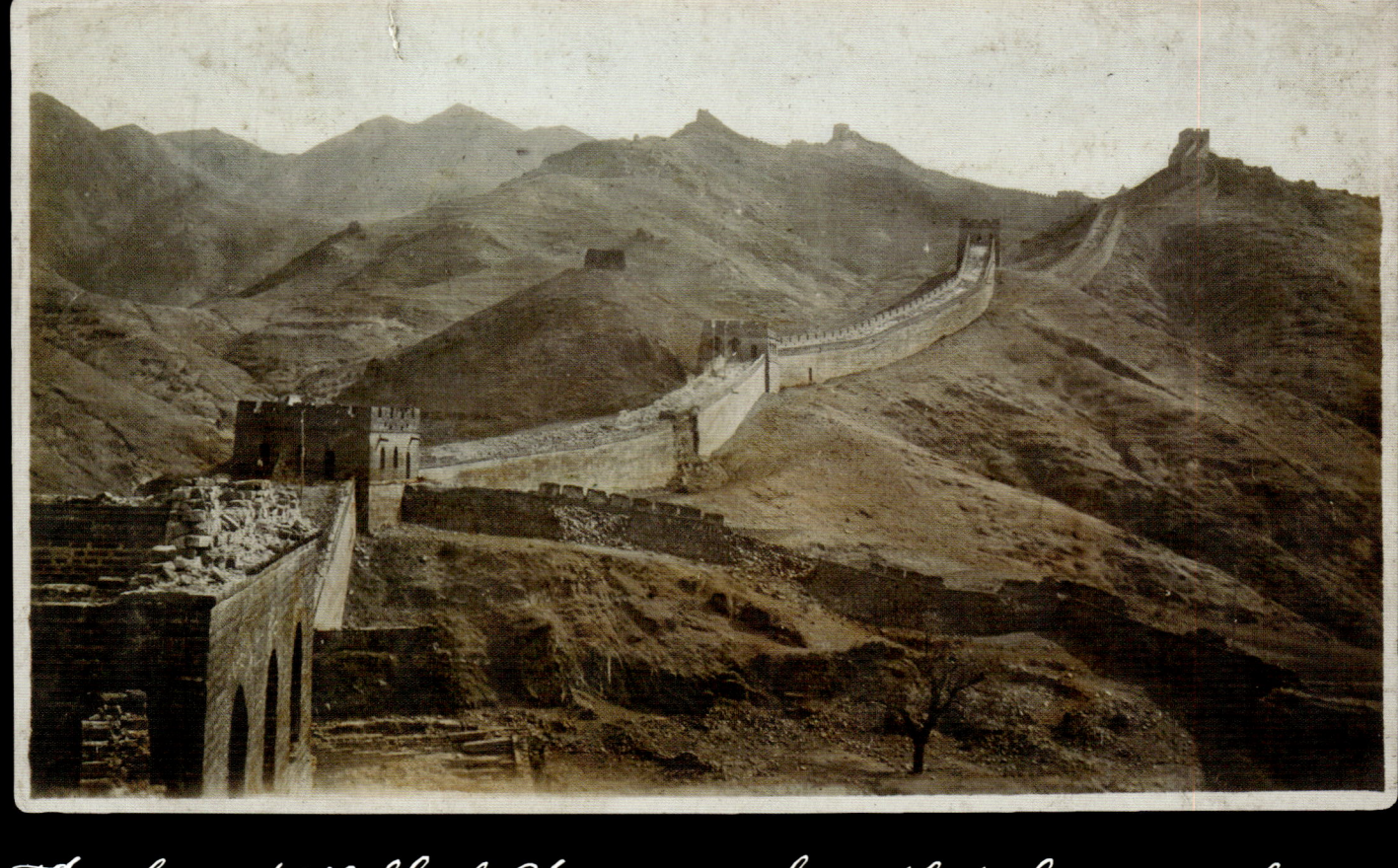

The Great Wall of China—a breath taking sight for as far as the eye can see!

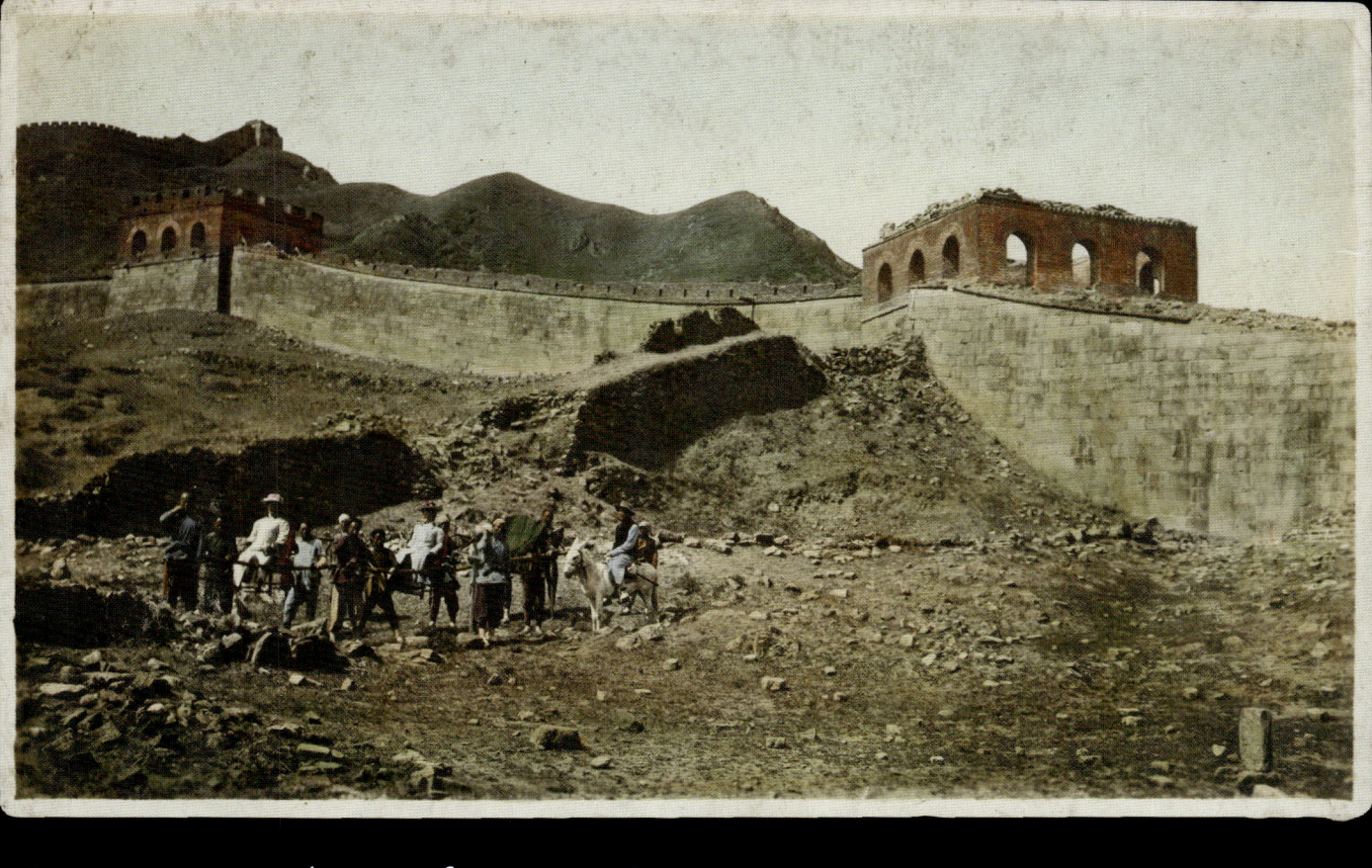

Even in sedan chairs the approach was arduous over the rough terrain.

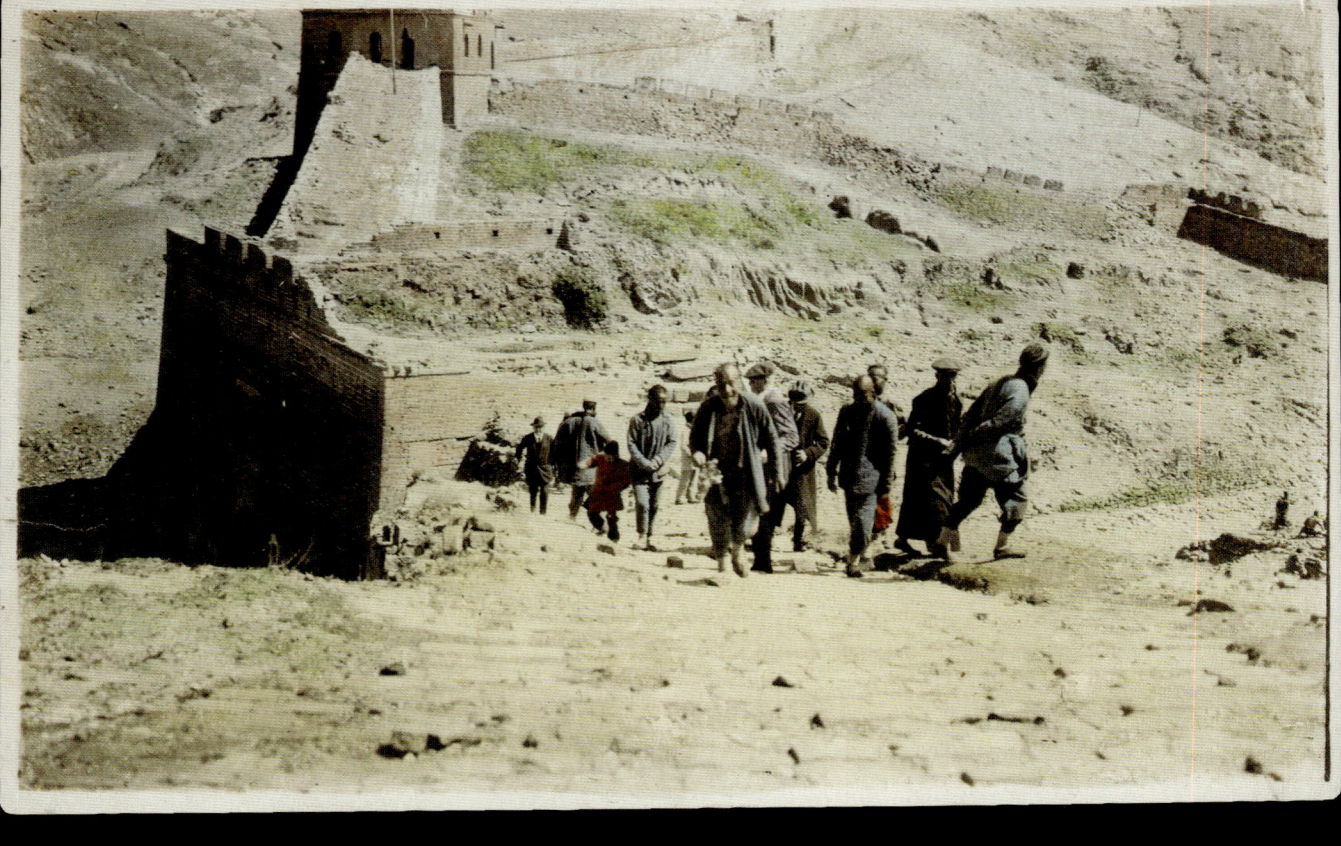

Relieved of their burdens, the coolies scattered.

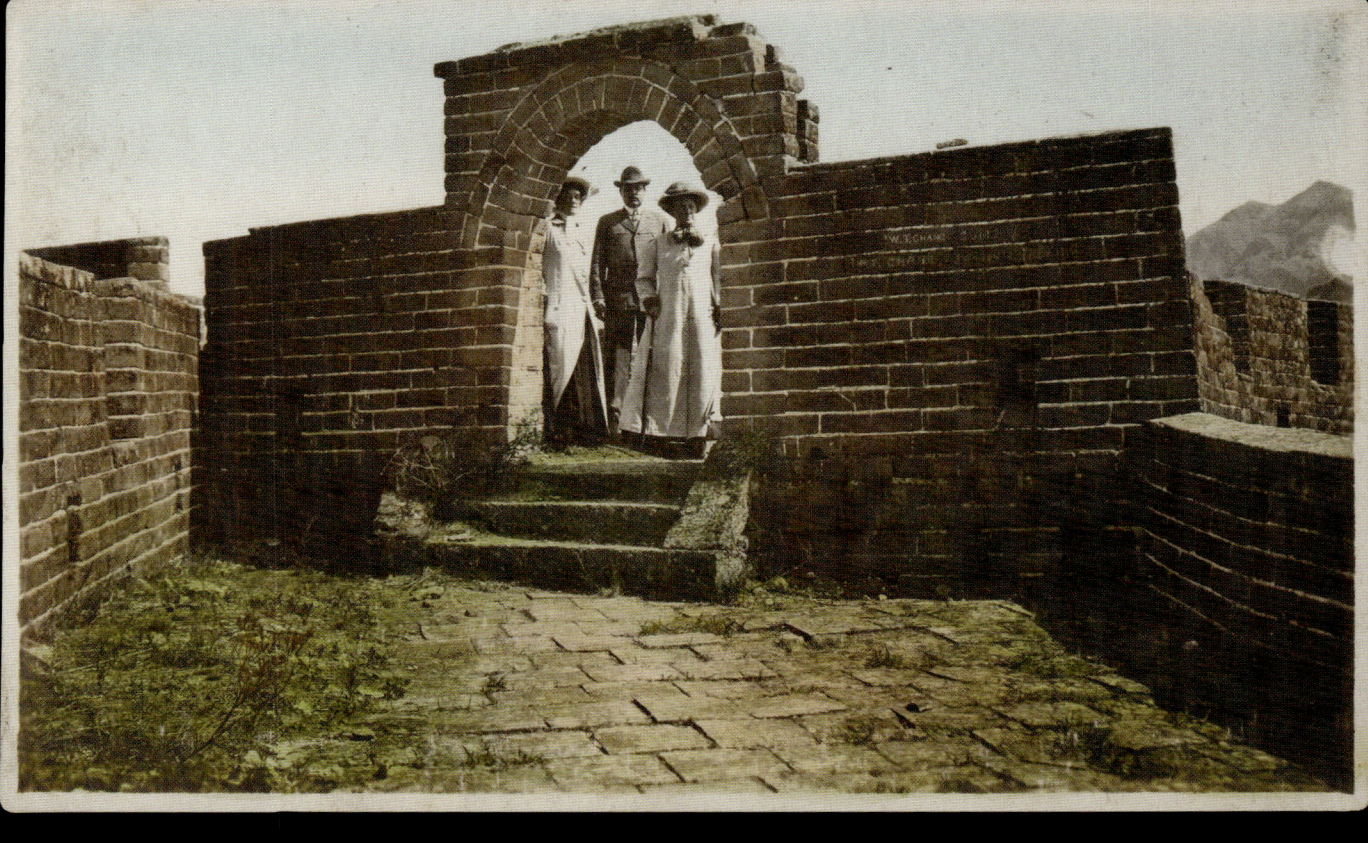

We three, the intrepid trio, on the battlements.

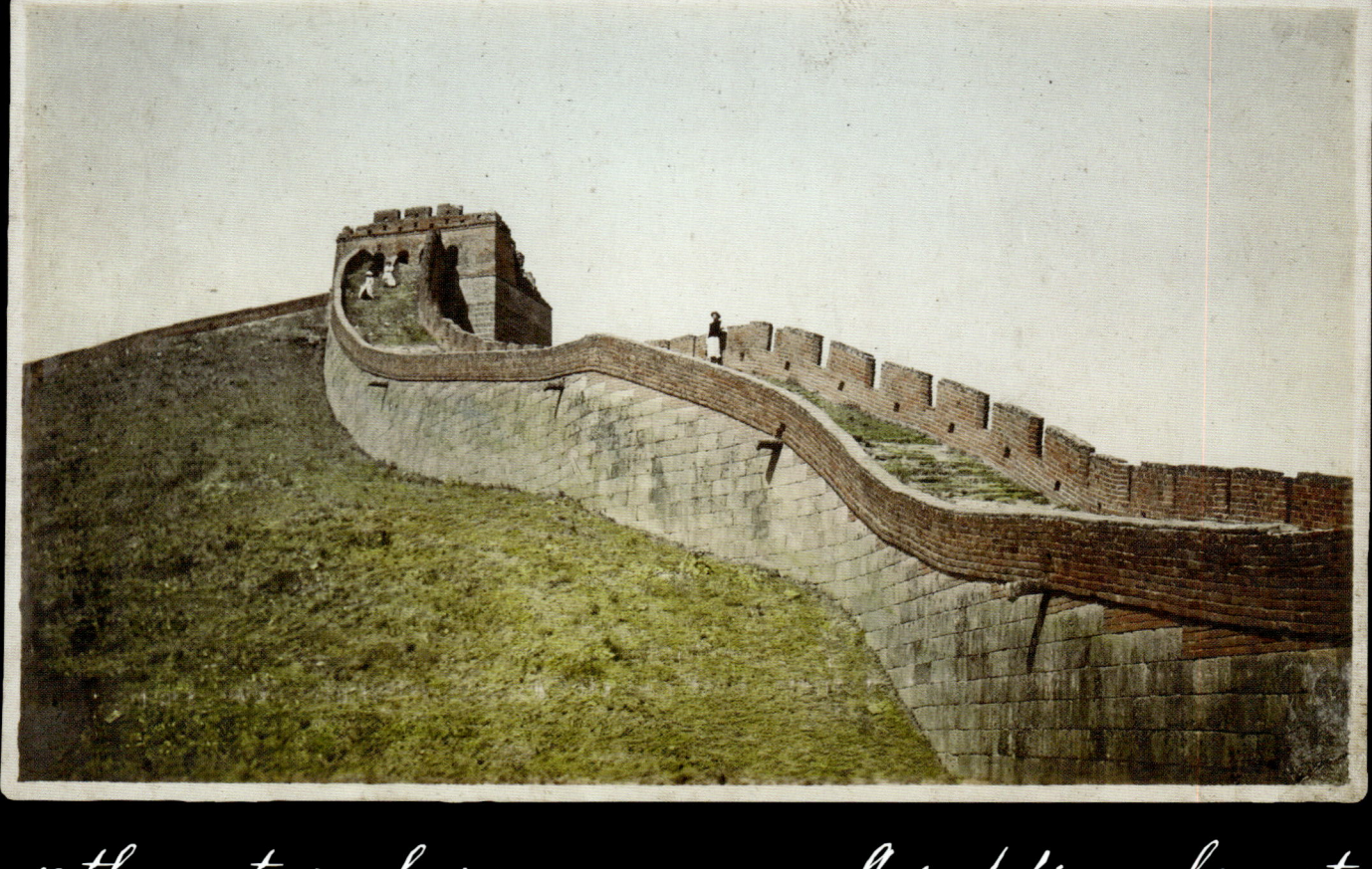

13th century horsemen once galloped five abreast on the serpentine ramparts.

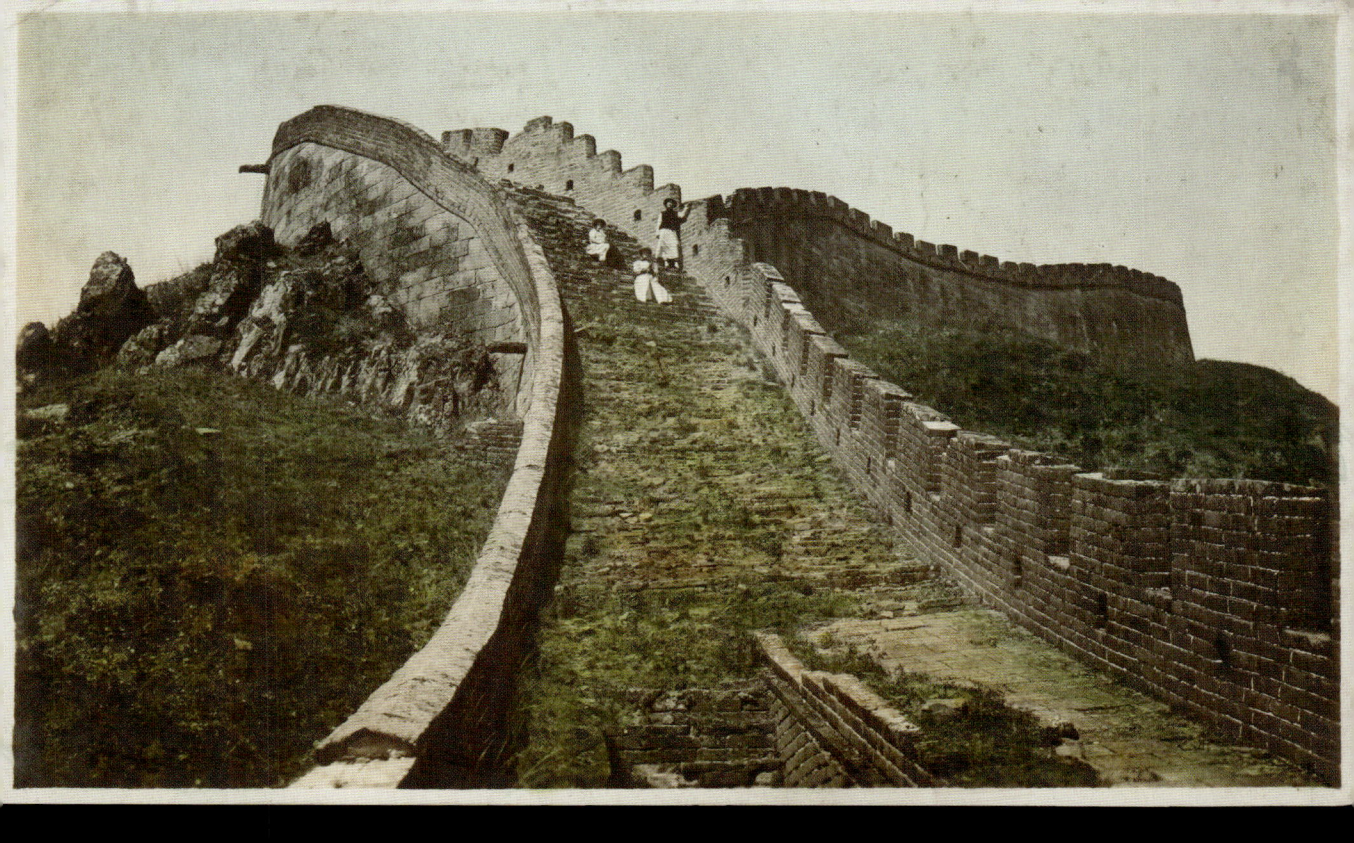

The wall is solid on one side and crenellated for
Mediaeval archers on the other.

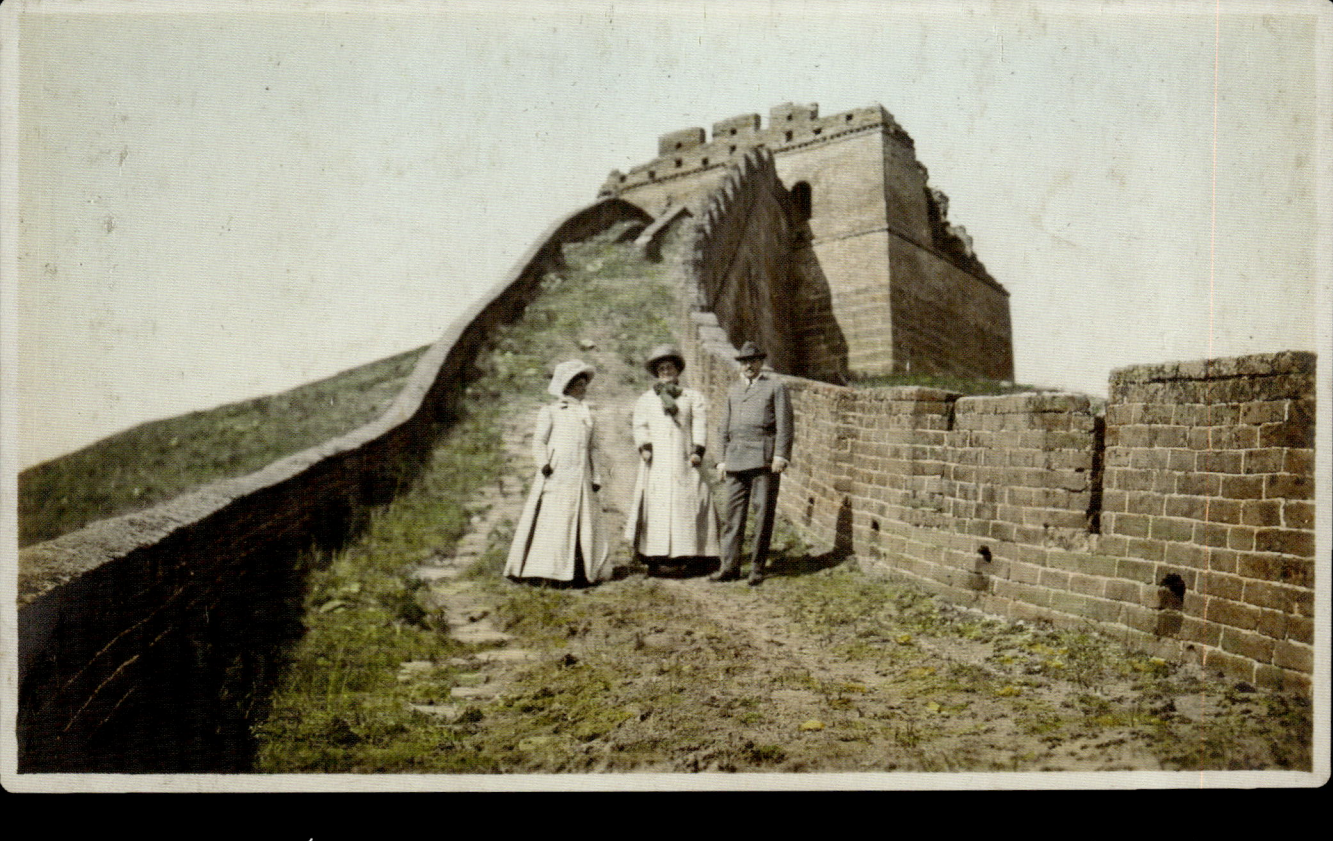

We stopped for a portrait upon one of the Seven Wonders of the World.

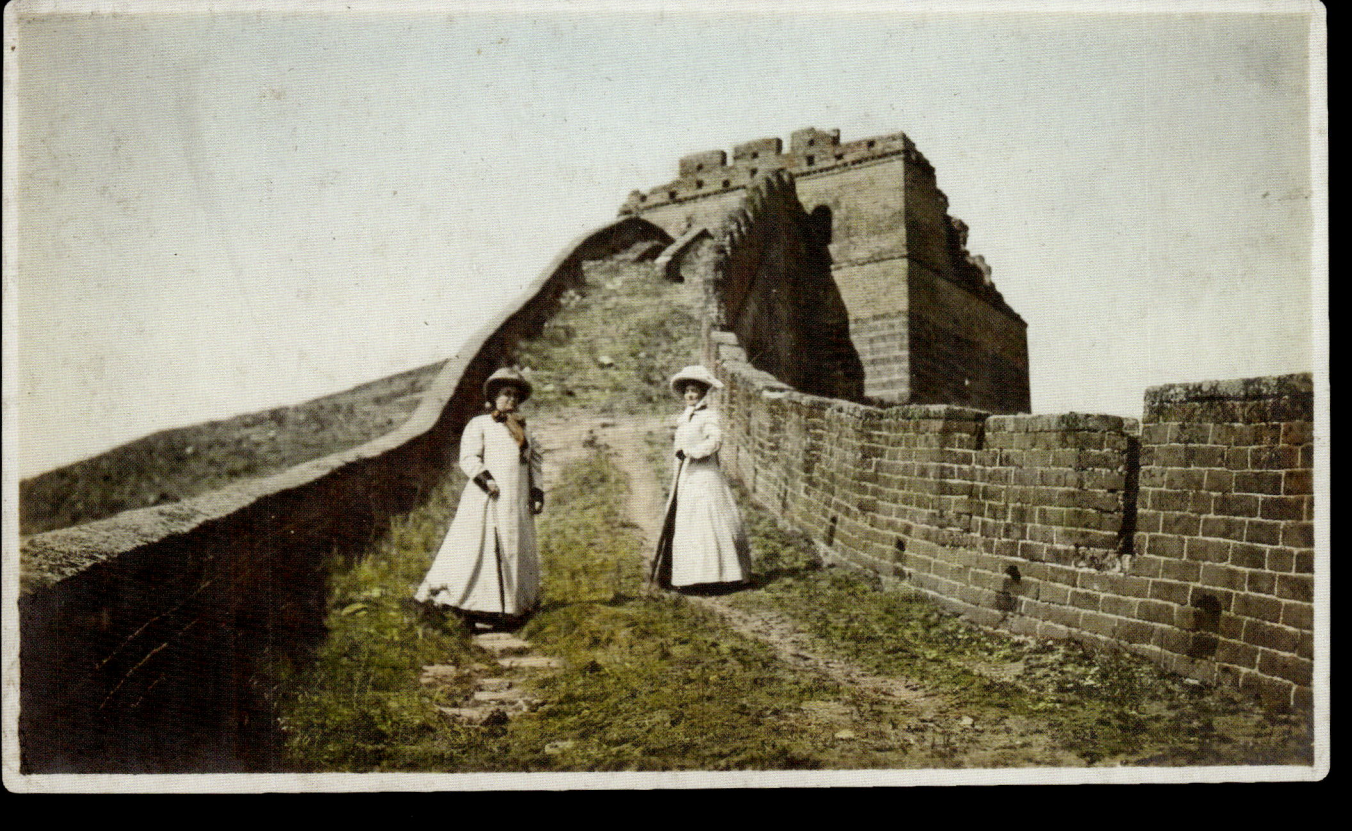

We could not appreciate the immensity of it until we were standing on it.

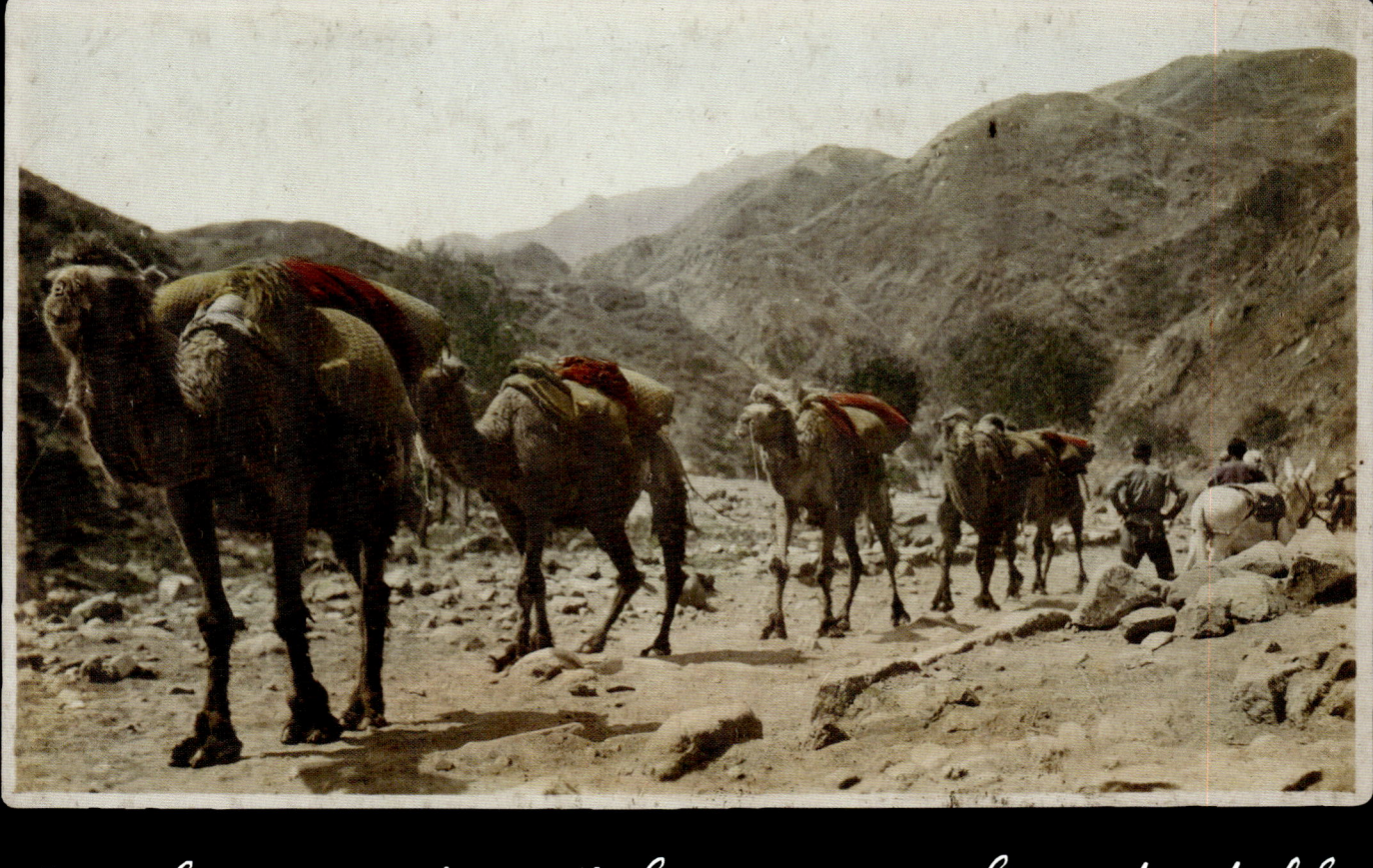

Camel caravan from Peking was making for fabled
Thibet—Nankow Pass

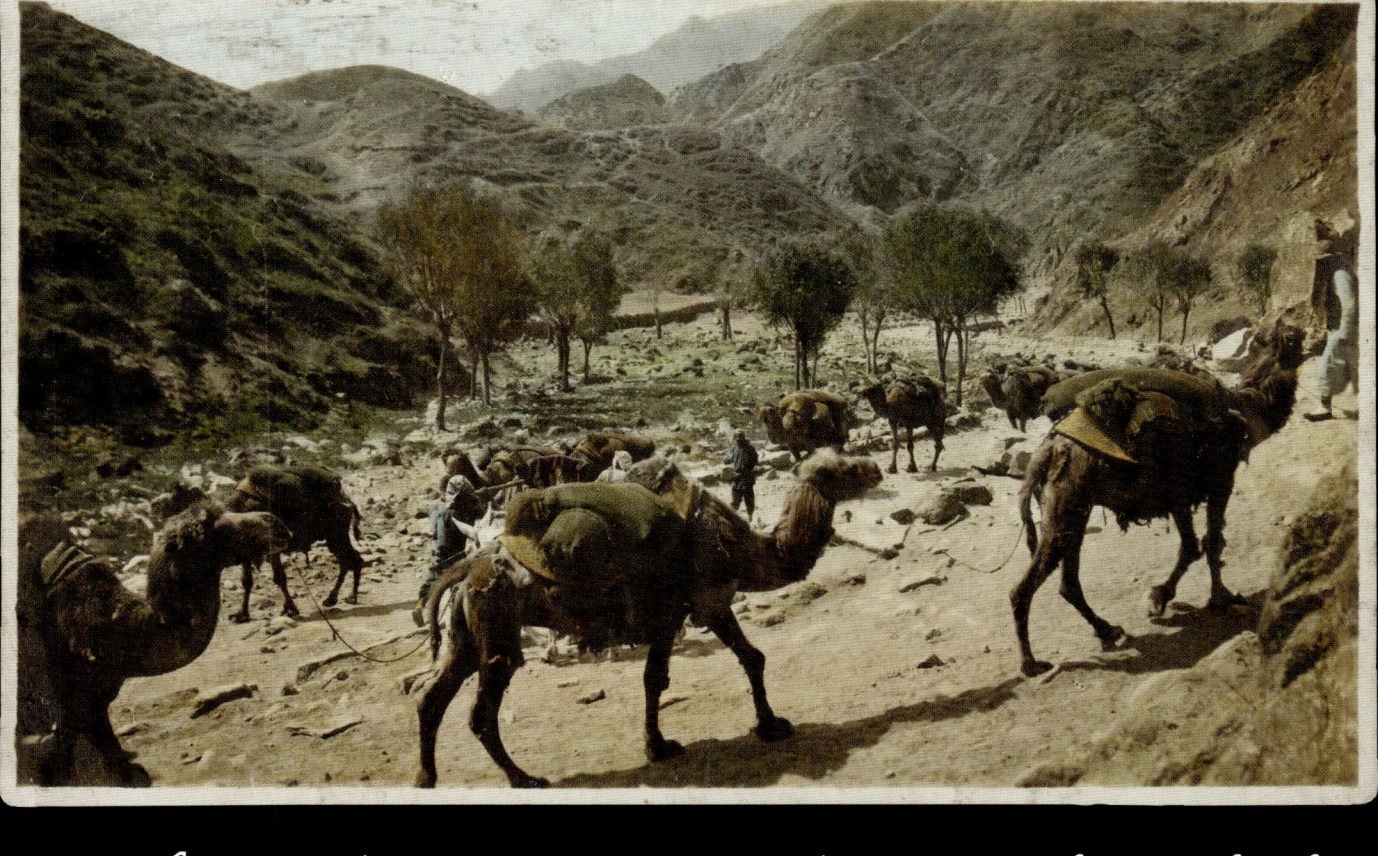

Camels roped in tandem paced slowly through the dusty winding valley.

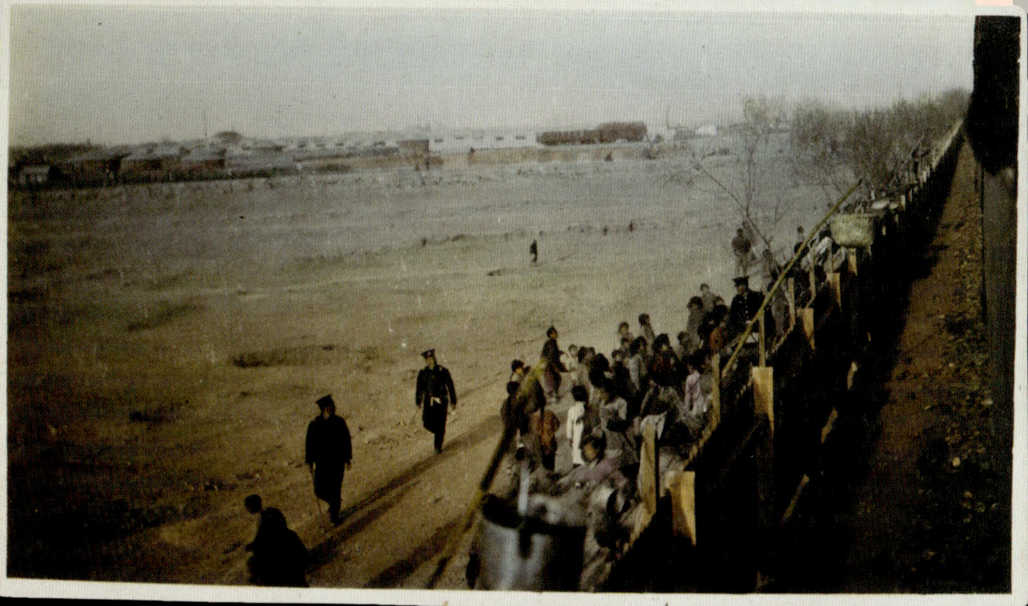

From the train between Pukow and Peking.

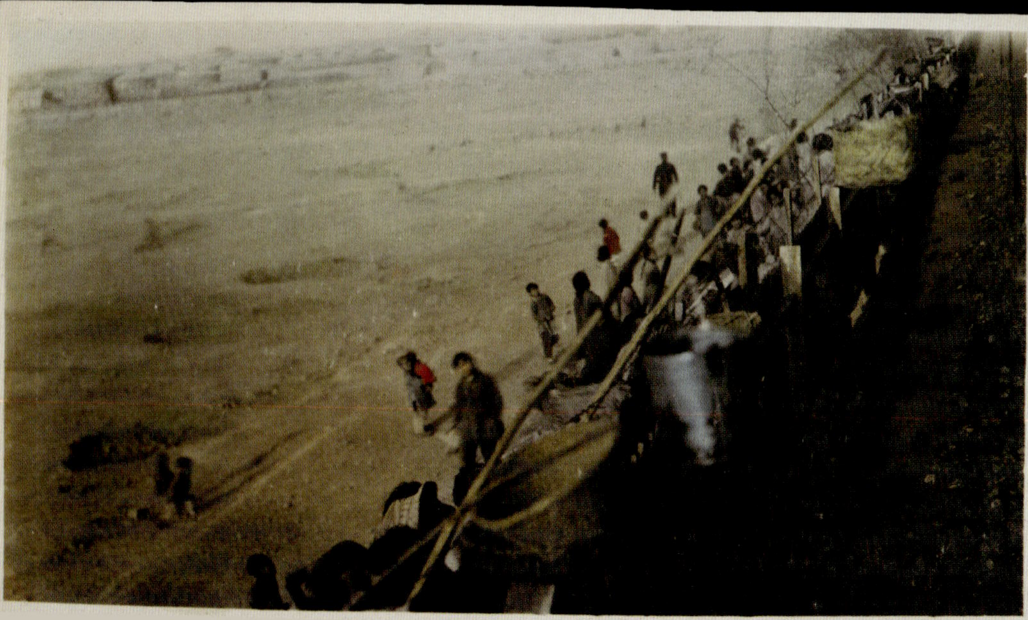

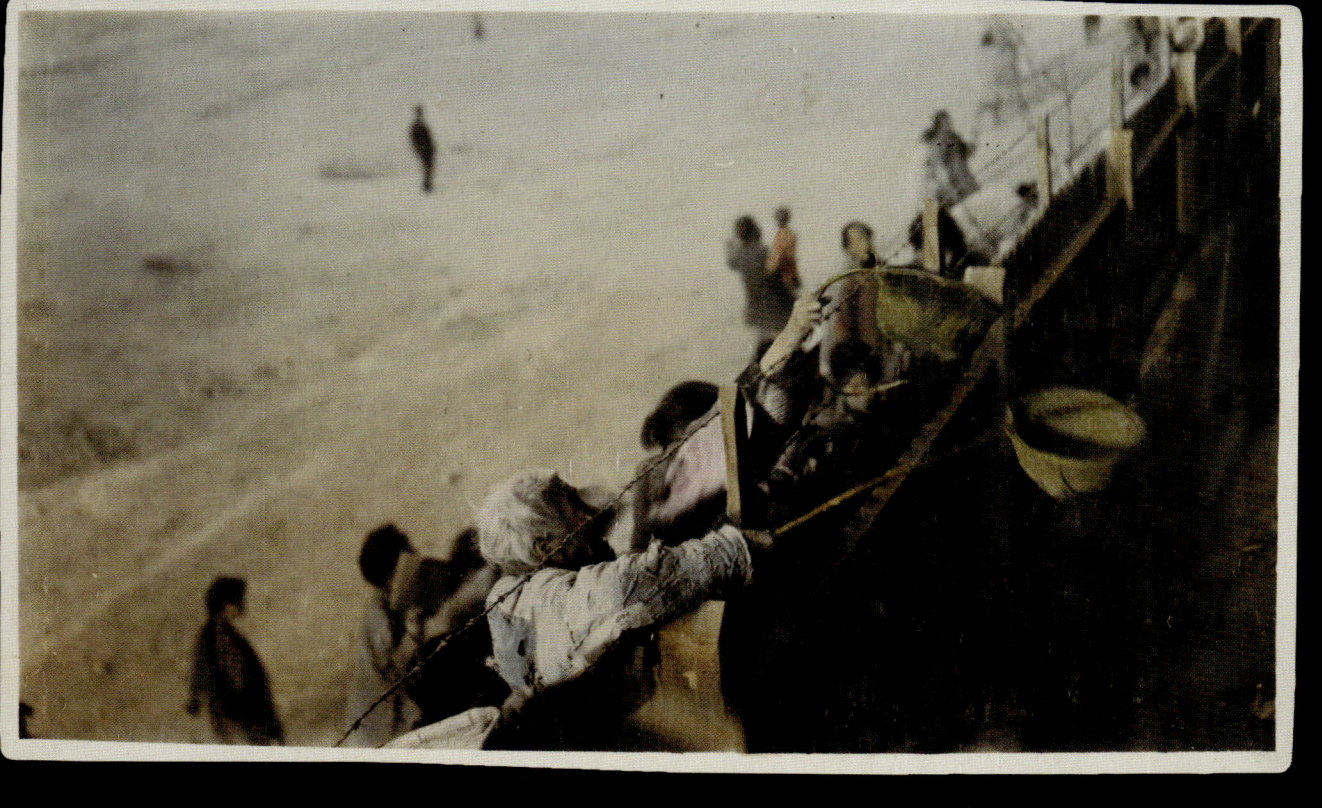

Beggars along the railway found a clever way to fish for handouts with pails on long bamboo poles.

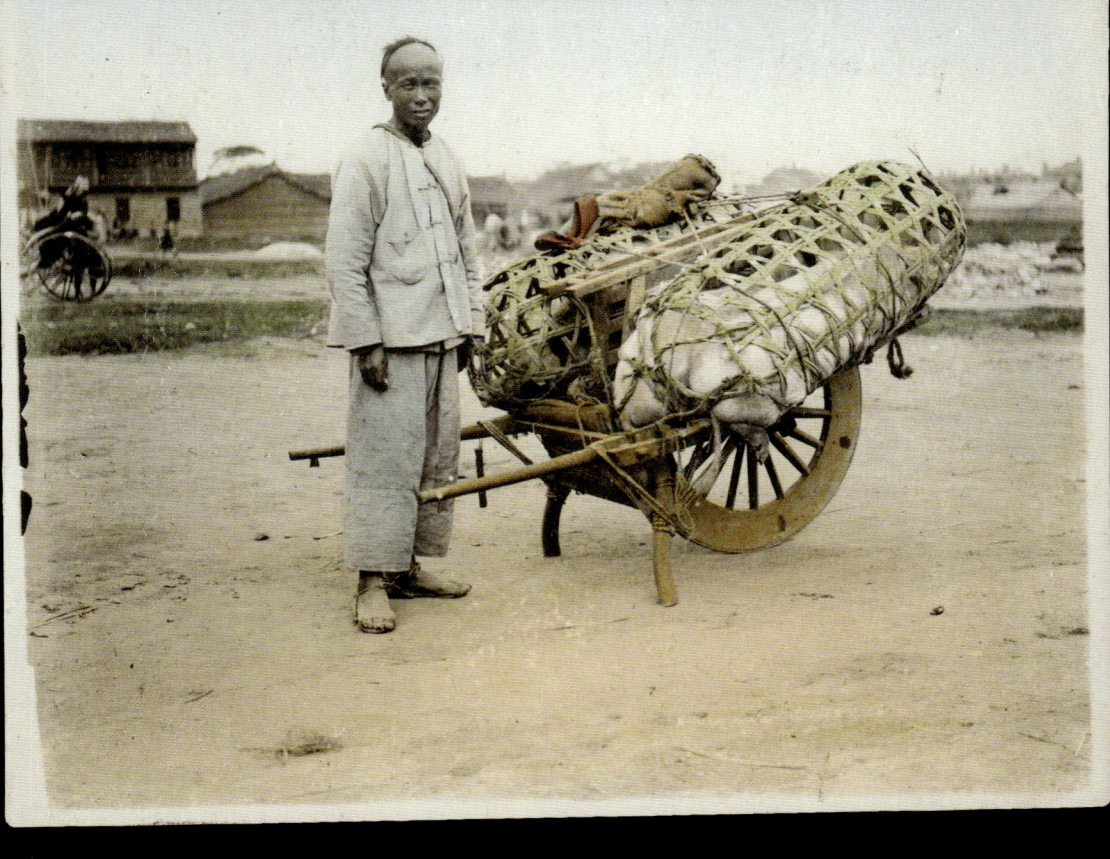

Hogs go to market in a wheel barrow.

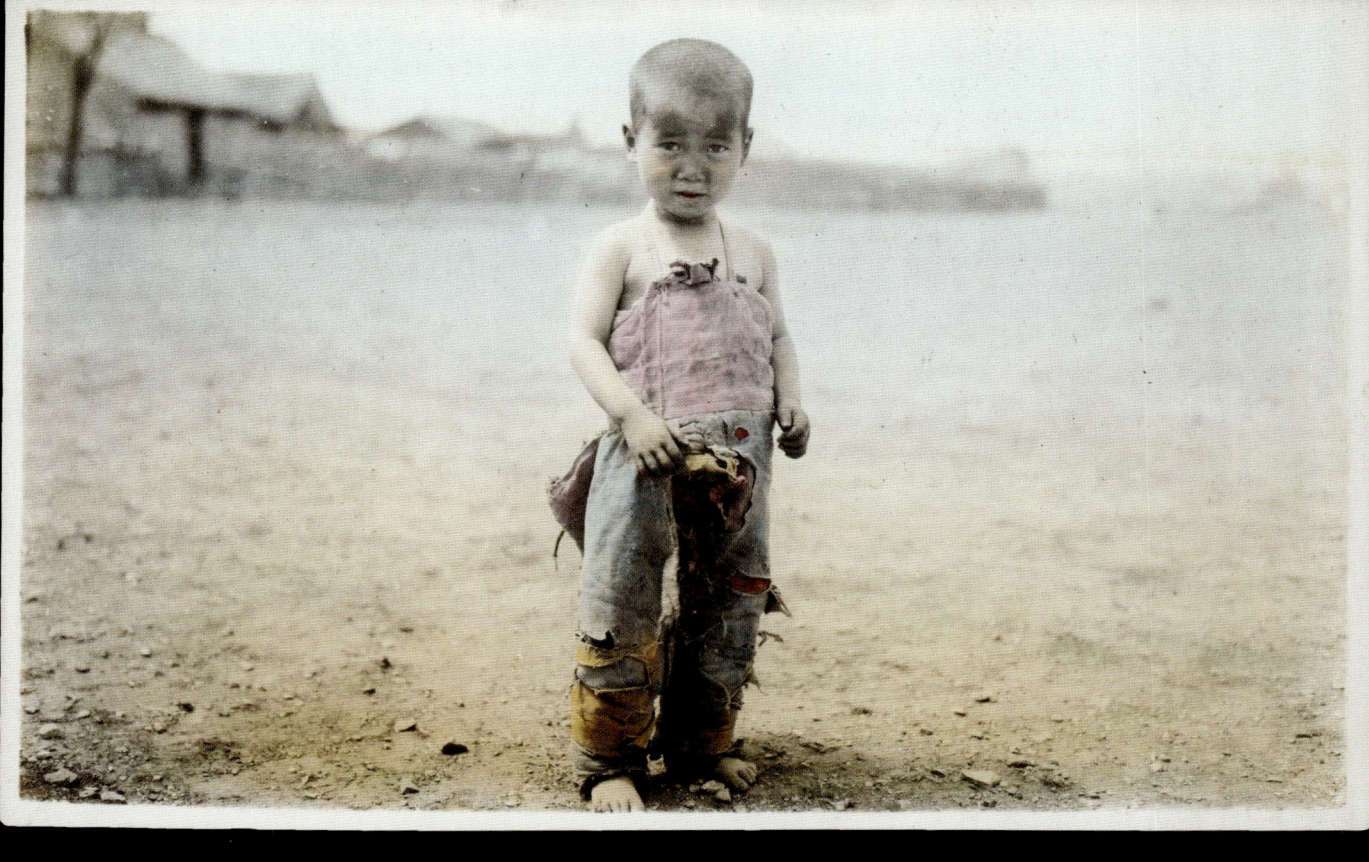

A little boy greets us in his Sunday best.

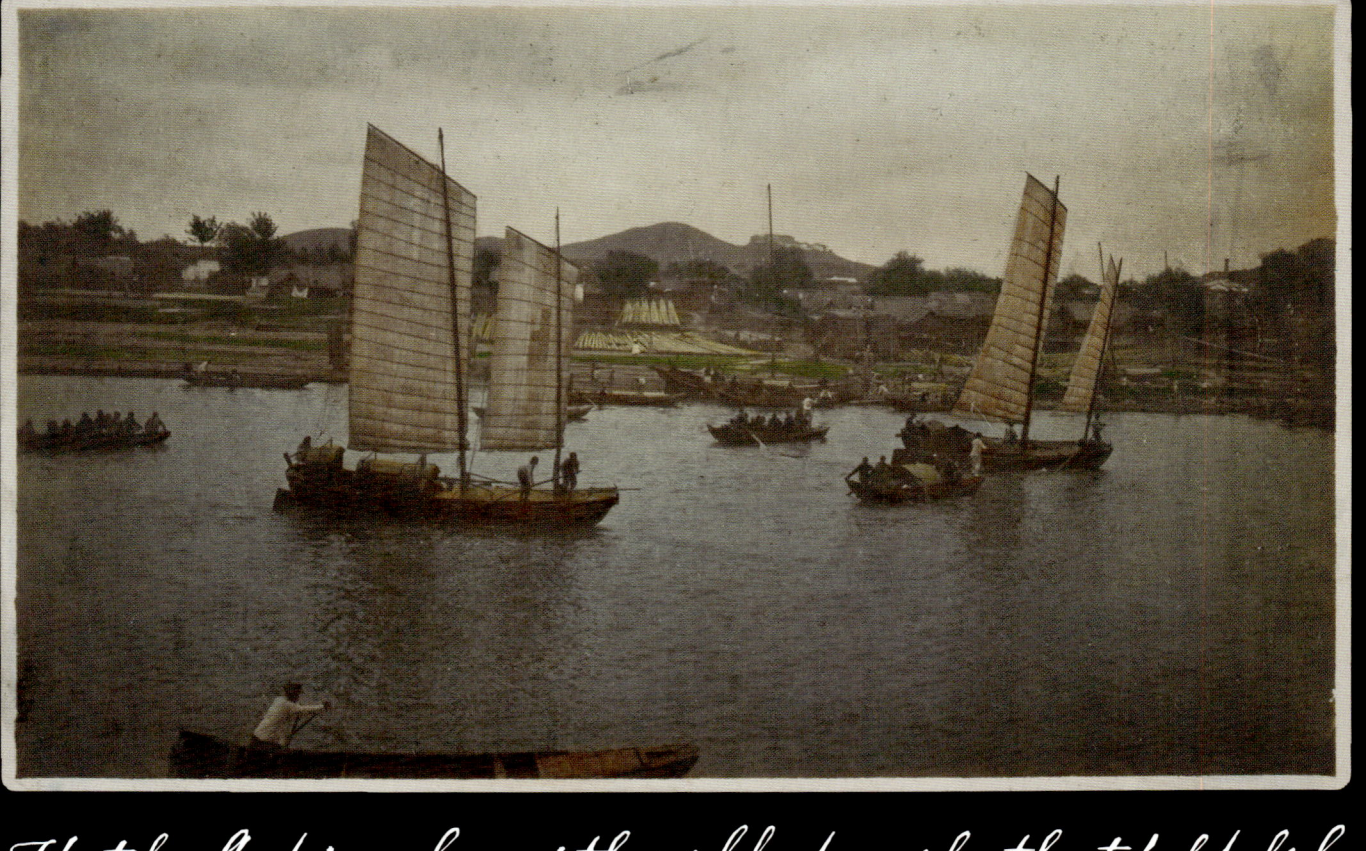

Flat hulled junks with ribbed sails that fold like fans ply the Yang Ste and Wu Hu Rivers between Shanghai and Hankow.

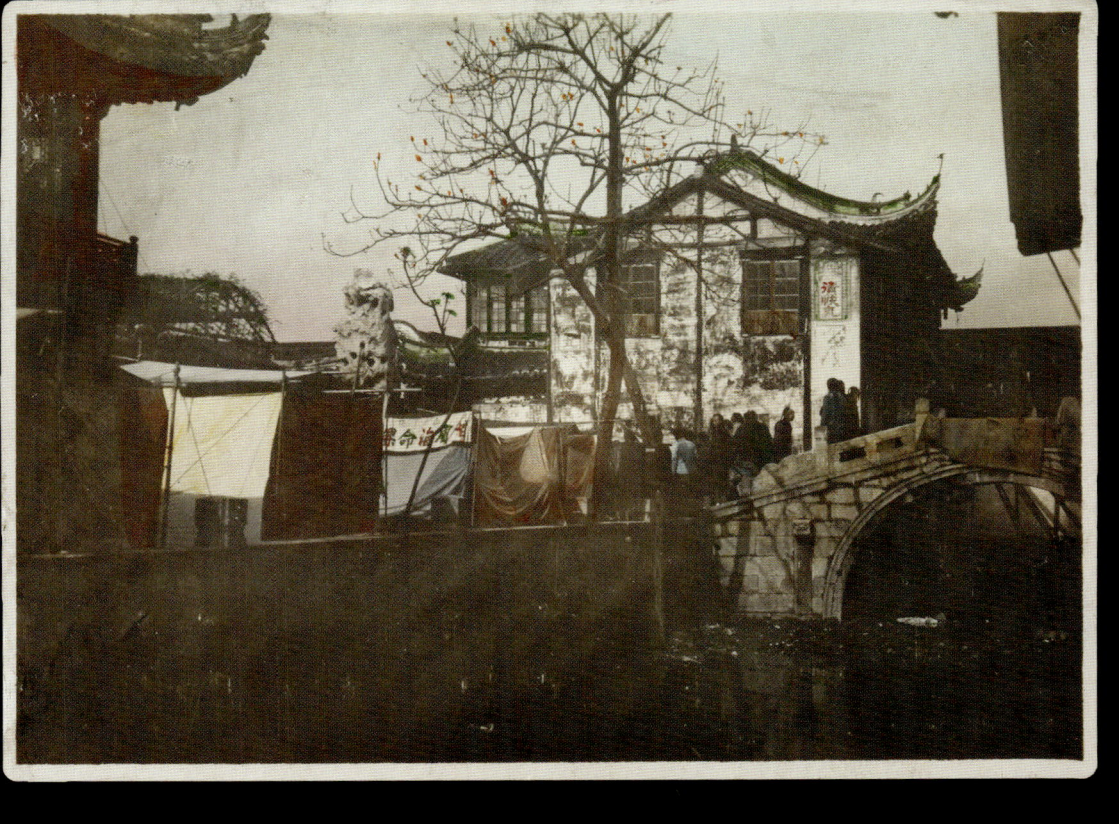

The city of Shanghai was built on land dredged from swampy river banks and is laced by canals and bridges.

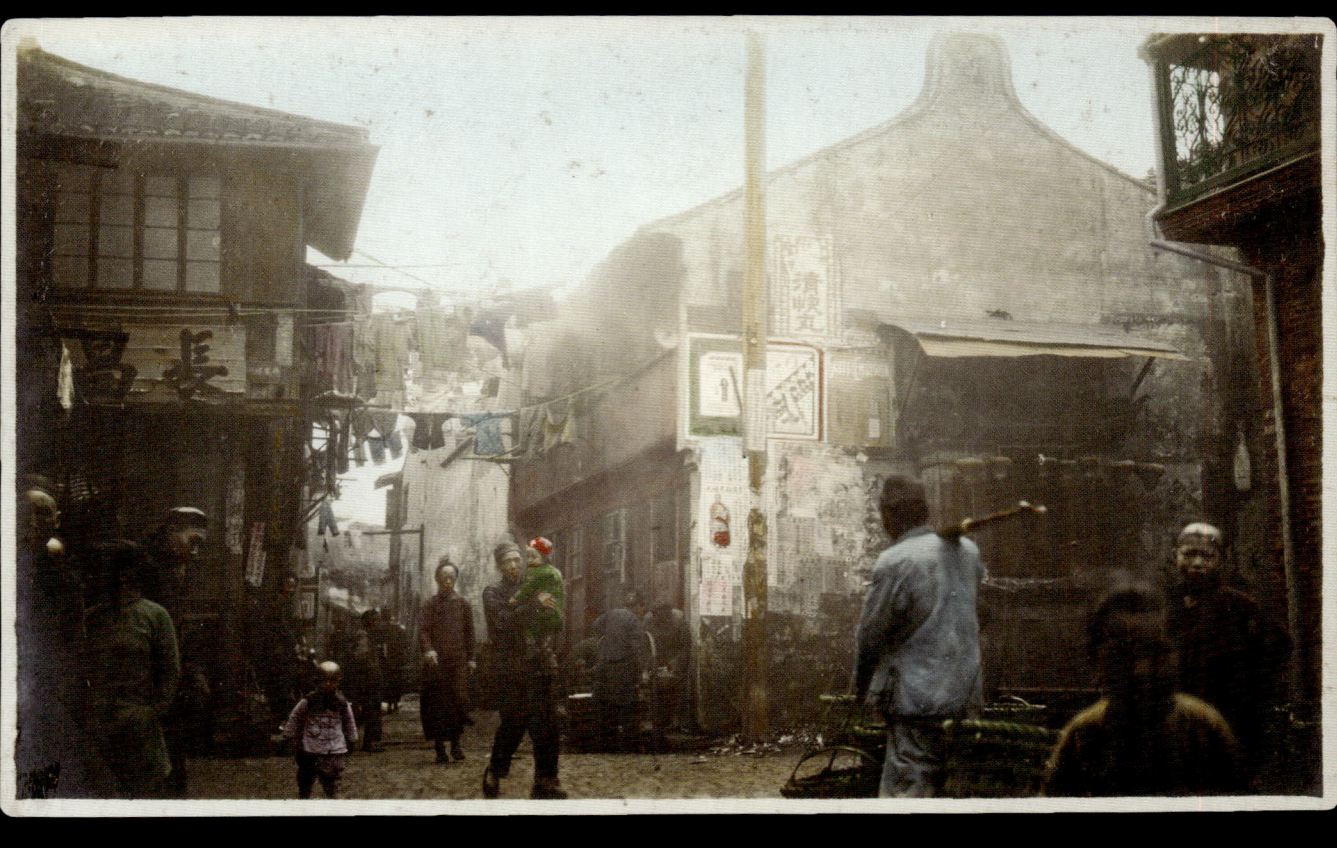

The Native City lies behind a 16th century wall and it is where many of the poor and working Chinese live.

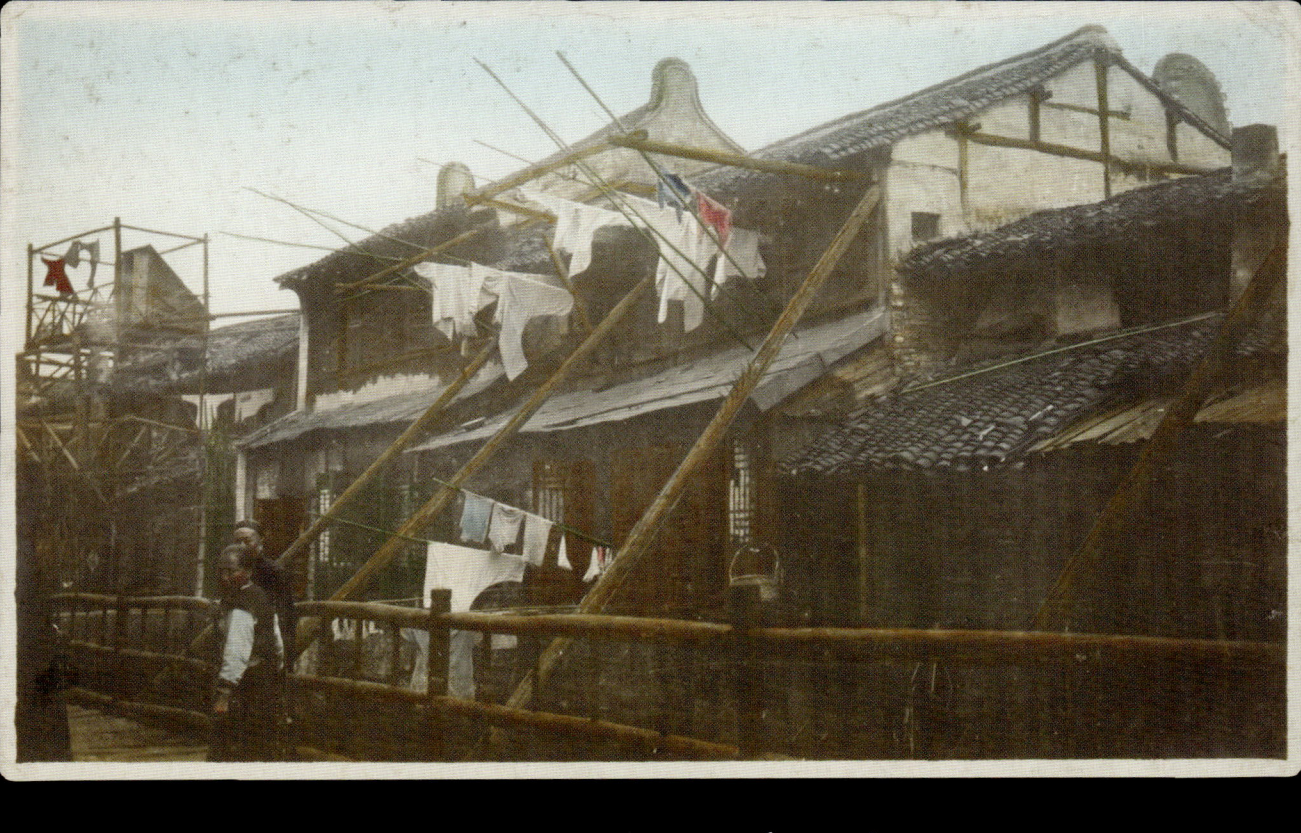

Narrow lanes and canal embankments are everywhere gaily festooned with laundry hung like flags.

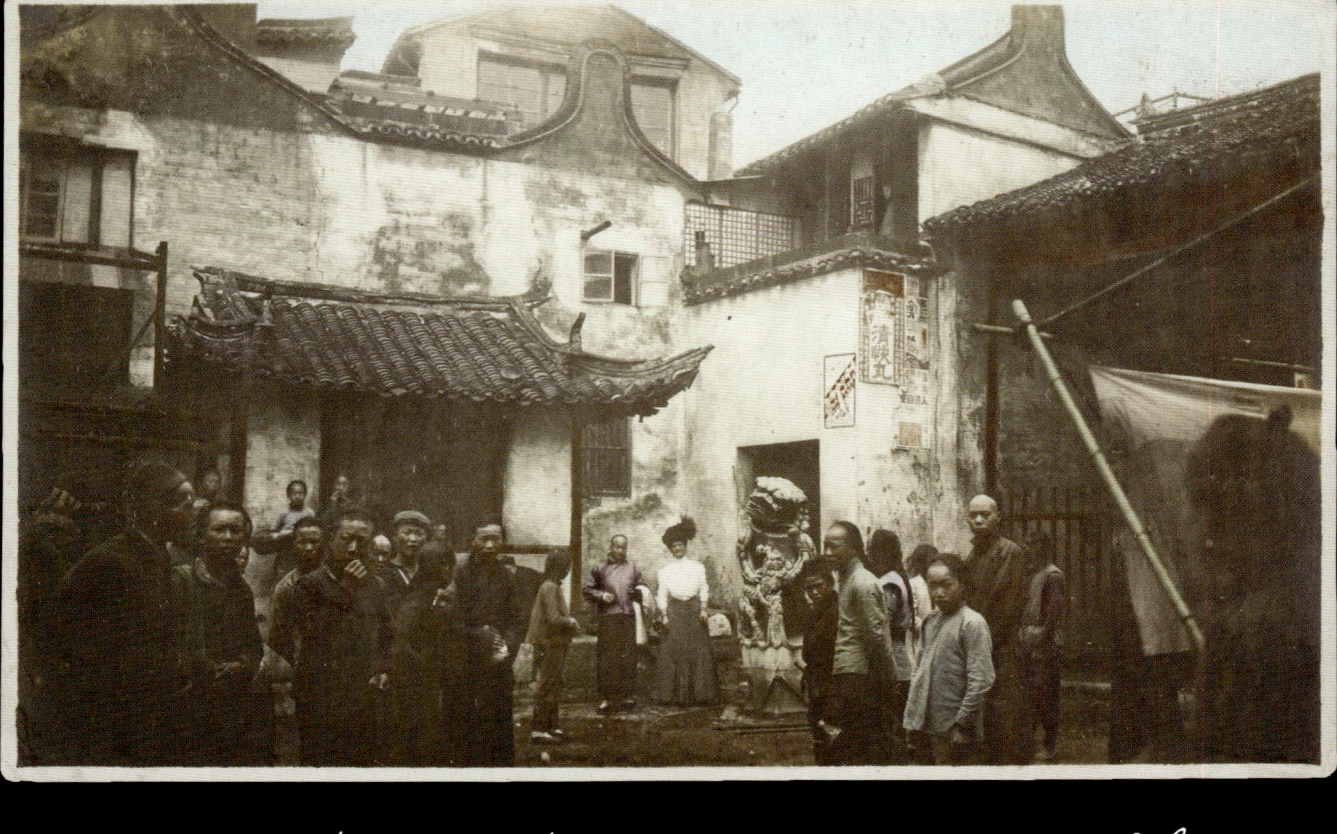

We attracted an audience of curious neighbors when we visited Mr. Hu and his family.

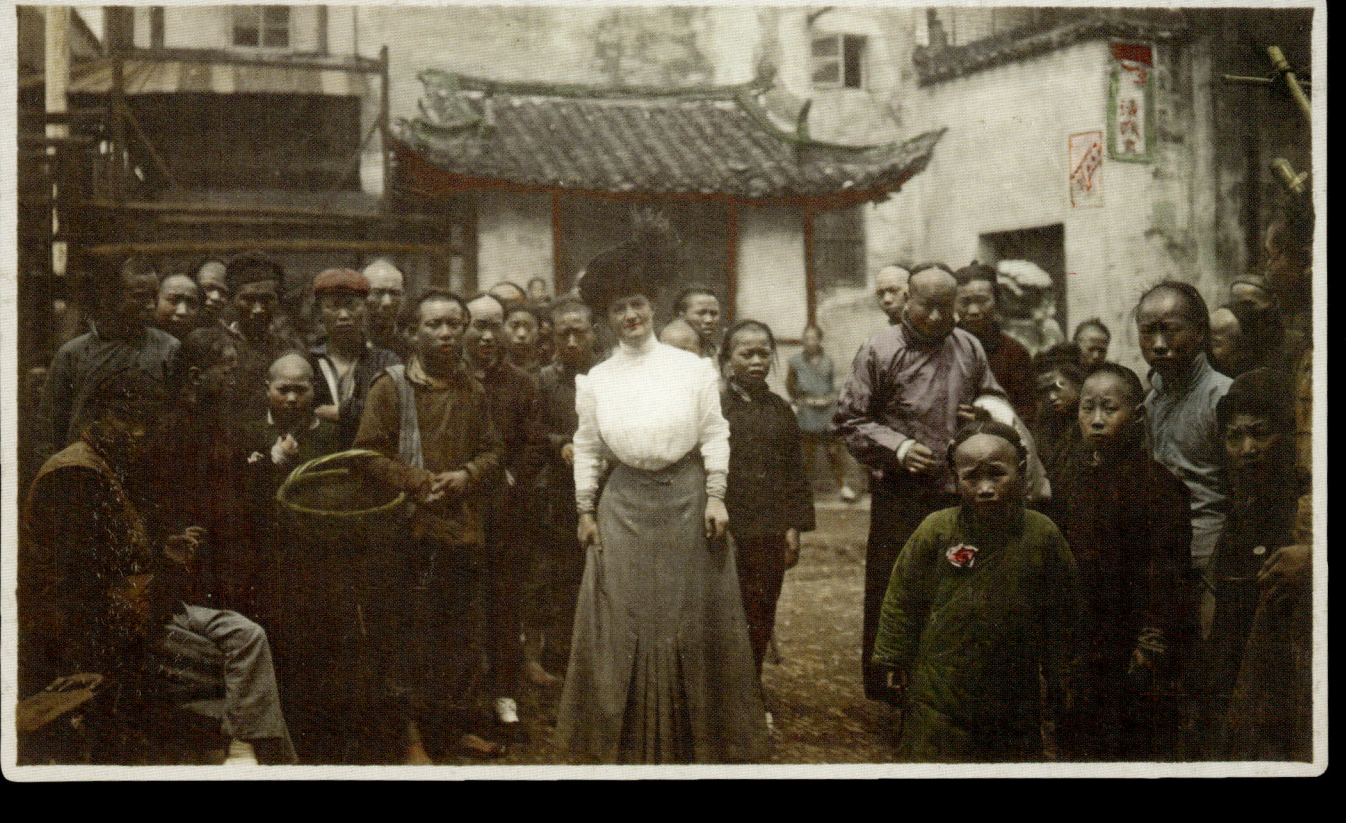

Curiosity shifted at once to the photographer the moment the crowd became aware of his camera.

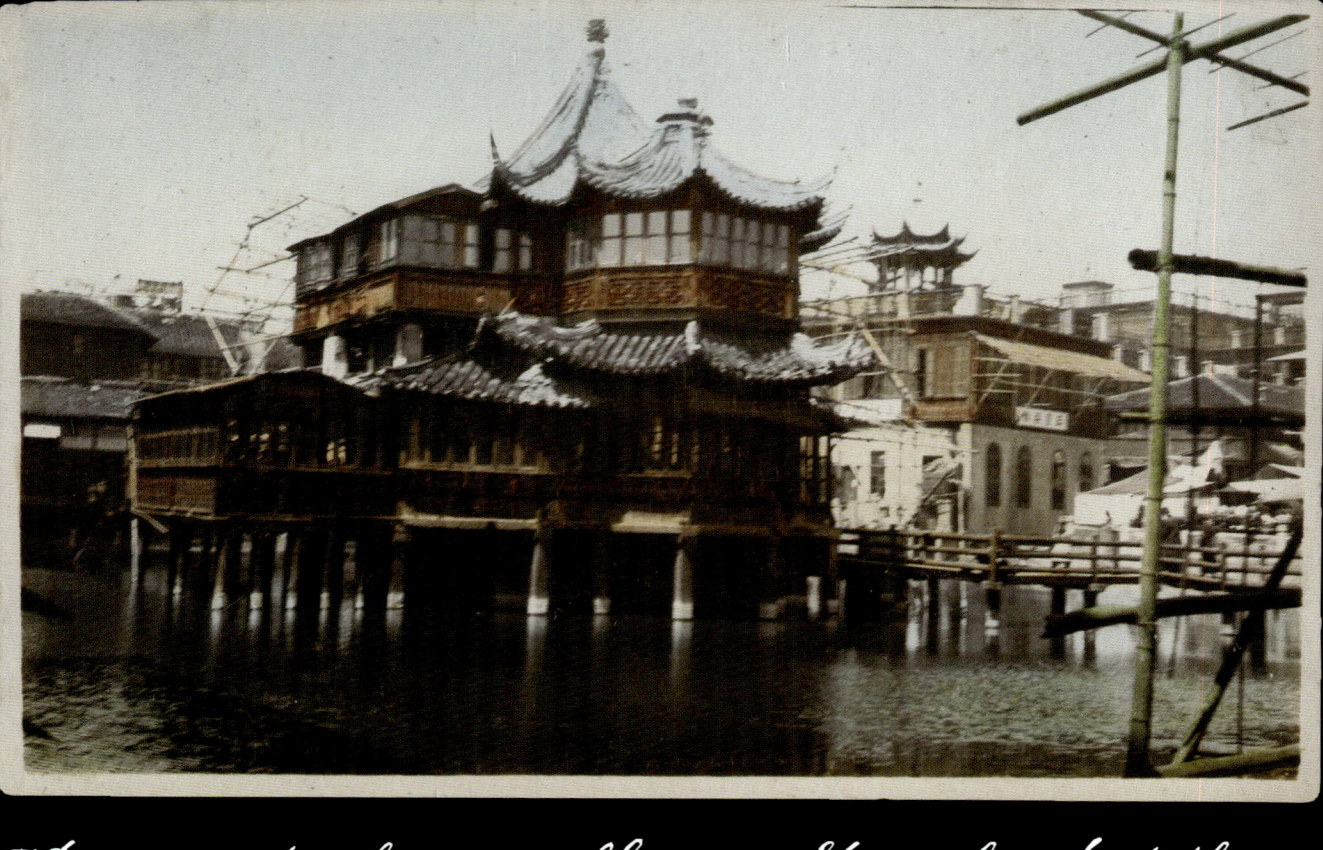

There are tea houses all over Shanghai but this famous Tea House must surely be among the prettiest.

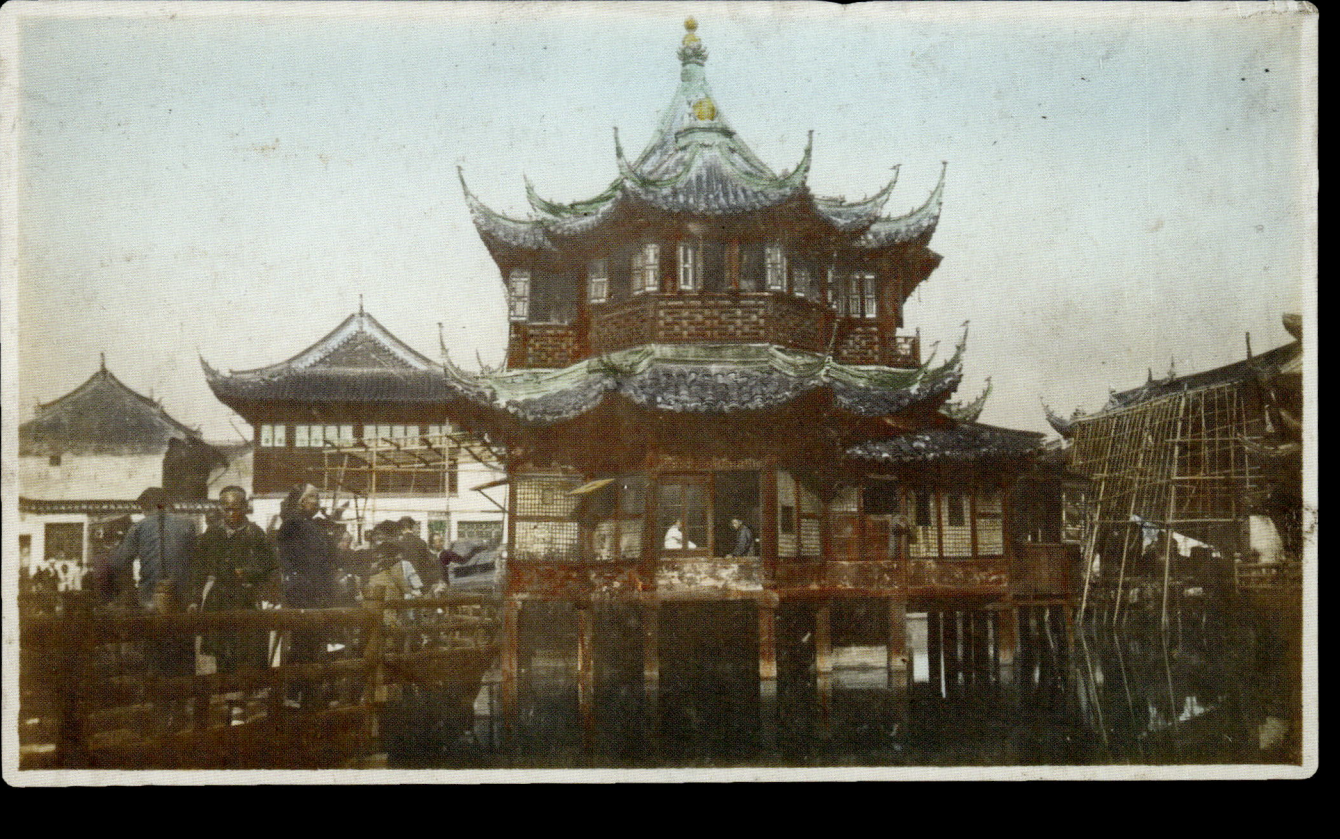

Tea House with delightful swallow tail roofs is reputed to have inspired the famed Willow Pattern porcelaine.

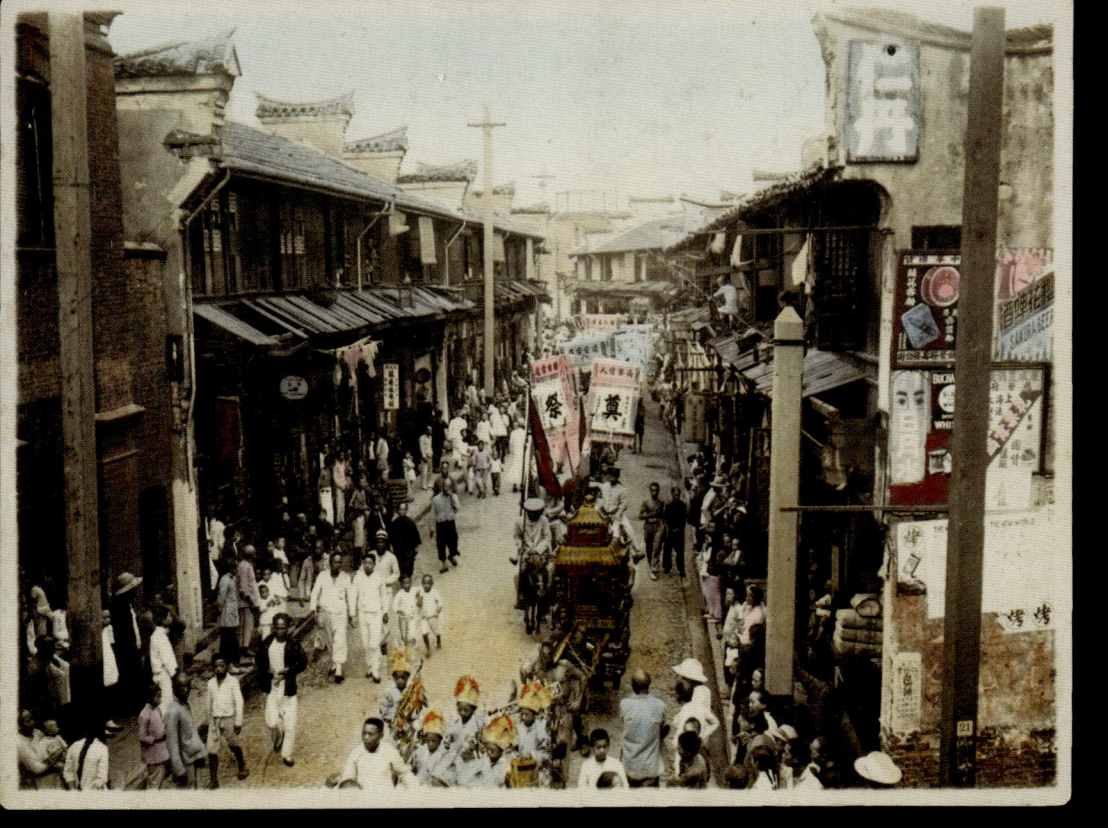

A Shanghai funeral is more like a parade with music and brightly colored banners.

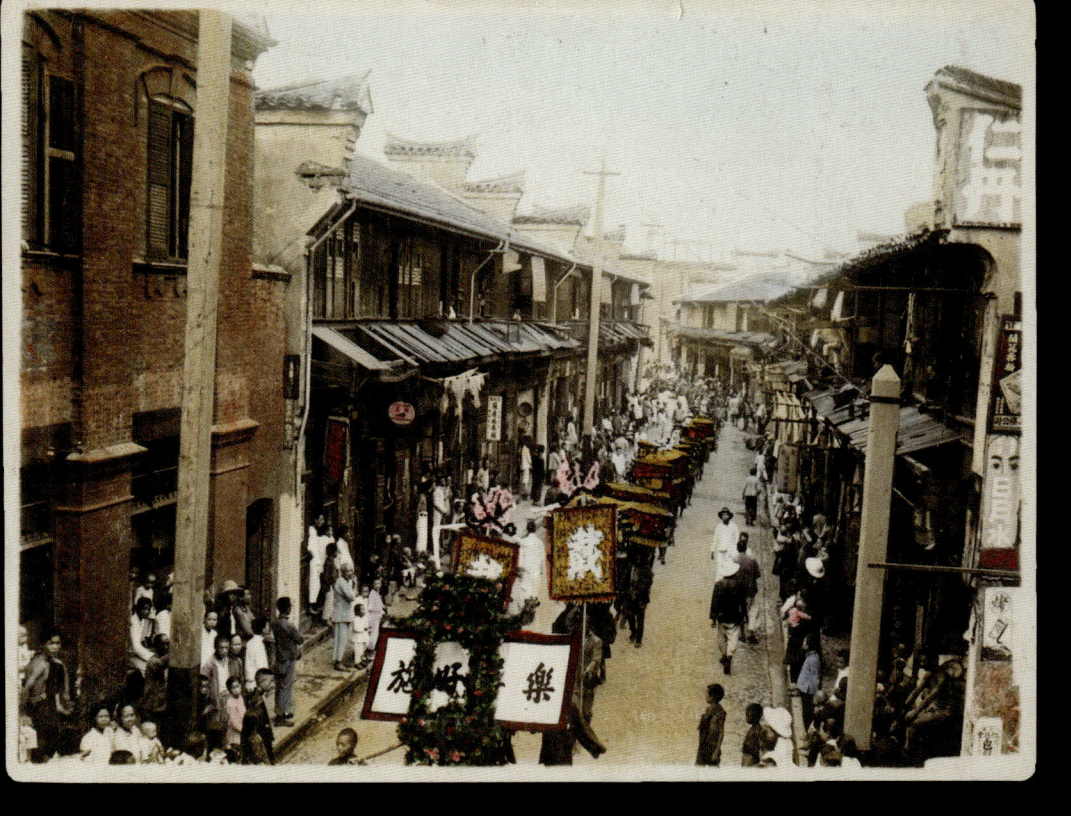

Hardly a day passed when our paths did not cross a funeral procession.

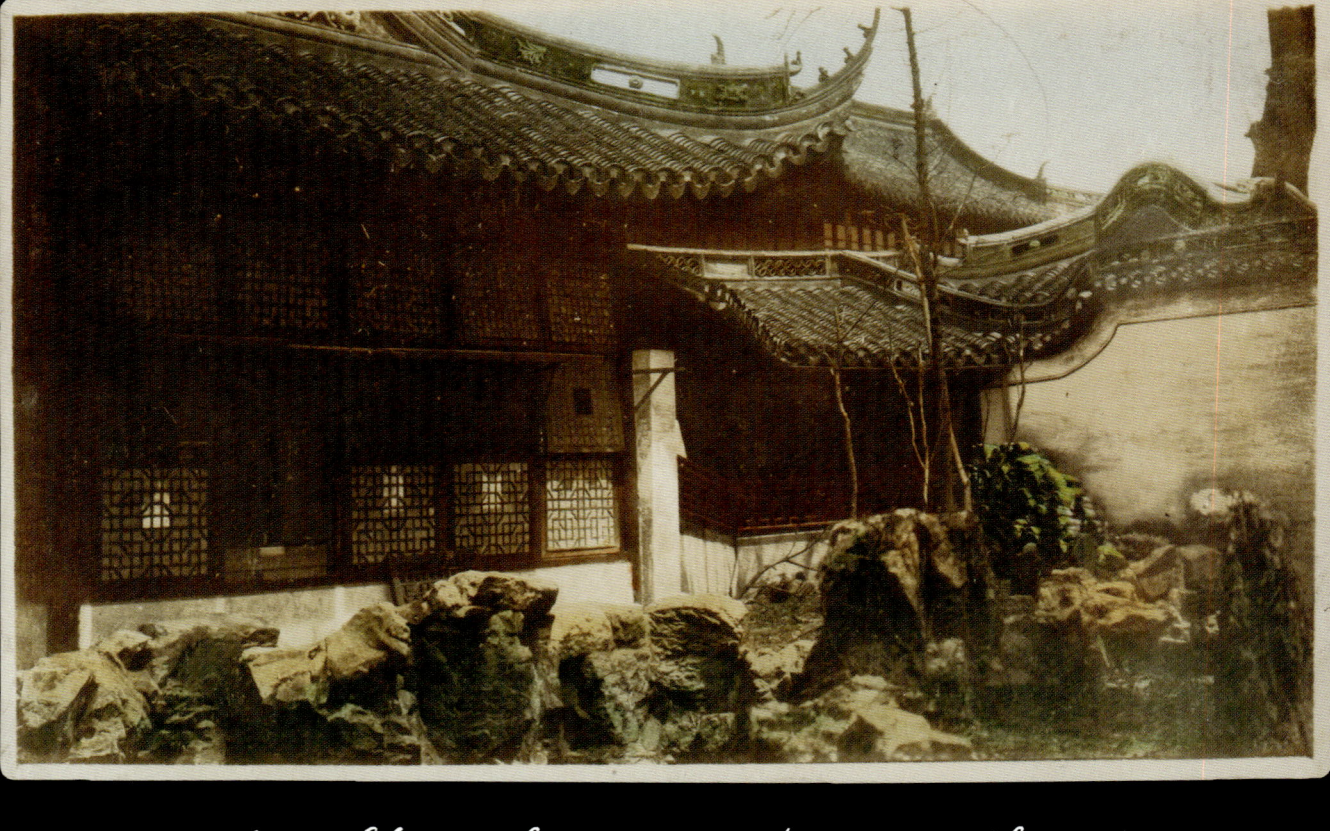

House of a Shanghai Mandarin—the stones in the rock garden were specially chosen for their fantastically grotesque shapes.

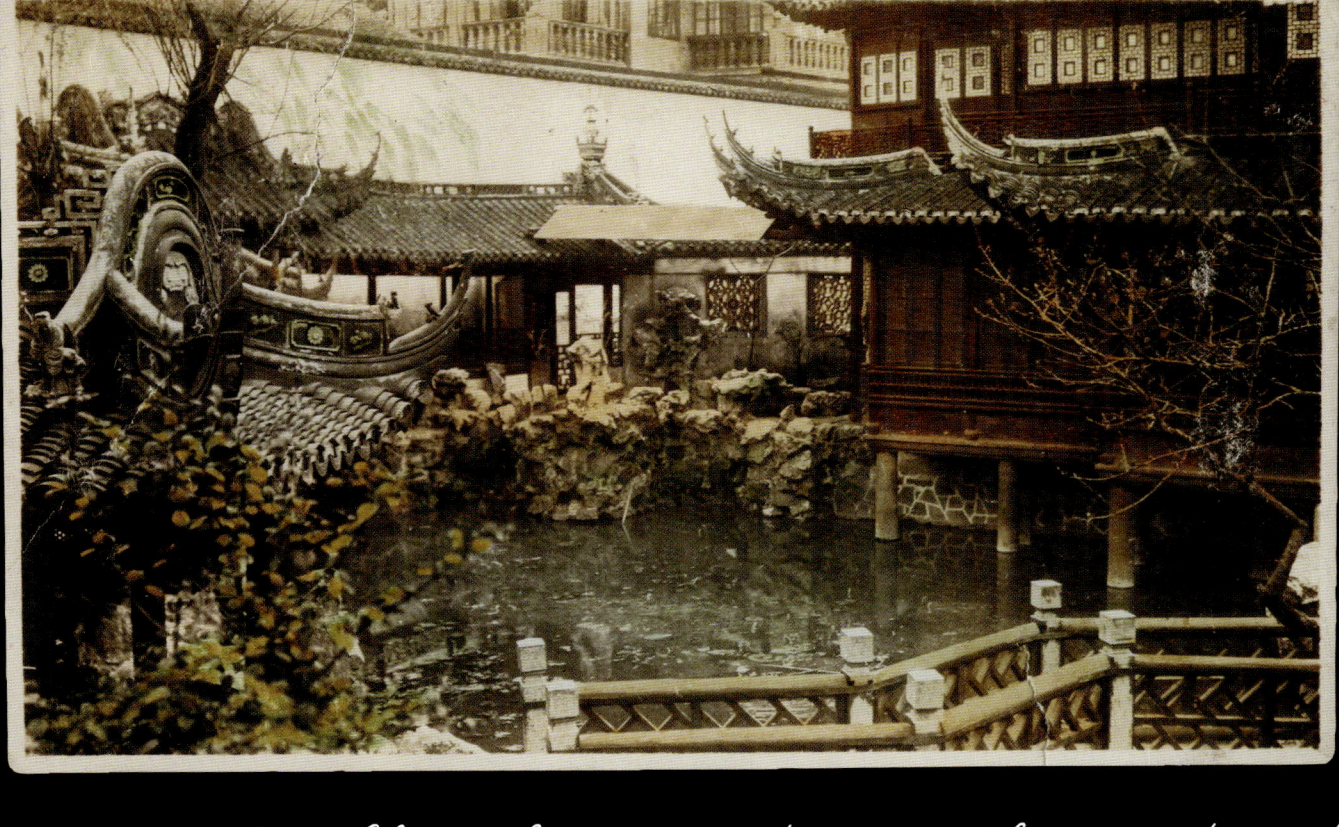

House of a Shanghai Mandarin—the pond and walking bridge and grottos were a serene haven within the high white walls.

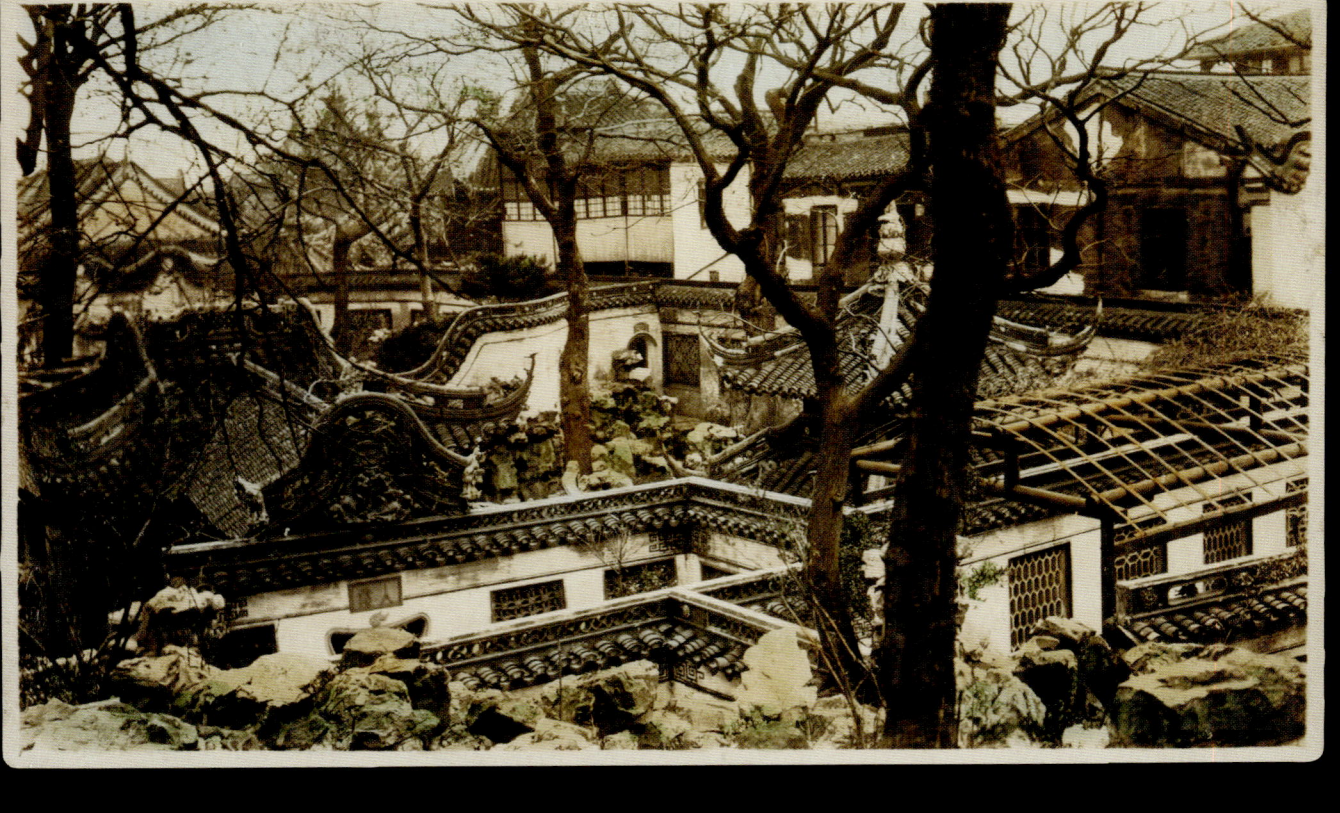

House of a Shanghai Mandarin—the compound was comprised of pavilions and courtyards.

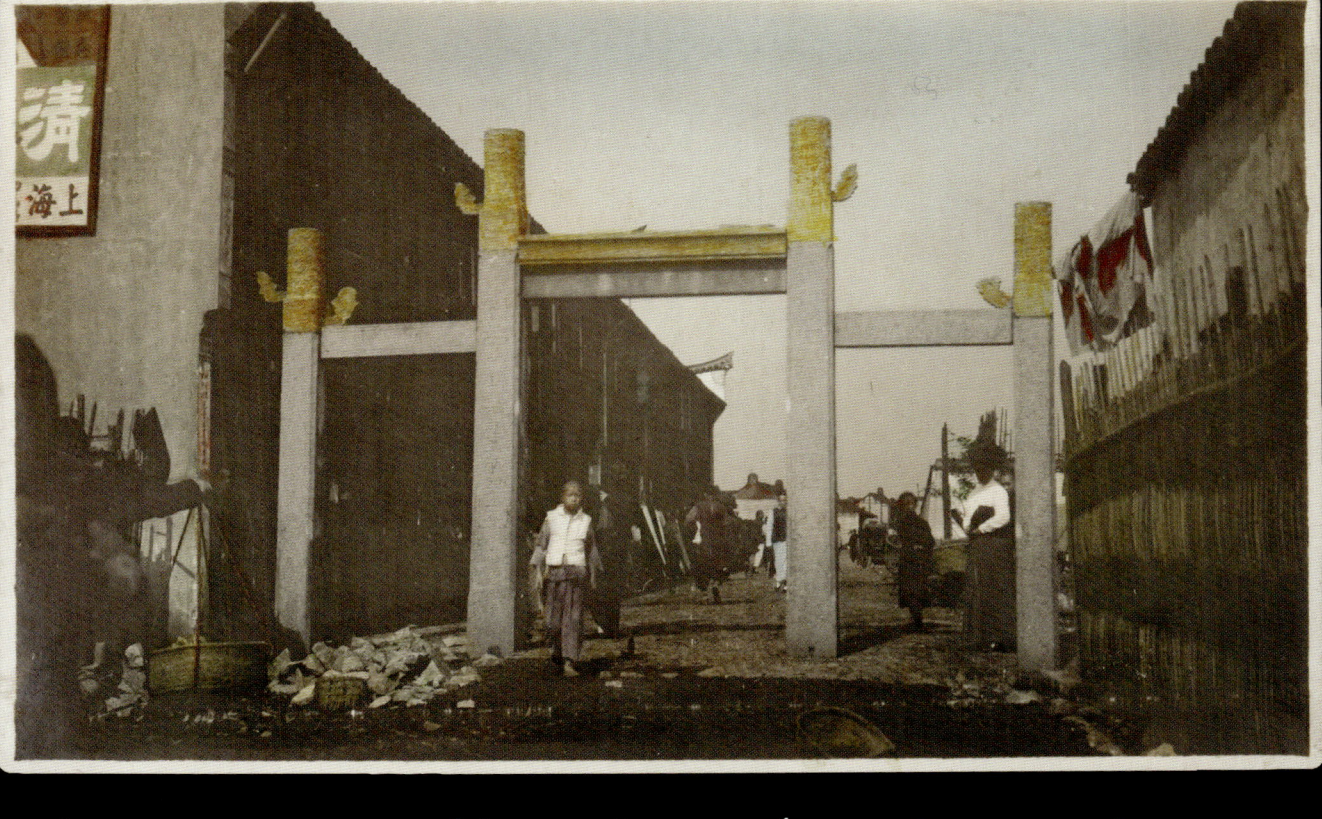

Street scene—Shanghai. A pailou used for hanging the severed heads of executed criminals!

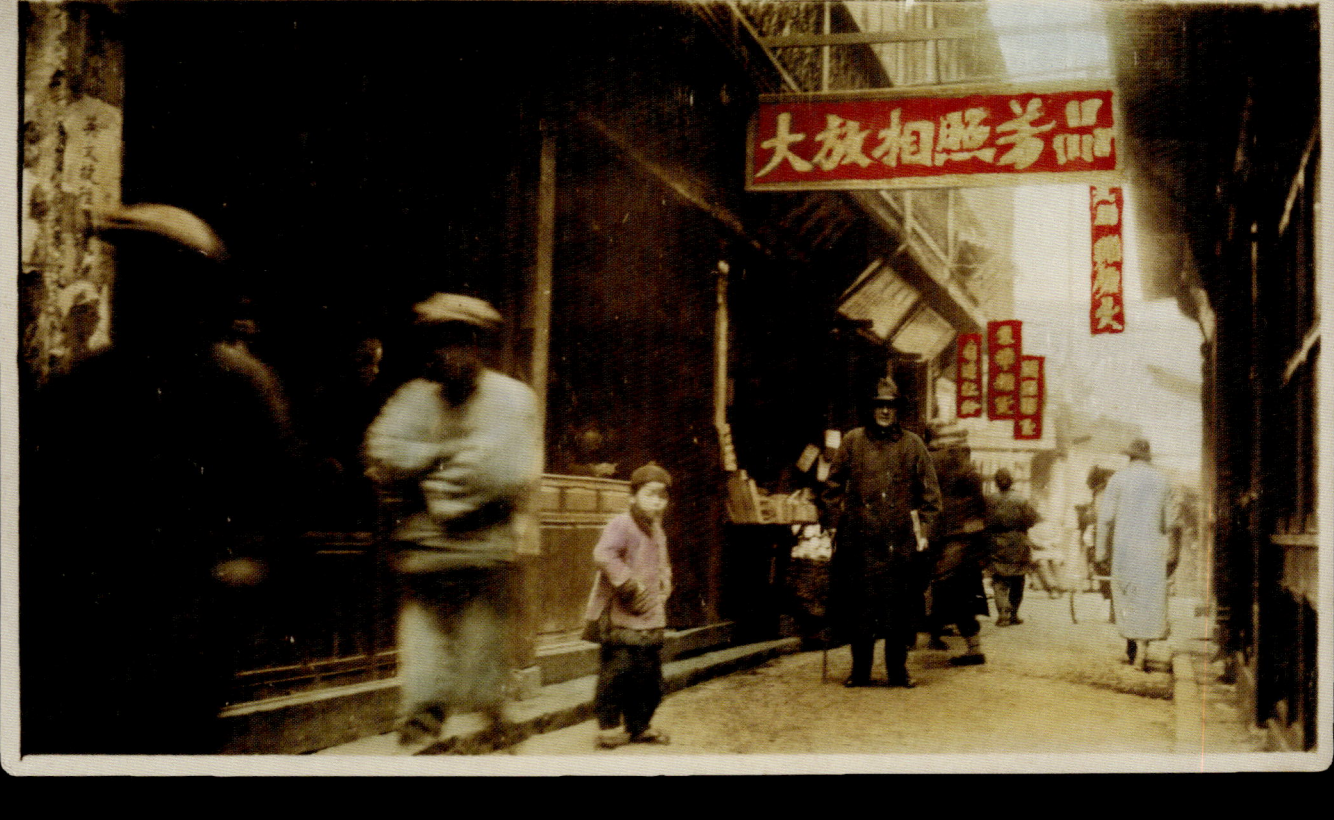

Street in Old Shanghai lined with banks and apothecaries.

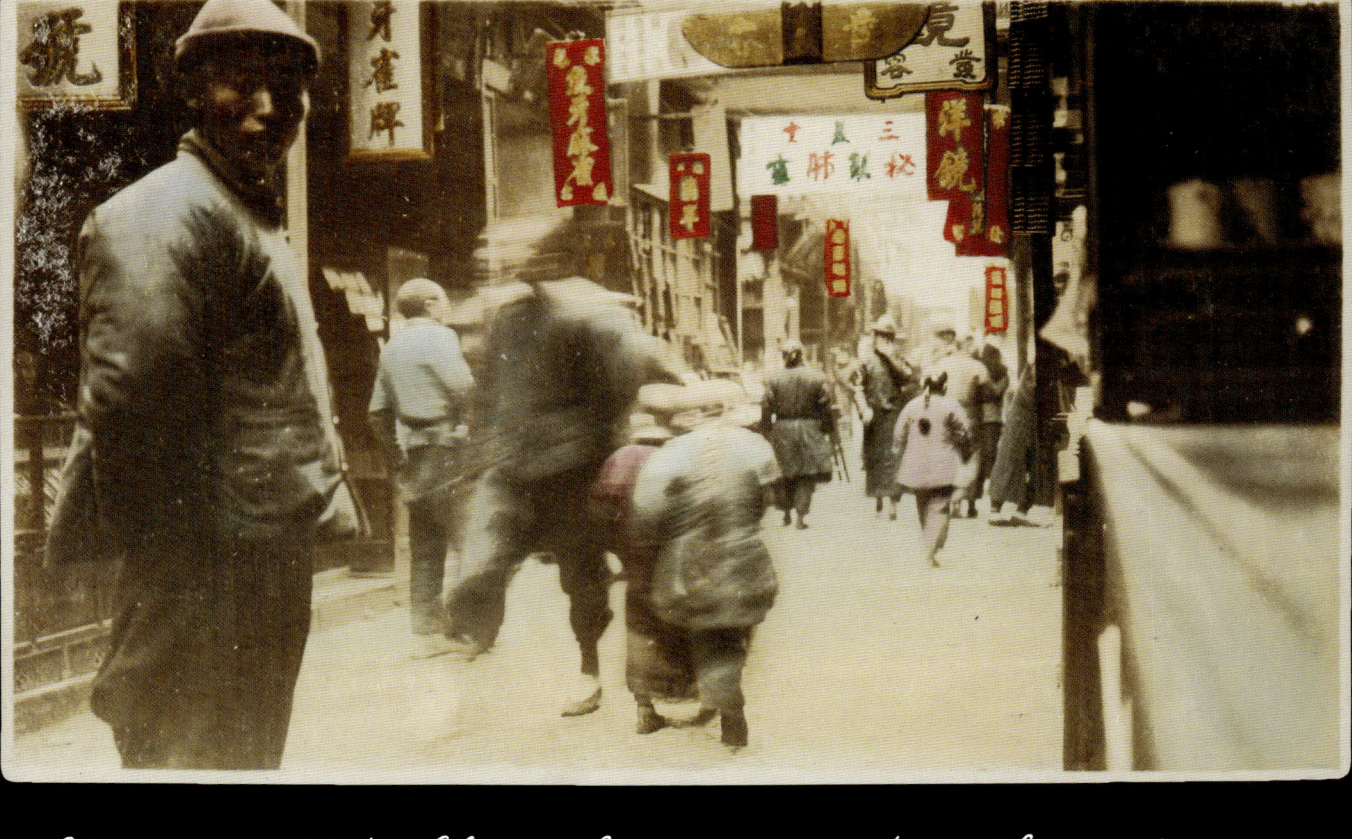

Street in Old Shanghai crowded with restaurants and tea houses.

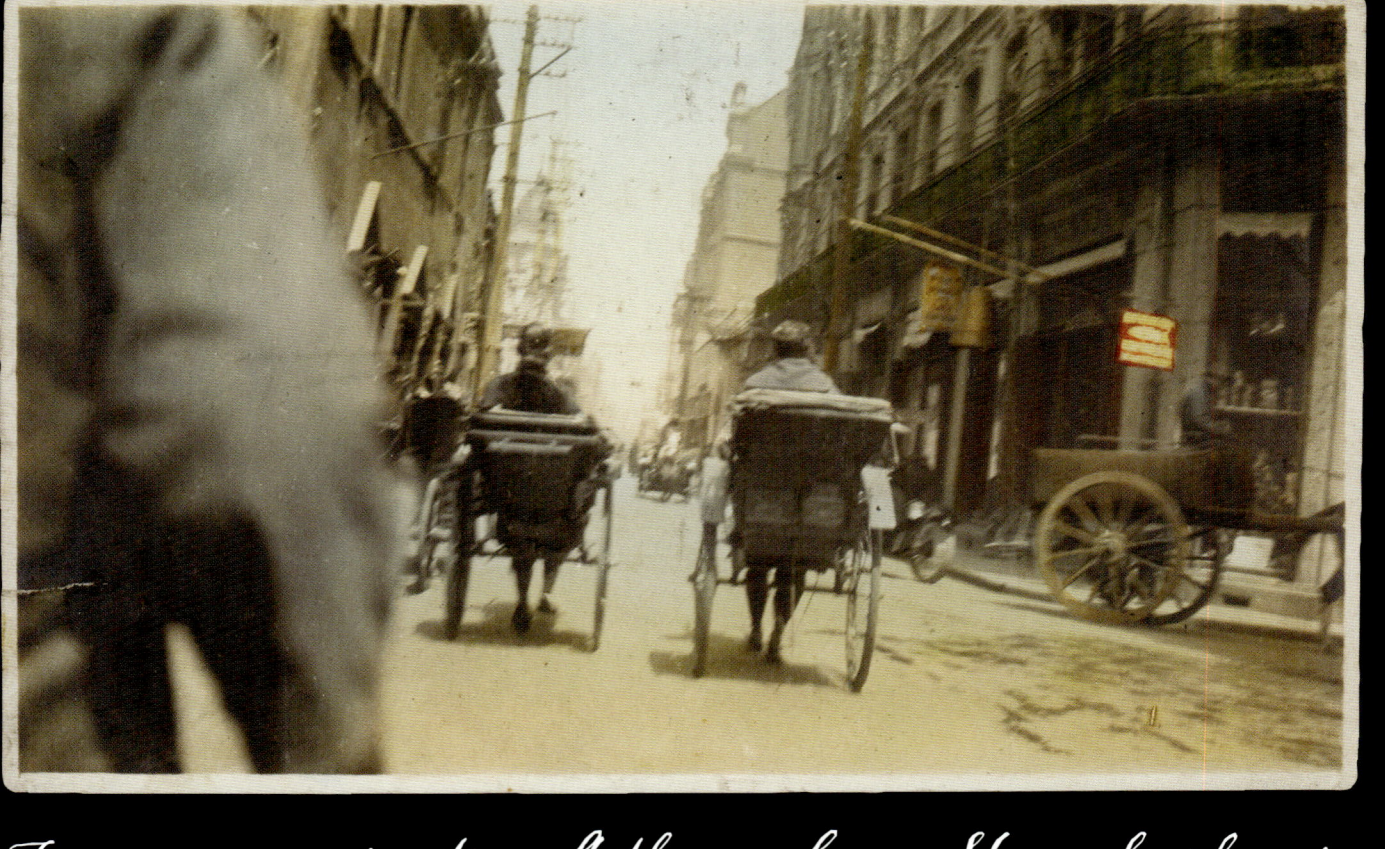

Foreign residents call themselves Shanghailanders and have made the city the most sophisticated in the Orient.

The Chinese are
called Shanghainese
and even the poor
districts bustle with
markets and shops
and peddlers.

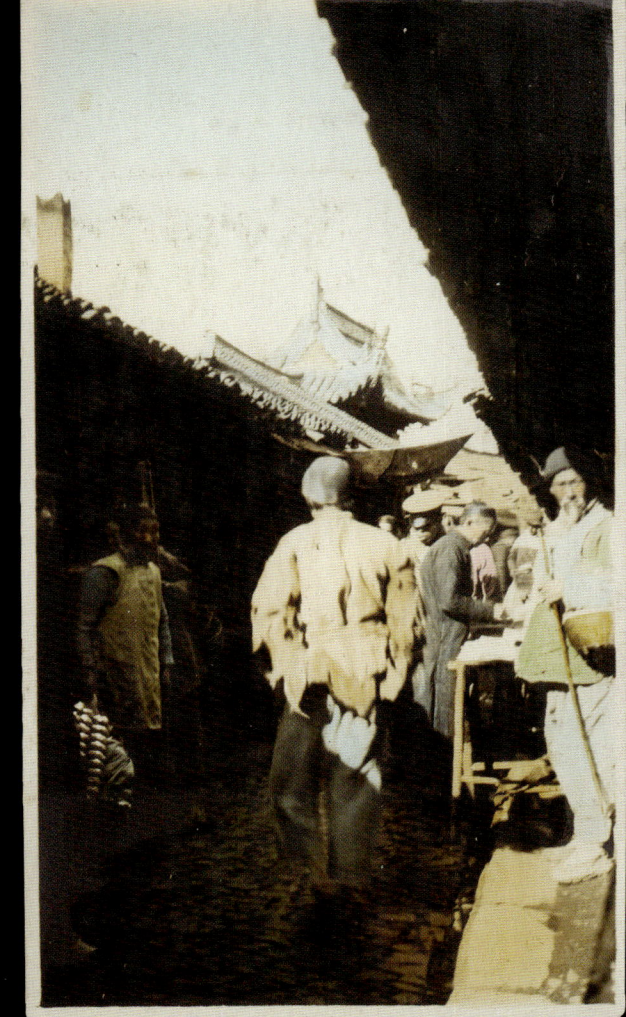

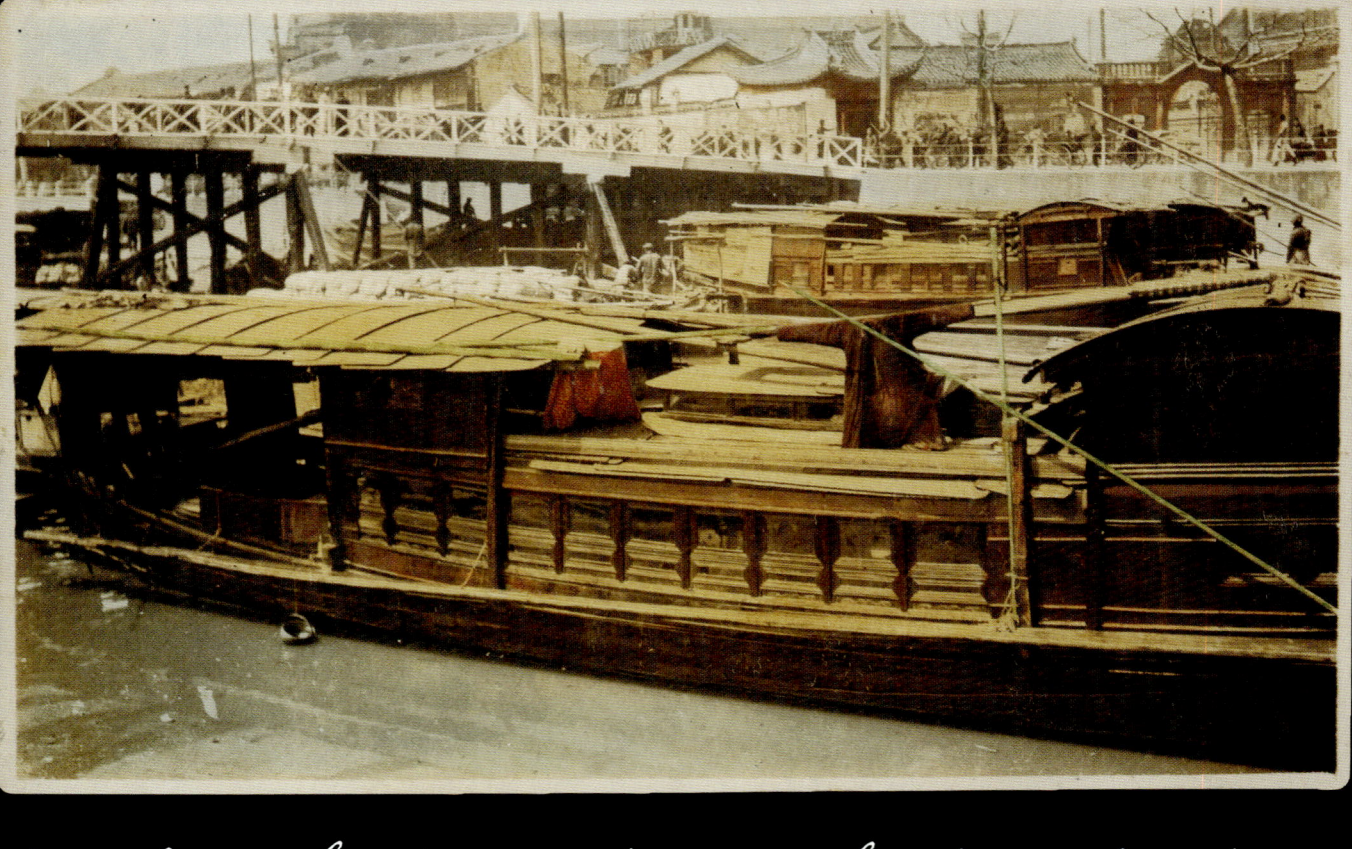

On a house boat moored near a bridge, a handsome
robe is hung out to dry in the sun.

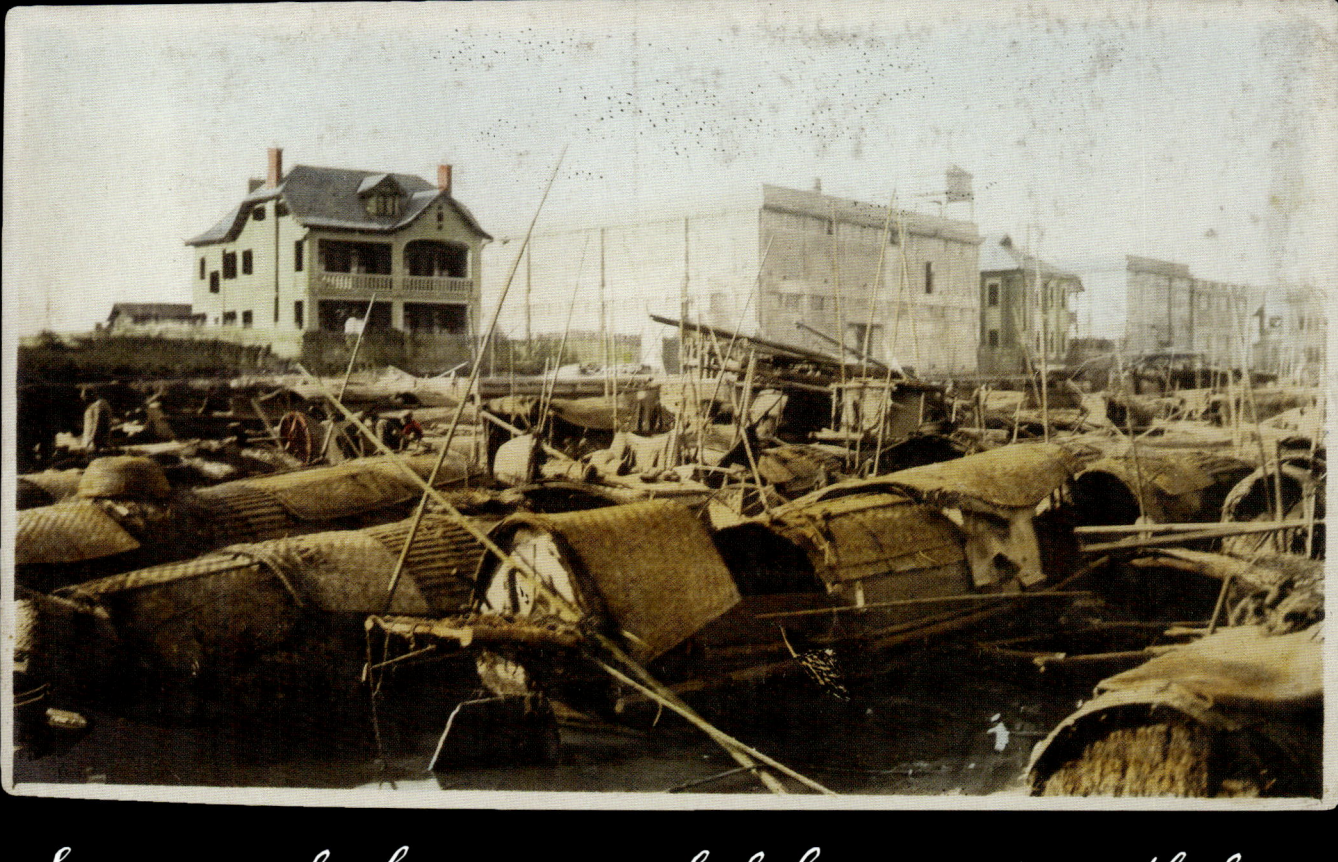

Sampans look very much like insects with long feelers on a canal lined with warehouses.

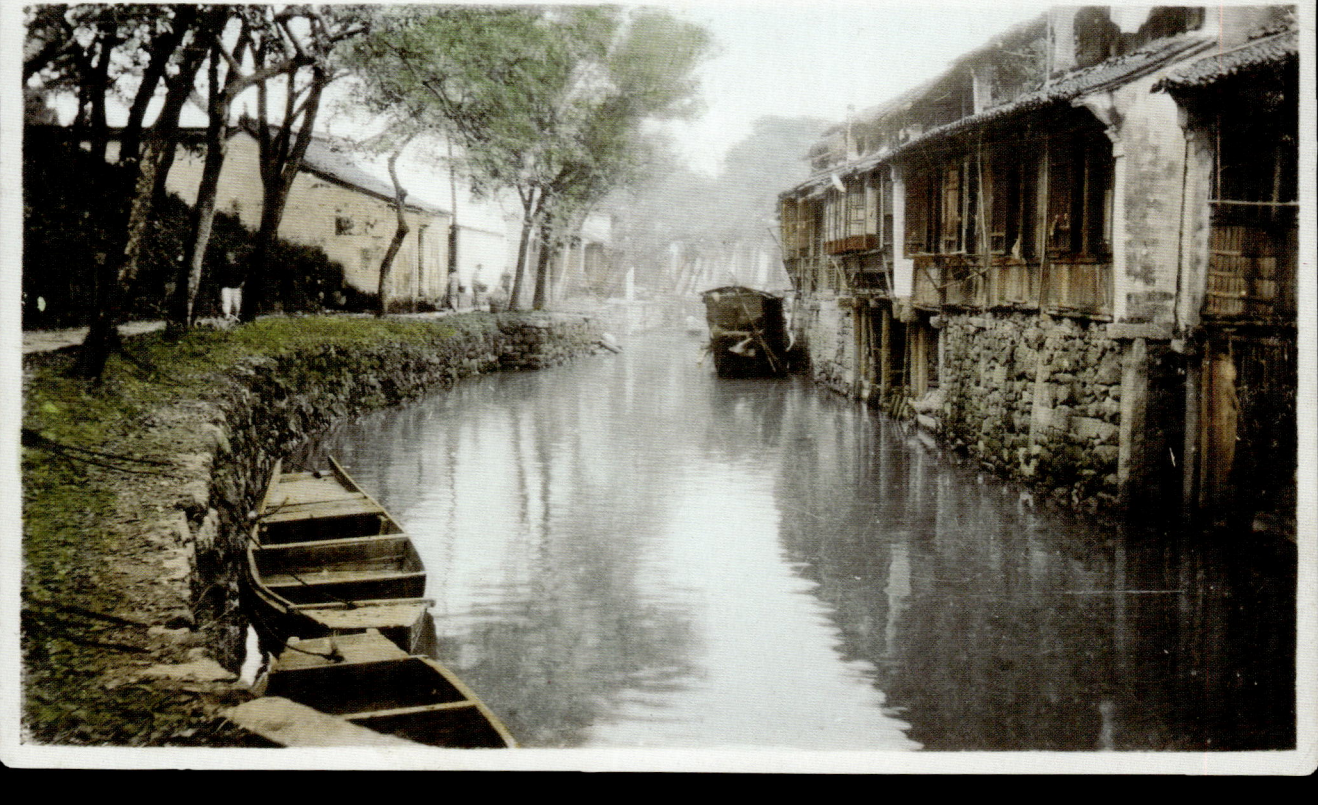

Misty morning canal scene — Soochow Creek

Chinese junk with tattered sail is a scroll painting come to life.

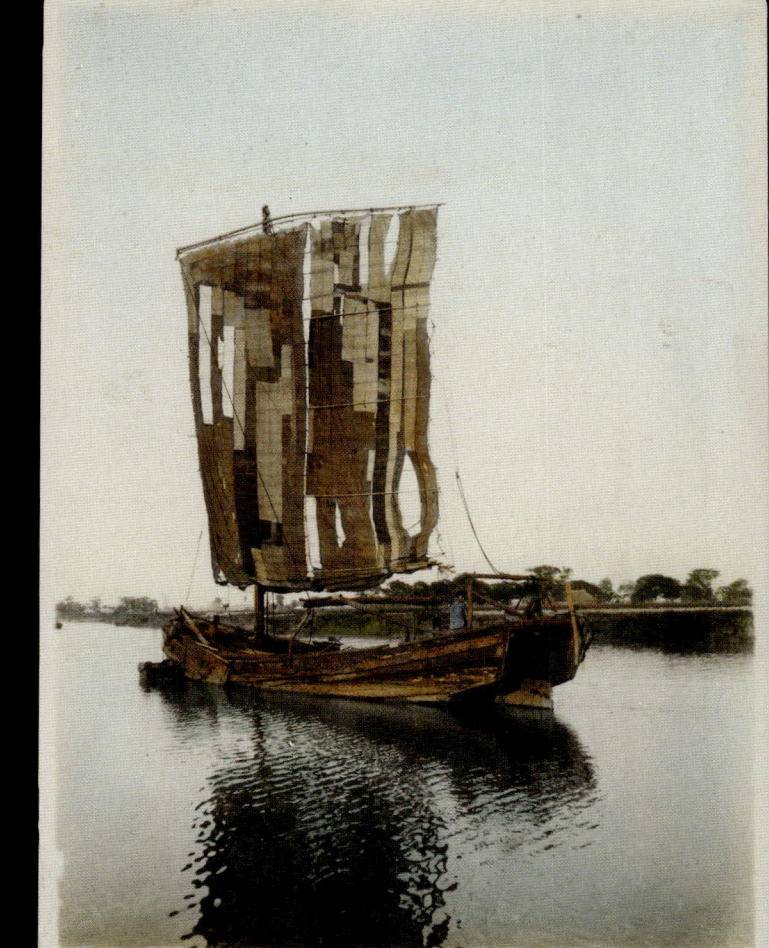

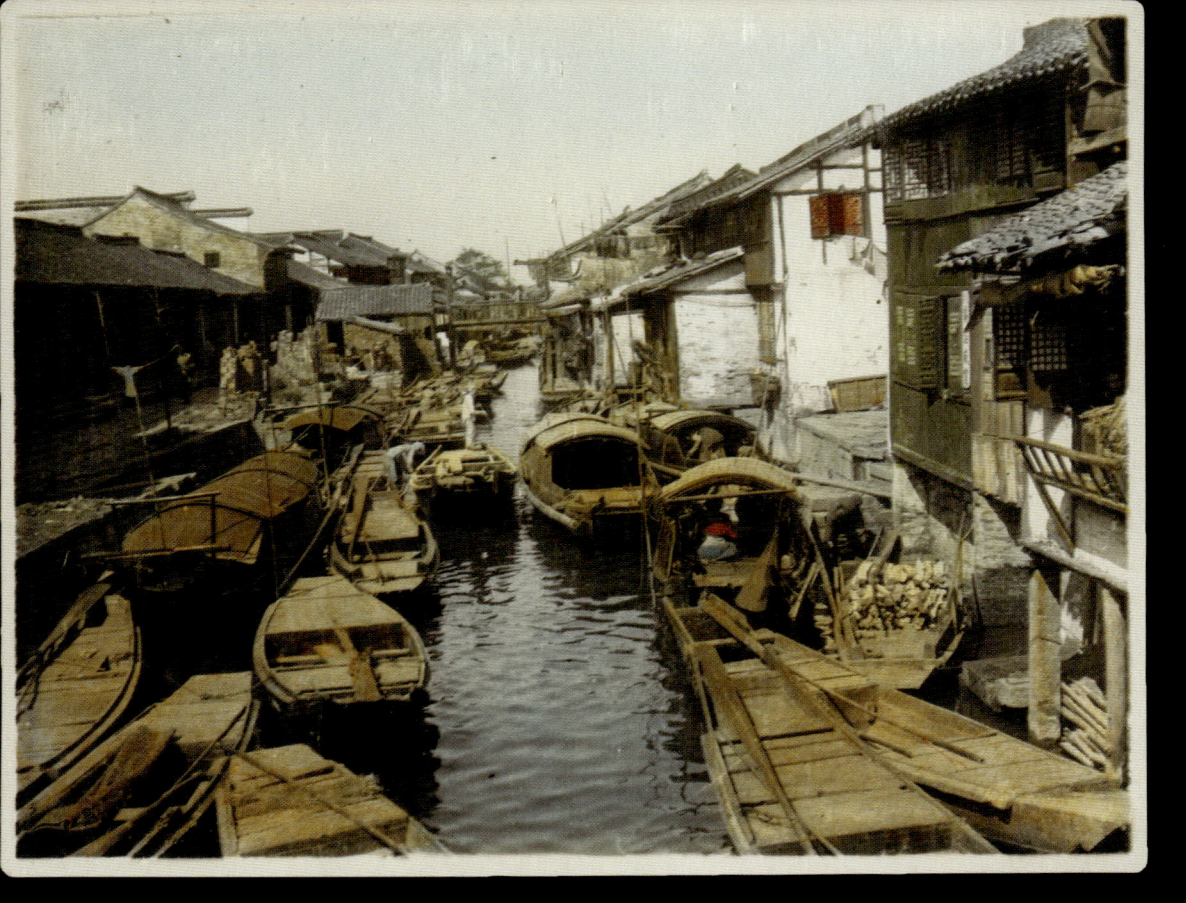

Sampans navigate a mercantile district along a Shanghai canal.

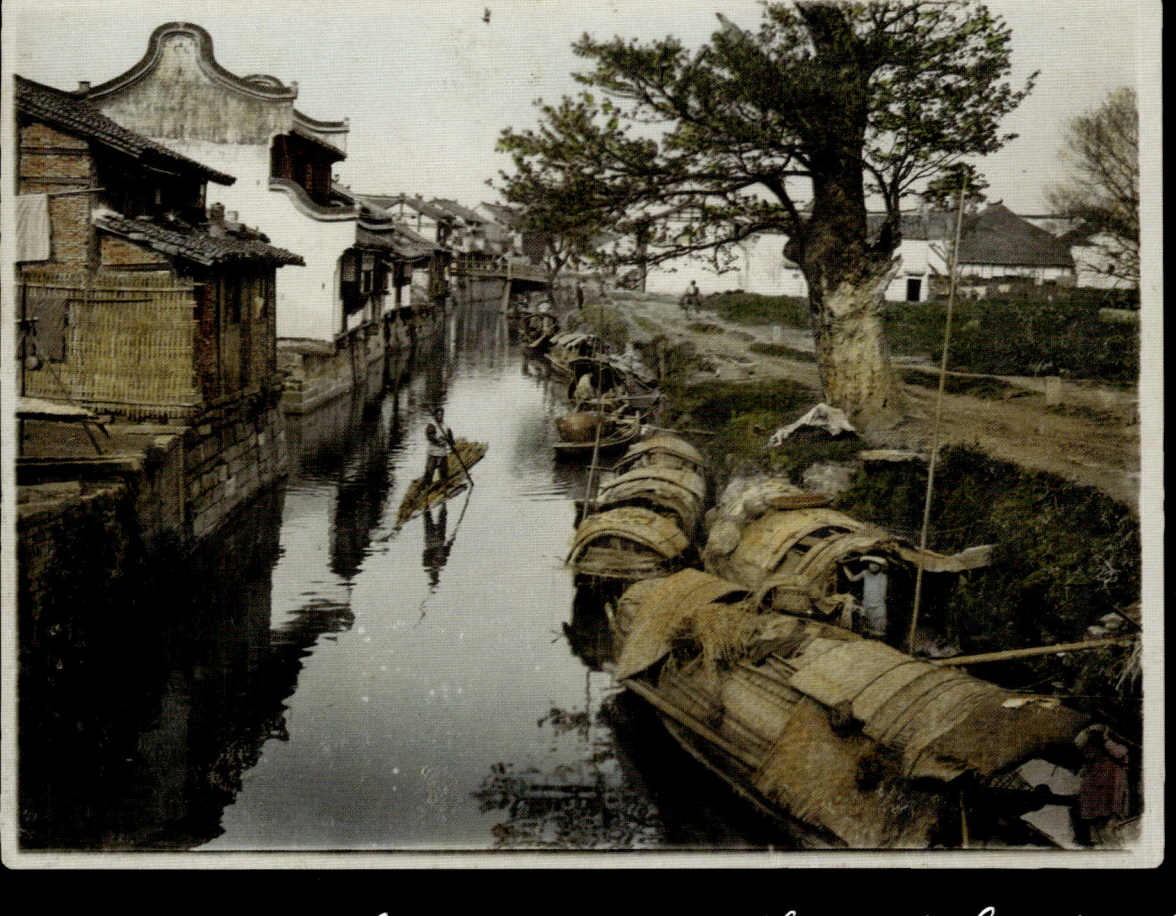

Bucolic canal scene nearer the outskirts of the city.

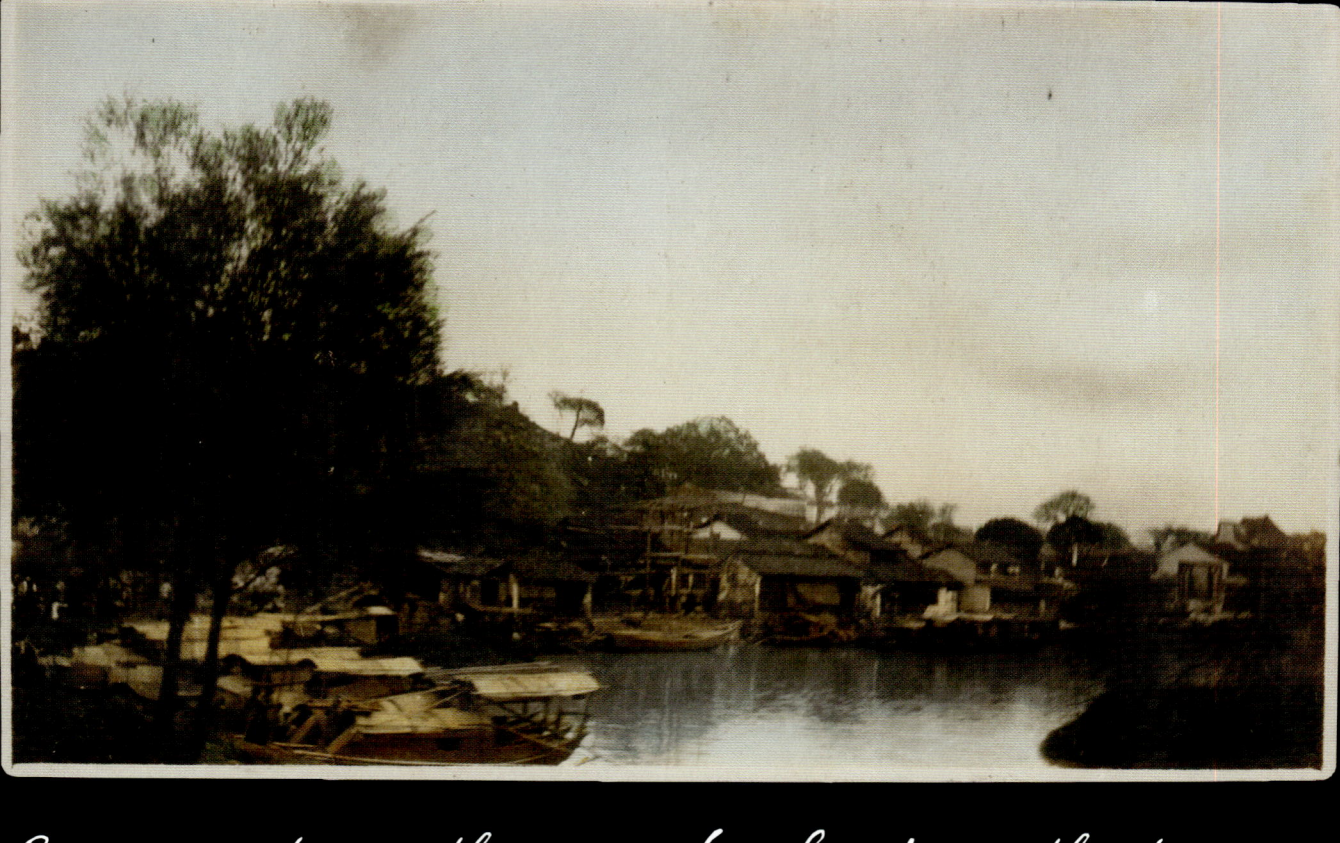

Community on the river banks, from the train between Shanghai and Hangchow.

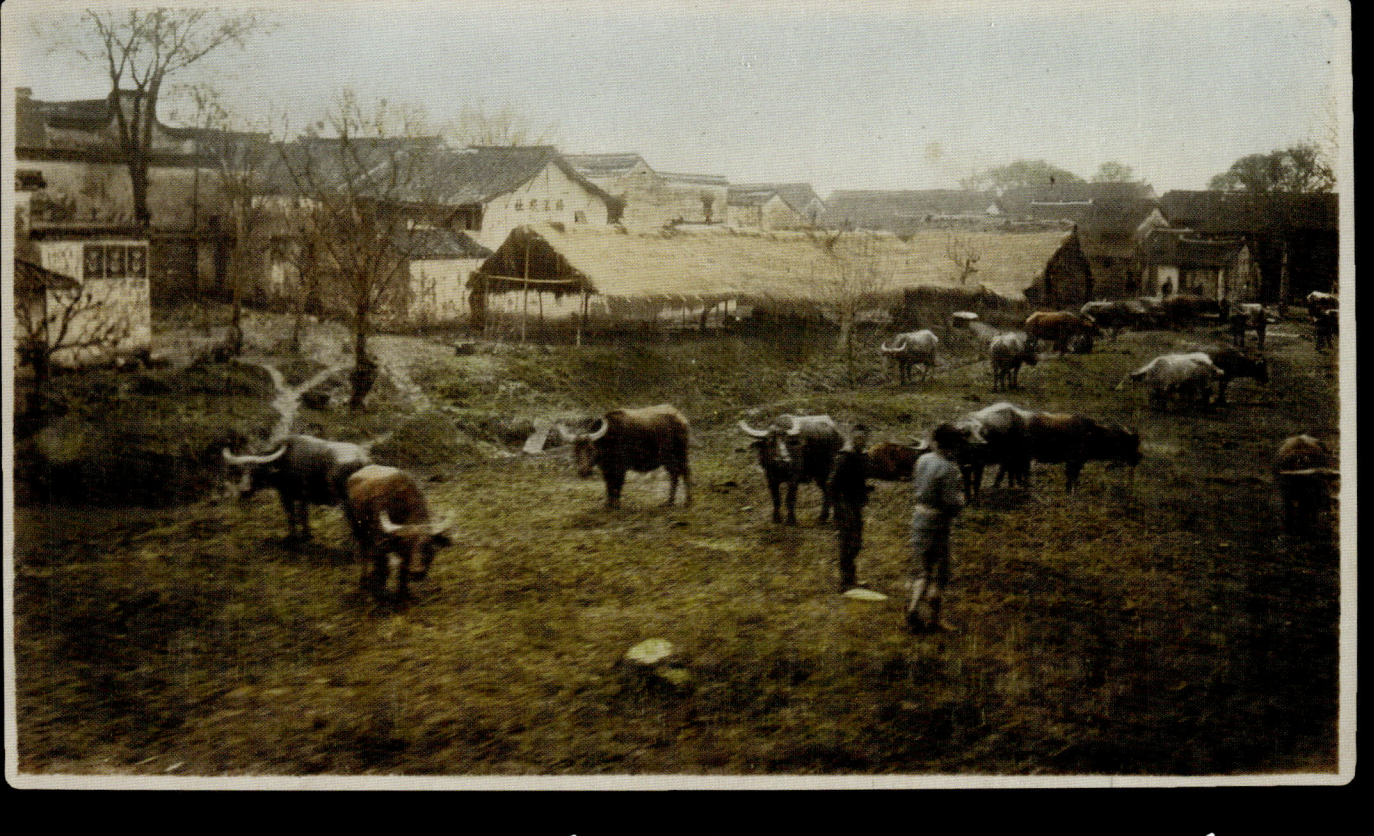

Farmers and water buffalo, from the train between Shanghai and Hangchow.

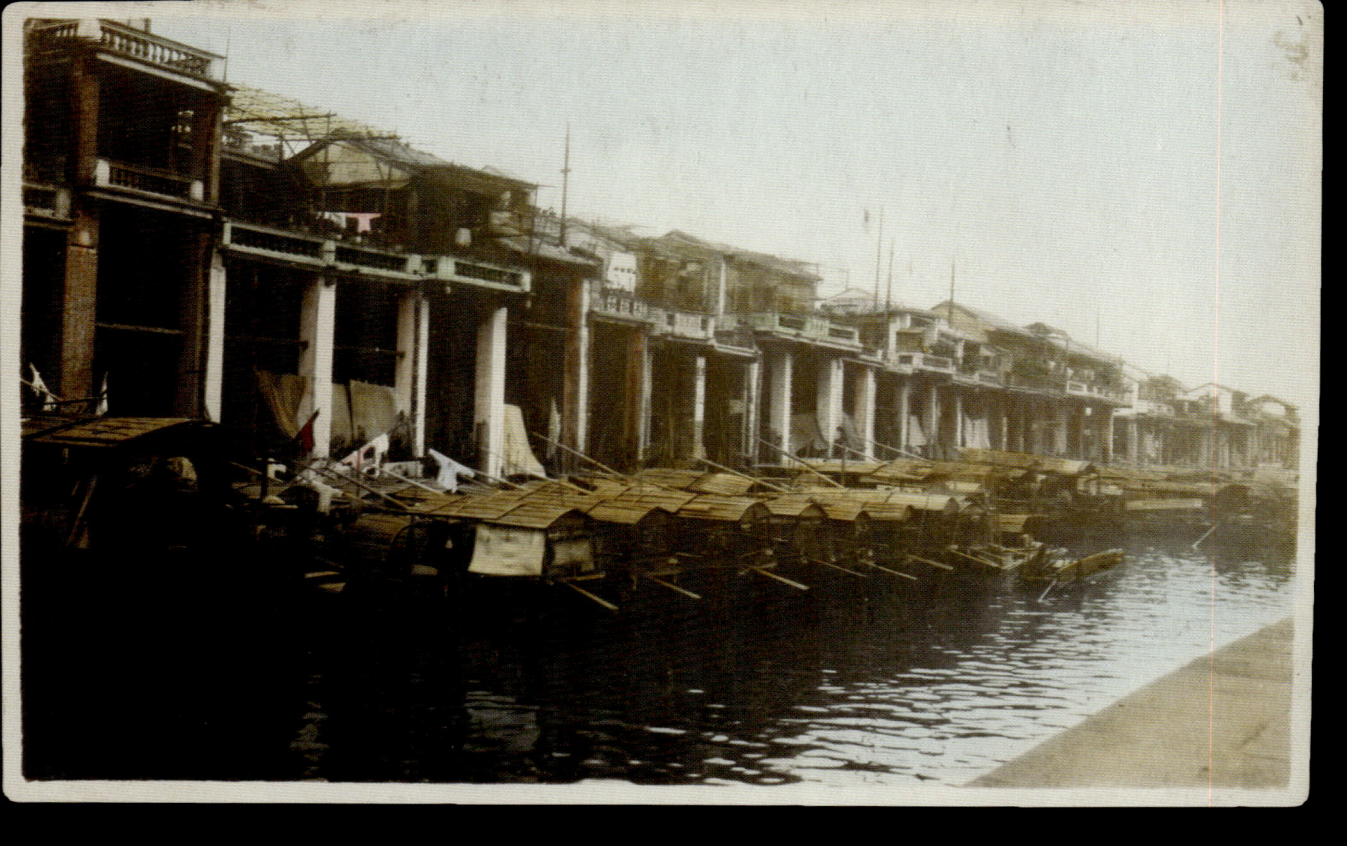

Sampans moored in orderly fashion along a canal —Canton.

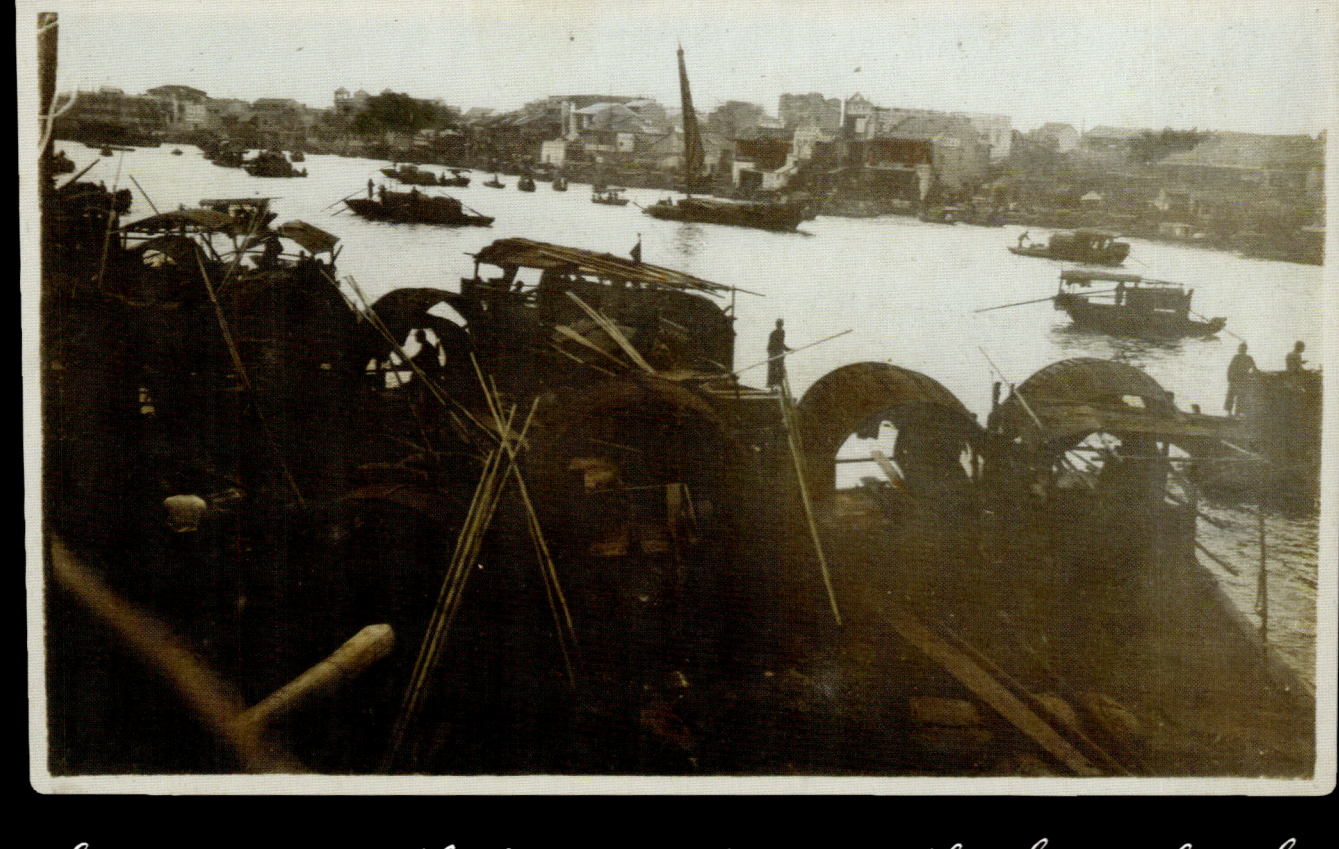

Sampans jostle for position in the busy harbor — Hong Kong.

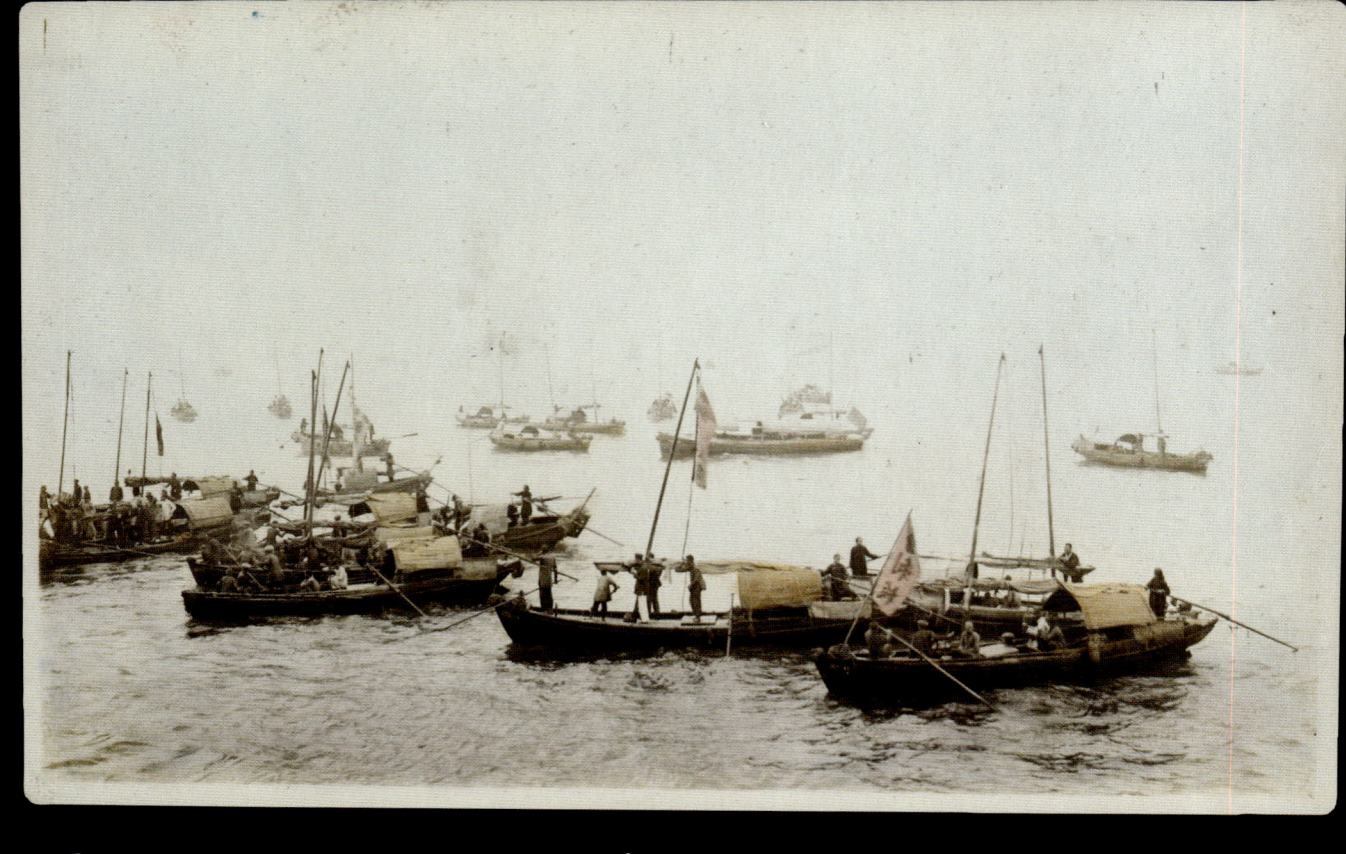

Sampans advertise boarding houses— Hong Kong.

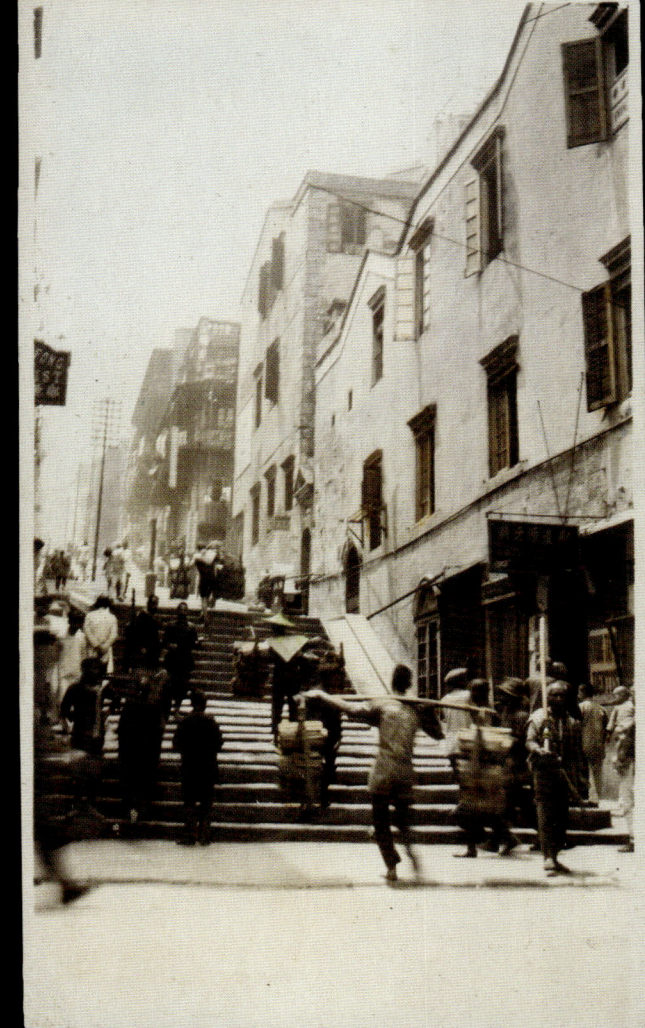

Step street in Hong
Kong. Much of the city
is built on the slopes of
a very steep mountain
called Victoria Peak.

Ten years later we returned to China—Peking, 3/-15/-1921.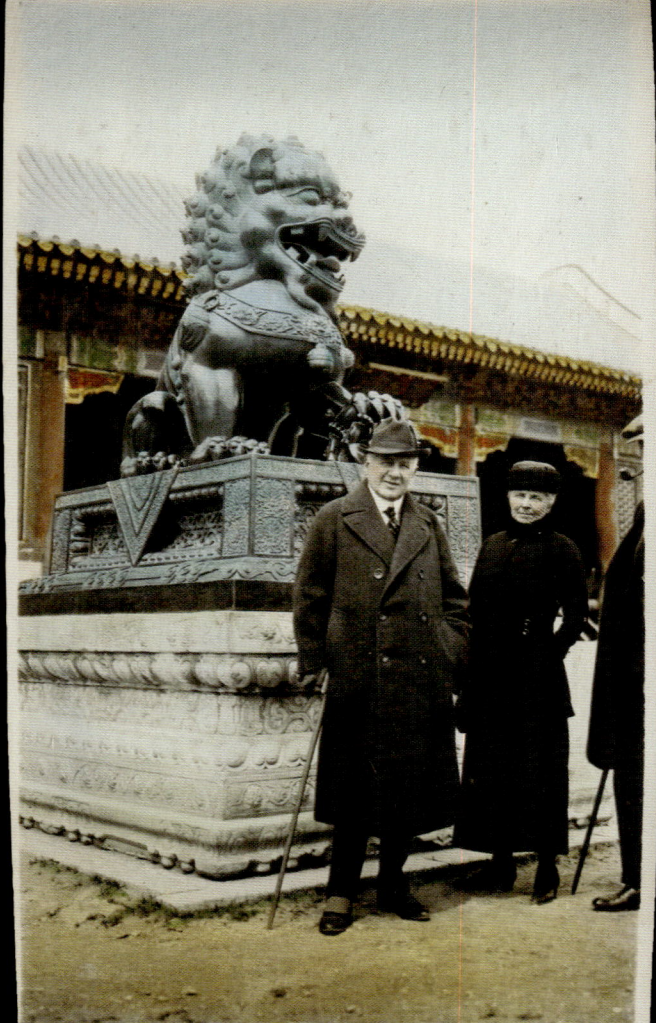

Afterword
by Hania Tallmadge

One of the few possessions from childhood that I have treasured all my life was the gift of an old photo album. I received it in 1949 from Christian Rub, a close friend of my aunt, the late Mme. Ganna Walska. Christian was a character actor in Hollywood movies for three decades. His best-known role was as the voice of Geppetto, the puppeteer in the animated film *Pinocchio*. He gave me the album because there were several postcards in it, which he knew I enjoyed collecting. I don't know when, where, how, or from whom he acquired the album. I was a child at the time and never thought to ask him.

Every few years I took out the album, poured over its elegant black pages, studied the graceful white script, and dreamed about the exotic places I hoped to see for myself some day. As I grew older, I came to appreciate the delicately hand-tinted photographs far more than the rather garish postcards. The photos seemed to tell a story, a wonderful, rather mysterious story of four Americans on a Grand Tour of Asia in the spring of 1910.

The intrepid quartet visited Japan, Korea, and China. They traveled by sea and by rail, in rickshaws and sedan chairs, on foot and on horseback. They turned up in crowded city streets and grand, but empty, palaces. They strolled beneath Tokyo's bloom-laden cherry trees and hiked the rugged ramparts of China's Great Wall. The women somehow managed all this in huge hats, tight corsets, and voluminous

Gibson-Girl dresses, while their male companions must have sweltered in stiff collars and heavy tweeds.

The album also is filled with the people they encountered: a kimono-clad mother with her child on her back, a man with a long braid glancing over his shoulder, a little boy in rags, and another in silk—their faces all turned toward the camera with curiosity. This led me to wonder about the person who took the pictures.

My recent research suggests that the photographer was probably an American man of some means, as photography was not an inexpensive hobby in 1910. This talented amateur had a marvelous eye for composition, as the more formally composed photographs demonstrate, while the more candid snapshots perfectly capture the action and atmosphere. As a child, I recall thinking I could feel the wind on the road to the Ming Tombs, and smell the mist on Suzhou Creek, and hear the peddlers' cries along Beijing's narrow lanes. This ability to seize the moment in an image is all the more impressive when one remembers that taking a photograph in those days was not as simple an enterprise as it is today. Even the portable box cameras of the era were bulky and heavy.

Nearly sixty years have passed since I received the album, and although I have fulfilled my girlhood dreams and visited most of the places caught in the lens of the mystery photographer, his images seem as magical to me as ever. It is very exciting to have the opportunity to share them. I hope you find them as fascinating and dream-provoking as I did—and still do.

Afterword

by Beverley Jackson

People often ask me, where does the idea for a book come from? This book was born when my good friend Hania Tallmadge called one day and announced, "I just found an album of wonderful photographs of the Orient I've had tucked away for fifty years. There might be something in it you can use for the book you're working on."

As I turned the pages of the album, I was instantly captivated by the carefully colored images, many of which recalled the lyrical elegance of Japanese woodblock prints. (This was probably not a coincidence, as photo-tinting in 1910 was frequently executed in Japan.)

Having traveled extensively throughout Asia over the last thirty years, I recognized most of the locations; some are virtually unchanged, but, sadly, not all. I knew at once the photographs were an invaluable record of the past, and that they had to be preserved, and, if possible, reproduced in some way. I realized the album itself was a treasure and worthy of becoming a book in its own right. My excitement must have radiated over the telephone because several days later Phil Wood, publisher of Ten Speed Press, was on a plane to Santa Barbara to see the album for himself. If anything, he was even more excited than I.

Hania and I had great fun playing detective while tracing the album's possible origins. She became a super sleuth, wielding a magnifying glass and minutely scrutinizing every single image. One discovery alone put her in the Agatha Christie category: In the lower right corner of one photograph, written in the tiniest hand-writing either of has had ever seen, she spotted a name—Byron L. Smith. This tantalizing clue, however, inspired more questions than answers and sent Hania to the public library. After several days, the trail led to a Byron L. Smith, founder of the Northern Trust Bank in Chicago. Further digging led to an article in *Chicago Record Herald* dated July 14, 1910.

This newspaper article revealed that Mr. Smith (we hoped *our* Mr. Smith) had returned to Chicago from a four-month tour of the Far East on July 13, 1910. He informed the Herald reporter that "Opportunities for American trade of the most profitable sort were seen in China." In fact, more than any other country China impressed the Chicago banker as the place toward which American manufacturers should direct their attention.

"I was amazed," Smith continued, "at the industry of the Chinese and could not help feeling the conviction that it would be well worth our while to get better acquainted with them and make a serious attempt to obtain some of their trade. If there is any place on the earth that is worth the careful consideration of the American man of business, it is China. Opportunities there are limitless."

It is startling when one remembers this really was written in 1910—not 2006!

Bibliography

Arlington, L.C., and William Lewisohn. *In Search of Old Pekin*. Henry Vietch, 1935.

Bogan, M. L. C. *Manchu Customs and Superstitions*. Tientsin & Peking: China Booksellers, 1928.

Brown, G. Waldo. *The New America and the Far East, Vol. 2 & Vol. 7*. Boston: Marshall Jones, 1907.

Crawford, Leola. *Seven Weeks in the Orient*. Chicago: Howard D. Berrett, 1914.

Davidson, Robert J., and Isaac Mason. *Life in West China*. London: Headley Brothers, 1905.

Der Ling, Princess. *Two Years in the Forbidden City*. New York: Moffat, Yard, 1911.

Franck, Harry A. *Wandering in Northern China*. New York: The Century, 1923.

Fraser, Mrs. Hugh. *A Diplomat's Wife in Many Lands, Vol. I & Vol. II*. New York: Dodd Mead, 1910.

Gernet, Jacques. *Daily Life in China*. Stanford, CA: Stanford University Press, 1962.

Haga, Hideo, and Gordon Warner. *Japanese Festivals*. Osaka: Hoikusha Publishing, 1977.

Hardy, Rev. E. J. *John Chinaman at Home*. London: T. Fisher Unwin, 1905.

"Journey into China." *National Geographic*, 1982.

Lawson, Lady. *Highways and Homes of Japan*. London: T. Fisher Unwin, 1910.

Little, Mrs. Archibald. *The Land of the Blue Gown*. London: T. Fisher Unwin, 1902.

McCormick, Elsie. *Audacious Angles on China*. Shanghai: Chinese American Publishing, 1922.

Rand McNally. *International Atlas of the World*. Chicago & New York: Rand McNally, 1922.

Seagrave, Sterling. *Dragon Lady*. New York: Alfred A. Knopf, 1992.

Sears, Robert. *Pictorial History of China and India*. New York: R. Sears, 1853.

Smith, Arthur H. *Chinese Characteristics*. New York: Fleming H. Revell, 1894.

Stoddard, John L. *Lectures, Vol. 3*. Chicago: George L. Shumand, 1897.

Village Life in China. New York: Fleming H. Revell, 1899.

Ten Speed Press
PO Box 7123
Berkeley CA 94707
www.tenspeed.com

Distributed in Australia by Simon and Schuster Australia, in Canada by Ten Speed Press Canada, in New Zealand by Southern Publishers Group, in South Africa by Real Books, and in the United Kingdom and Europe by Publishers Group UK.

Cover & interior design by Brad Greene
Composition by BookMatters, Berkeley

Library of Congress Cataloging-in-Publication Data on file with the publisher.
ISBN-13: 978-1-58008-434-5
ISBN-10: 1-58008-434-6

First printing, 2006
Printed in China

1 2 3 4 5 6 7 8 9 10 / 10 09 08 07 06